They Died In Silence

A Woman Steps Forward

James Casey

Dillard Publishing
Carlsbad, California

They Died In Silence

Copyright © 1992 by James Casey

Published by
  Dillard Publishing
  300 Carlsbad Village Drive Suite 108-A
  Carlsbad, California 92008-2999

Published and printed in the United States of America.

All rights reserved under International and Pan American Copyright Conventions.

No part of this book may be reproduced or transmitted in any form or by any means, electronic or mechanical, including photocopying, recording, or by any information storage and retrieval system, without written permission of the author.

Library of Congress Catalog Card Number: 92-73486

ISBN 0-9633858-0-1

Contents

Preface	v
CHAPTER ONE No Longer A Teacher	1
CHAPTER TWO Dressmaker Courier	29
CHAPTER THREE The Uprising	55
CHAPTER FOUR The Americans	79
CHAPTER FIVE Into The Mountains	99
CHAPTER SIX Survival	123
CHAPTER SEVEN Nazis Up Close	147
CHAPTER EIGHT The Russians	183
CHAPTER NINE Lieutenant Maria	219
CHAPTER TEN Citizen Maria	255
Epilogue	283

Preface

In 1944, the Polish Home Army attacked German forces in Warsaw. The Red Army, across the Vistula River, stood by while SS troops savagely defeated the Poles and razed most of the city.

At the same time, General Omar Bradley's 12th Army Group broke out of their beachheads and swept east toward Paris and the Rhine.

US Lt. General Mark Clark's 5th Army moved up the Italian peninsula. The converging Allied advances led to the defeat of the Third Reich.

In Czechoslovakia, Maria Zima—twenty, beautiful and a teacher in a tranquil, mountain village—was forced into becoming a courier for the Czechoslovakian Forces Interior. The Czech Government ordered an uprising of all Czech military and civilians. Their plan was to attack the Germans on all fronts, forcing them to send in reserves and pull away from the Allied forces closing on Germany.

The Americans and British sent in intelligence units, anti-tank weapons and small arms to lend support to the Czechoslovakians.

Since Maria spoke several languages, she was ordered by the commanding general of the Czech forces to act as interpreter for the Russian forces. She translated battle reports for the Russians in Banska Bystrica, a city held by the Slovak Liberation Army. She met members of the American Dawes Team—fifteen Americans sent by the OSS—and thirty-two downed American and British pilots the team was escorting home.

The Partisan uprising began and rapidly failed. When the city fell, Maria had to flee to the mountains with the Dawes Team and six hundred members of the Czech Army.

The winter trek over the mountains took three months. Eighty-three men froze to death, hundreds more were killed or captured by the Germans. Maria and the men suffered severe hardships from exposure and starvation.

They Died In Silence is the story of this young woman who stepped forward and offered her life to her country and the military forces of the US and Britain. She followed orders; she was a soldier and a hero to Czechoslovakia and the United States.

In 1946, by order of the President of the United States, Major General William Donovan pinned the US military Bronze Medal on Maria's dress. This was the first time in the history of our nation that a woman was so honored. She stood at attention as the West Point Cadet Corps passed in review. An honor that the people of Czechoslovakia and the United States should always remember. This is her story. It must be told.

James Casey
Carlsbad, California

Chapter One

NO LONGER A TEACHER

Julius Goldberger was gazing through his office window, the one that overlooked the lumber yard. His heart sank as he watched the arrogant Nazi lieutenant maneuver himself through the stacks of lumber ready to be shipped for the Reich. How he hated this man. Before the lieutenant could reach the office, Julius made his way from the window to his desk so he could sit and assume a nonchalant position.

The lieutenant flung the door open and slammed it into the wall. He gave his usual greeting, "Ah, Julius, you're looking well."

Goldberger lowered his eyes and dropped his head, saying nothing. Several times, he peered over his pinched-nose glasses and watched the lieutenant stroll around the office, peeping behind pictures, under papers and between the file cabinets. Finally, he asked, "Is this one of your social calls, or is there something that I can help you with?"

The lieutenant answered, "I am looking, Julius, always looking. Soon I will find her, but rest assured I will never stop looking until that day comes."

He leaned forward, looked closely into Julius' face and said, "I will find her, Jew." Then the lieutenant walked to the door. Turning back, he added, "Like always, Julius, I will be back, maybe tomorrow or maybe next week, but I will be back."

He gently pulled the door closed behind him. Just before it latched he gave Julius a deliberate smirk.

Julius sat behind his desk and dropped his head into the palms of his hands. He had survived the past five years by keeping his nightmares out of his daily life. He had, in fact, avoided looking too closely at anything, real or imaginary, that would remind him of his fragile position. Goldberger had been the only Jew allowed to remain in Maly Sulin. The others—Heller, Herschkovics, Bergman—had all been carted away, with their wives and children, to serve the *new order*, by dying.

Goldberger had more to lose than the others, so, as is usual, he was left with more: his life, and the job of managing the lumber mill and timber tracts he once owned. The expropriation of his business and land, the freezing of his bank accounts in Bratislava and Prague and his baptism as a Christian was sufficient payment for his life.

He learned quickly to live only to work, eat, sleep and weed out humiliation from his thoughts and feelings. He congratulated himself that his youthful enterprise let him survive when others could not. He complimented himself on his ability to negotiate with a hostile force. One that hated Jews. Very well, he would cease to be a Jew.

For years, this strange transformation of self-image was to serve him well. It was only now, worn out from his fear of exposure, that the reality he had denied came back to haunt him. He felt helpless and alone.

He had to get rid of Anna.

With some effort, he stood up and walked into the small outer office and asked Olga Zima, his bookkeeper, to come into his office. Olga was eighteen, tall, blonde and large-boned, without being heavy. She stood and followed Julius.

"Please, Olga, sit. Bring that chair over here and come sit by me. We can talk quietly."

The precaution was unnecessary. Nothing could be heard over the drone of the heavy machines of the lumber mill.

"I need help and I don't know to whom or where I should turn. I know I can trust you. Can you keep a secret? If you don't want to hear it, just say so and that will be the end of it."

"Don't be ridiculous, Julius! Are you ill?" Olga liked Goldberger and felt comfortable with him. She had known him all her life. Before the War, they shared the same hometown,

Jakubiany. Julius had been a frequent visitor at the parish house. Her father, a Greek Catholic priest, baptized Julius at the beginning of the War. As a favor to him (he was stripped of his state salary for refusing to sing the national anthem at the beginning of mass), Julius hired Olga at the mill.

Olga was concerned. It was not like Julius to be distraught. She asked, "Does it have anything to do with the lieutenant that just left?"

"Yes, Olga. I am in trouble." Julius explained, "You see, he came to threaten me again. When they rounded up all the Jews in the village a year ago, my sister and her son, David, were reported missing. To this day, they haven't found them and the lieutenant has been pressured to check me out. He told his superiors that he would search the woods, my house, the sheds and the mill. Anyway, he had the decency to tell me what he plans to do. I told him to go ahead, that I hadn't heard from my sister in years, that I hadn't had much to do with her since our parents died, and that I had no idea where she was."

"Is that all?" Olga asked.

"No, Olga, that isn't all—she's here, in my cellar."

"Oh my God!" Olga couldn't keep still.

Julius went on, "She's been here the whole time. She rapped on my window in the middle of the night. What could I do? You should have seen me building that phony wall down in the cellar and ripping up the floorboards. I'd never worked with my hands before.

"Then, I had to fight to keep her down there. She wanted to be in the house. I got tired of her nagging, bringing her meals and doing her laundry. She is my sister and I really do love her. So, I allow her to come into the house sometimes in the evenings. I shuttered the windows and we speak in whispers. Then, do you know what? She wanted to go out, go into the village and get some air. Can you believe it? Soldiers all over the place, worse than that, the gossips! I tell you, God is going to get those people, the people of our own city. I can't believe it when I think about it.

"Anyway, I put my foot down. I told her if she kept talking nonsense, she would have to stay in the cellar all the time. Not that she didn't still come up during the daytime. She'd never admit it, but I would find silver out of place, a lamp moved, food missing. I'm sorry to burden you with all of this, but if you only knew what a pain in the ass this woman is. You wouldn't believe it. I don't know what to do any more, and I haven't told a soul."

Olga tried to comfort him, "You are a good man, Julius. Better than you think."

"Good man? I'll be a dead man if I don't move her in a week. If the lieutenant decides to move in sooner, it will be less than a week. Who knows? I'm dead regardless."

"Do you really think he knows?" Olga inquired.

"How should I know? I think he suspects, but doesn't want to make his move yet. Remember, our young lieutenant was a Slovak. It won't do him any good if the Germans find out; and it won't do him any good if they have to find someone to take my place to run this mill. Maybe I should ask him to move her to save his own hide." This notion pleased him. He went on, "Even if I could think of a place to move her, it would be impossible for her to travel without papers."

"She got here without papers," Olga reminded him. "Papers can be bought."

"That's true." He smiled, "Then she'll have something to show the lieutenant when he tears up the floorboards. That ought to impress him."

"I'm trying to help and I can't think clearly with your sarcasm," she scolded. "It's just a silly cover for being scared and it's not doing you or me any good."

Goldberger was shamed into silence. Olga took the lead. "Maybe," she continued, "my father could help."

"Please! That is out of the question."

"Maria?" Olga offered.

"Who?"

"Maria, my sister."

Julius shook his head, "I can't involve your family."

Olga insisted, "She could help you. She has a room of her own and she's far enough away from the district. It would only be for a couple of months until school is out, then you could find Anna another place. Two months wouldn't be such a hardship for Maria. Why, the War may be over by then."

Goldberger was moved by her excitement. He shrugged his shoulders, "I suppose it wouldn't hurt to ask."

That afternoon, Olga and Julius made plans to travel the following day to Hrinova, the village where Maria was teaching. Goldberger cleared their absence with Schiller, the German overseer, on the pretext of finding some parts for broken machines. Olga left early to seek a friend of a friend who knew where to buy forged identity papers.

Goldberger worked late, long after the mill had closed. When it became too dark to see, he put on his hat and coat and walked down the narrow path toward his home. For Olga, it was a foregone conclusion that Maria would agree to help; Julius prayed she would. Would everything turn out all right? He wondered.

Maria Zima, at twenty, was taller than her sister, less fleshy, more angular. She wore her thick, blonde, luminary hair long. Her blue eyes were set off by her high cheekbones and thin straight nose. Everything about her suggested length: her height, hair, face, legs and arms. Each feature complemented the other. And she did not appear to lack a physical center, as tall people sometimes do. She was beautiful.

Maria had reached her present height at an early age, and for most of her life had imagined herself ugly. A tall and thin figure was not considered fashionable in central Europe at the time. Feeling deficient, she adjusted by padding her chest and wearing several pairs of thick stockings to increase the size of her legs. For years she ran away when she saw older boys in groups. She didn't know why, they just frightened her. Several times during the last year, young ministers were presented to her as suitors by her parents, but she was not interested in marriage. She was not about to spend the rest of her life in the provinces; she did not want her mother's life; she wanted to be a professor of history in a large university.

Maria's youthful views reflected the conflicts of her time. The feudal system in Slovakia had ended only five years before her birth, and feudal conditions were still common in her village. The peasants only subsisted on the land; very little grew. There was no electricity, no roads. Education beyond the village school was restricted to a small middle class that had only recently matched the aristocracy in economic and political power. The changes over the last 150 years in Western Europe were force-fed to Slovakia by the world's events during the 1920s and 1930s. Children were reared in a world that had disappeared by the time they became adults. The Treaty of Versailles ended Maria's parents' world before she could enter it. The Munich Pact of 1938 and fascism destroyed the old ways.

Maria was born and reared in the Slovakian mountains largely due to political circumstances. The fall of the Austro-Hungarian empire and the closing of the borders occurred while her father, Edwin, was a divinity student in Presov, in eastern Slovakia. Upon graduation, he was forced to stay within the borders of the new Czechoslovakian Republic. He accepted his parish largely because it was only seven kilometers from his wife's hometown of Stara L'ubovna, the nearest town with road or telegraph connections. Only two wagon ruts served as a path to his new home. It must have been like a missionary outpost to this man, who had grown up near Vienna and was educated in Budapest.

The contradictions between the pedestrian conditions of the peasant village and the upper-middle-class background and education of Edwin Zima did not create problems for Maria until she started school. A school much like the one in which she was now teaching in Hrinova. She began school where there was one room and one teacher for 150 students, ages six to fourteen.

It became clear, quite early, that if Maria was to be educated as well as her parents had been, she would need a private education. Zima withdrew her from the village school at the end of her second year and attempted to educate both his girls at home. It was impossible. He was distracted by his other duties. As he grew impatient with the children, they became too frightened by his outbursts to learn from him.

The following year, Maria was sent to a private school in Stara L'ubovna, where she lived with an elderly maiden aunt, then to successive boarding schools, both Greek and Roman Catholic, in Presov.

Isolated from the peasant children by class differences, she now experienced new and different kinds of isolation: from living with an aunt in dark musty rooms, to living in a cubicle at the end of a room with forty other girls in a ward, militarily guarded by a nun.

Every summer, Maria would return to Jakubiany. During the first week, there was always a battle between Maria and her parents. Maria brought the outside world and its tensions home with her—to her father's discomfort and her mother's apprehension. Maria never wanted to return to the school she had just left. She complained of the narrow-minded hypocrisy, the words of freedom mouthed by the faces of authority. Where she saw constraint, her parents saw permissiveness. They were upset by the democratic familiarity with which she spoke of her teachers. In later years, they would be disturbed by Maria's worldly dress and manners.

When Maria changed schools, it was her father who acquiesced and made the arrangements. He was a conservative man, bound to the rigid traditions of his faith. But he was also principled and intelligent and not satisfied with his own lot. There was a part of him that wanted to encourage Maria's honesty, spirit, and intellectual curiosity. He thought these were dangerous attributes in his daughter. What could she do with them? But he had no son, and seeing himself reflected in her, he yielded.

Maria's mother's wishes were simpler, less conflicting. She had gone to Teacher's Training Institute and had married after graduation. She wanted the same for Maria, she even hoped that Maria would marry a priest—Greek Catholic priests were allowed to marry as Maria's father had—someone she could assist and build her life around. She wanted her children and grandchildren close at hand. She could not understand her daughter's constant dissatisfaction. She resented scraping the money together to send Maria to yet another school.

Maria's happiest year was the one spent away from school, when she lived with relatives in the Vienna suburbs. Here, she worked in the city as a student apprentice in a dressmaking shop. She had more a glimpse than a real taste of life in a Western city. She was well-chaperoned by her aunts and older cousins, but it was her first experience outside the mountain villages and provincial towns of Slovakia. She felt she belonged in Vienna and wanted to return.

Germany annexed Austria and then Czechoslovakia. After the Germans granted semi-autonomy to the Slovakian province and made the chief of the local fascist party its leader, mobility and personal choices were severely restricted. As a result, Maria enrolled in the Greek Catholic Teacher's Training Institute in Presov. She was a first-year student when the Germans completed the takeover. They annexed Czechoslovakia's western provinces and created a puppet state in Slovakia.

Maria would never forget the announcement. Students were called to a general assembly in the school's auditorium. Their surprise was evident from the muttering heard in the hallways. The portraits of Masaryk and Benes were removed and replaced by the sausage-like countenance of Msgr. Tiso, the Roman Catholic priest who headed the fascist party. The flags were changed. In the place of the Czechoslovakian lion was the party banner of three round hills and a cross.

The rumbling died down when the Institute's director reached the podium. His praises for the *new order* were out of character, even for him. The sobbing began, isolated at first, then became a collective effort. The director became confused and shuffled his papers. A party official seized the microphone and addressed the students, glaring at the director.

He attempted to explain, "I can see that you young people require some reeducation, and that we will take care of shortly."

There were changes; books were banned or altered and all reference to the old republic ceased. Strict curfews were imposed and the teachers grew increasingly timid. The War began six months later, with it came mobilization, troop movements, shortages, rationing and deportation of the Jews.

In the spring of 1944, it was clear the Germans would lose the War. There was little support left for them among the Slovaks. Even politically unconcerned persons began to see their republic as an occupied country. The ranks of the Partisans swelled as young men fled to the mountains rather than be drafted into the army or work in German factories. Personal resentment against the German soldiers and bureaucrats, for their arrogance and privileges, was widespread. Although there had been no actual fighting in their region, the normally poor people had been made almost destitute.

It was against this background that Maria had taken a teaching position, after graduating from the Institute, at a village school in Hrinova. The school was much like the first school from which she fled. Hrinova and Jakubiany were similar. It seemed ironic she was beginning her adulthood just the way her childhood had begun. She forgot about it for the time being. All personal choices had been eradicated. Her wish to become a history professor: gone forever.

If teaching in a village school in Hrinova would have been unthinkable to Maria in her early adolescence, it was better than settling down with a minister in some remote mountain village. After all, Hrinova had its attractions. The valley and surrounding mountains were extraordinarily beautiful; the town was quiet.

Maria was required to teach forty peasant children between the ages of nine and twelve. There were two other teachers: Jan Puchy, the headmaster, and his wife, Helena. Maria liked them and frequently had dinner in their home at the rear of the school. It was Helena, a fat woman with a full, attractive face that always had a smile, who comforted Maria and told her not to fret over her duties.

Compulsory education was in effect, but it could not be taken too seriously; what went on in the classroom had nothing to do with the lives that the children would almost certainly lead. They disappeared from school during planting or harvesting season. Only a sporadic effort was made to enforce the attendance rule. One family, with only one pair of shoes for their three children, sent each child every third day. Fathers could be arrested for their children's absences, but their sentences were willingly served; jailhouse meals were better than those served at home, and they were free.

Helena's husband was soft-spoken, his sad eyes were accentuated by the lines in his face. He was a tall, lanky man who seemed to walk with a forward tilt. School was boring to him and he did not come alive until the evenings, when he could indulge his tastes for *slivovitz* (Czechoslovakian vodka) and the village women.

Puchy immediately pawned off his propaganda and military indoctrination duties on Maria. When she arrived, the textbooks had not been censored yet and the boys were not being drilled. Maria performed her tasks with her customary sense of responsibility and dedication, although instead of fear and esprit de corps her field commands provoked sexual glances from older boys.

Maria loved the school. The attractiveness of the structure, stones covered with white stucco and a roof made of slate that reflected the sun, added to the picturesque setting. The mountain air was pure. The woods that surrounded the school contained much wildlife and she often sat and watched deer dart to security after hearing a woodsman's ax.

This day was gorgeous. A mild breeze crested through the valley; the tall grass swayed and pulsed with each diminutive gust. Maria sat at one of the student tables under a large oak tree on the side of the school. A mountain stream cut through the corner of the schoolyard, flowing down the mountain. From time to time, Maria would lean back against the tree so the sun could warm her face. The War, with all of its troubles, was thousands of miles away. Today, her mind drifted with the warm breeze.

She tried to keep herself from dozing off. Her eyes were almost shut. Suddenly, she snapped her head back, sat up, squinted and placed her hand over her eyes to block out the sun. Maria noticed two figures in the distance, approaching the entrance to the schoolyard. She watched as they drew closer, then jumped to her feet. With her hand still blocking the sun, she walked slowly toward the silhouettes. She beamed with joy; it was Olga, the most beautiful of her five sisters.

Maria had not seen Olga in months and ran to greet her. She threw her arms around her sister and said, "What are you doing here at the school? I never see you or hear from you and then you show up out of nowhere."

Olga giggled and immediately told Maria she was too thin. Maria forgot her manners for only a second and said, "Julius, what in the world are you doing up here?"

"I have to ask you for help, Maria." Julius explained, "I have no one else to turn to. I have tried to reason out this problem and it seems that you have the only solution. If you say no, I will understand and that will be the end of it."

"Well, what is it?" Maria asked. "You look so serious."

Julius began, "It concerns my sister, Anna. You know her. Well, I'm indispensable to the Nazis because of my lumber management, so they leave me alone. Anna isn't. I am hiding her at my home—in the cellar—but I think that they are finally on to me."

Olga interrupted, "Oh, Julius, you are starting to babble again. Let me tell Maria. You get everything confused." Olga continued, telling Maria the whole story, concluding Anna must be moved as soon as possible.

Maria listened attentively, realizing the situation was grave. She took Julius by the hand, trying to relieve some of his anxiety, "There is only one way I can help you, Julius, and that is to tell Jan and Helena. If they agree, our troubles are over."

"Can you trust them?" Julius was nervous.

Maria was frank, "I know that they are not Nazis, but they, too, would be taking a great risk."

He gave in, "I guess we could ask, it wouldn't hurt."

"You and Olga stay here." Maria directed them. "I'll ask right now. There is no use wasting time, it seems you have reached the critical point."

Maria vanished into the schoolhouse and returned in minutes. "They don't want to know anything about it."

"What does that mean?" Julius wanted to know.

"It means 'yes,' but they don't want to see or hear anything."

Julius took Maria by the hand, "God will never forget you for doing this. If it is all right, I will bring Anna and her son, David, by as soon as possible. Probably in the next day or two."

Surprised, Maria complained, "Her son! Julius, you never said a word about a second person! Do you realize how small my quarters are above the school? It will be impossible for three of us to live there."

Julius was nervous again. Fear crossed his face. Maria was his last and only hope. If she faltered, all would be lost. Olga, noticed his disappointment and took Maria aside to dispel her hesitation, saying it would only be for a couple of months. By that time, school would be out.

Maria realized that their problem was greater than her temporary discomfort. Her fear was for the others, Jan and

Helena, not herself. She turned to Julius and said, "Of course, you are right, Julius. I'm just uneasy about it."

With the situation temporarily resolved, Olga glanced at her watch and said, "We should be off. It is getting late and we don't want to miss the last train back." With that, she kissed Maria on the cheek and disappeared down the road. Maria watched as they turned and glanced back. She waved until they were no longer visible.

That evening, she walked back and forth in her small room wondering if she had made the right decision. She was afraid to tell Jan and Helena about David for fear they might call off the entire plan. If that happened, where would they be? Either way, she felt she had got herself into a predicament that she would regret.

It was Saturday, school was out and Maria was returning from an early morning walk in the forest. She was startled to see Anna and David carrying a large well-worn suitcase that Julius had given them and twice as many rag-wrapped bundles as they had hands. Their newly-forged documents identified them as Slovaks, but there was no disguising Anna's Jewish face and accent.

Maria and Anna exchanged greetings at the gate. Anna's hug brought smells of garlic and cologne. David, an eight-year-old with black hair and morose eyes, offered Maria his hand.

"You've had a long trip. Let me show you the room." Maria led David through the door of the schoolhouse and up the steps.

Anna pondered the horrors of the trip and of Maria's physical attributes: The trains had been late; Maria had nice eyes; the food had been inedible; Maria was too thin; there had been so many soldiers; such beautiful hair. Anna had just begun a discourse on the dangers and treatment of sunstroke when her eyes registered disappointment at the tiny room.

Maria, noticing, said, "Yes, I know the room is small, but it's warm in the winter and cool in the summer and, if we are well organized, it should be comfortable. You and David can have the bed, I'll take the cot over here."

Anna and David settled down in the small room, but Maria could tell that Anna was not happy with the arrangement. That evening, Maria warned Anna never to speak with anyone. The community was full of gossips who would jump at the chance to wag their tongues.

There was another problem: The head guard for the internal security forces was stationed nearby. He often visited the Puchy's home and had supper with them. Not only that, he was forever knocking on Maria's door, fabricating reasons why she should accompany him on his rounds. "I can't stand him. He is crude and obnoxious," Maria frowned.

Anna listened, smiled and said, "You're too good. Your bed? It looks cozy." She sat on the bed. "Is this filled with feathers or straw? Hmm, feels like straw. How my back will ache." Her eyes surveyed the room. She placed her bundles under the bed, saying, "You must be intelligent to teach children."

"You don't have to be an intellectual to teach children," Maria responded.

Anna patronized her, "Nonsense. Of course, you do. In the evenings, maybe you can give my David some lessons. He's growing stupid from living underground in holes with his mother."

"Would you like lessons?" Maria turned and asked David. He smiled weakly and shook his head no.

"Speak when you're spoken to!" Anna barked at him. "Certainly, you want lessons. He reads all the time. His father was a learned man, God keep him. Let us unpack and when we're finished you can help us rearrange the room so that we will have more space."

"Make yourself at home and I'll be up later," Maria told them as she closed the door behind her. In the few minutes that the three of them had been in the room together, the air grew stuffy and thick. Where could they put everything? She had no space. How was she going to live in such intimacy with these total strangers? Maria decided then to move her cot into the classroom.

In the morning, as the law required, Maria took Anna and David to register at the post office. She had not slept well and this trip had been a great source of worry. It was the first of many hurdles that she faced. Local authorities did not question Anna's documents and Maria took them on a short nervous tour of the village.

"Let's head back, I have much work to finish at the school," Maria suggested. They took a shortcut through the village and passed the office of Dr. Joseph Klein.

"Who is Klein?" Anna asked. "Is he German or Jewish?"

"Jewish. The Germans let him stay. All the other doctors are in the army."

"Have you met him? What is he like?" Anna wanted to know.

"Only once. I went to see him for treatment of a strep throat." Maria answered, "There isn't much to tell about him; he is just a nice doctor."

"I see," said Anna, not completely satisfied.

They turned right at the corner and walked toward the school.

The days that followed were uneventful, except that each day Miso Sopko, the local constable, passed the school on his rounds. Today, just as the children were dismissed, he waited at the schoolyard gate. He gave Maria a salute, grinning from ear to ear. She returned his salute with a wave and tried to manage a smile. He had always been a nuisance to her—he was certain that his uniform and position made him unfailingly attractive to women—and he was a dangerous man now that Anna was here. Maria had already managed to avoid him twice and hoped to again, this time by ducking quickly into the building. He called to her, she didn't escape him.

"Maria, I want to talk to you." Miso called.

She braced herself and went out to meet him.

"You've been avoiding me," he said, placing his hands on her hips.

"Now, Miso, that isn't true." She disengaged herself.

"Yes, you have, my pet," he replied, rubbing a finger down her cheek.

Maria turned away quickly. "Miso! If I avoid you, it's because you have the hands of an octopus. And no manners."

"My manners are fine for most girls." Miso insisted, "You won't admit to yourself that you like your octopus, little schoolteacher."

Maria wished he would find her response abrasive. It might make it easier to deal with him. But she found him pathetic, this skinny, thirty-year-old kid with bad teeth, parading around like some storm trooper.

He pointed upstairs and said, "Speaking of manners, you haven't introduced me to your aunt. Agh, look at you blush. Admit it, I could make you happy, make you feel like a woman." He drew her toward him.

She reached behind her and yanked his arm away. "Leave me alone, Miso, I told you, I don't . . ."

Miso was disturbed. Rebuffs to his advances rarely humiliated him, he was used to it. Maria, however, was afraid of him, as well as angry.

Miso tried again, "Introduce me to your aunt, Maria. You're not too good for that, are you?"

Maria regained her composure. "No, of course not, come upstairs and meet her." She wondered how Anna was going to handle this.

"Anna," Maria said, "I'd like you to meet my friend, Miso Sopko. Miso is the officer in charge of security for this area."

"Oh, so pleased to meet you," Anna gushed. "You startled me when you came in. You're a very handsome young man. So strong."

Miso looked over at David, who, as usual, sat reading one of his books.

Embarrassed, Miso mumbled, "Thank you."

Anna patronized Miso, "You'll be a lucky catch. Why didn't you tell me about this young man, Maria? She never tells me anything. So cute. David, shake hands with the gentleman. Good. Sit down. I'll make some coffee. You like coffee? I like real coffee, not this wartime—chicory soup I call it—mud. Ah! We haven't any sugar. Maria says she can't find any in the shops." Anna fluttered around every inch of the room, continuing her monologue. "Always reading, that boy. His late father, now he was a . . ."

David was visibly frightened and kept his nose in his book.

Miso found his official voice. "Why is this boy not enrolled in school?"

Anna blew her nose into her apron. "Excuse me. My allergy, every spring." She looked up at Miso innocently. "Maria is tutoring him in the evenings."

"It was too late in the year to enroll him," Maria added.

Miso watched them for a moment then demanded, "Your papers, please, madame."

Fishing the papers from her bag, she said, "Hruby. Here, it says so right at the top."

"And where did you just come from, Madame Hruby?" Miso inquired.

"Orlov." Anna's fluttering stopped.

"How long do you plan to stay?" Miso was getting more serious.

Anna continued the charade, "I don't know, who does these days, we may settle."

Miso seemed confused rather than satisfied. He returned her papers and wished her a pleasant stay. Anna's color returned.

"The water's boiling. Sure you won't stay?" Anna offered.

"No, I must get going." Turning to Maria he continued, "But I would like a word alone with you, Maria."

Maria was puzzled until they reached the bottom of the stairs where Miso cornered her by leaning his hand against the wall.

"What kind of jackass do you think I am?" he asked her.

"Jackass?" Maria knew then that he did not believe them.

"Those papers are forged. The post office in Orlov has no record of her being registered there," Miso reported.

Maria wondered if he was bluffing to make his point. She had no way of knowing. She offered an excuse, "Someone must have made a mistake."

"There has been no mistake. You can't tell me that woman is your aunt."

"She is," Maria insisted.

"On your Jewish side?" Miso tried sarcasm.

Maria's face was flushed as she said, "No, on my Austrian side. I'm no more Jewish than you are."

"I know you are not. That isn't the question, but you know that Austrians don't usually pepper their conversations with Yiddish." Miso concluded, "Anyway, that isn't for me to determine, only to report—if I have to.

"What do you mean . . . 'if you have to?' " She knew what was coming.

His smile returned. He let his free hand slide against her buttocks. "There are certain things that a girl could do to cloud a man's memory. That's what I mean."

Maria was horrified; she cast her eyes down to the floor.

Miso squeezed her. "Save that little ass for me, schoolteacher. If I hand you over to the army, they may not find you such a charmer. Take a couple of days to think it over. You'll like me, Maria. No one doesn't like Miso." He lowered his head and tried to kiss her, but she clenched her lips and tucked her chin into her chest. He drew back cheerfully. "If I were you, I'd beg for it. You just think about what I said and I'll be back, after I report this. Maybe tomorrow, next week, who knows."

After he left, Maria stood in the corner dazed. She brushed her hair out of her eyes, trying to think, trying to feel, trying to release the savage hatred she had for that man.

Anna called from the top of the stairs the moment Miso had parted. Maria looked up at her, blank faced. Anna screamed, "What did he want? Why did you bring him here, and into the room? You must be out of your mind, Maria!"

Maria blinked, trying not to think. She couldn't comprehend what had happened. "I don't know, he just came on his own. Please don't shout."

Anna accused Maria, "You told him! You want to get rid of us!"

"No, Anna. Do you really think that?" Maria's numbness gave way to anger. "Do you honestly believe that they would take you and leave me and the Puchys? For the last time, you are not keeping house up there. You are a fugitive! What do I have to do to make you understand? Nail your door closed?"

Anna was offended. "So that's what you would like to do? Now it comes out. If you feel that way, why don't you turn me in?"

"I can't turn you in!" Maria shouted back.

"No. You're too good for that. You'd rather lock me up yourself. No wonder the police are sniffing around. You're taking work away from them! You make everybody suspicious, the way you act about me."

"You're not normal!" Maria dropped her voice, "Miso knows that, everybody does."

"So what's the big deal? And don't tell me all these men are coming around here for nothing. You must be giving them something that they want!" Anna stormed back into the room and dumped herself into her chair.

Maria knew that something would happen now; it was just a matter of time. She felt like human refuse. Maria tried to plan for Miso's return, but she was stymied. Nothing in her experience had prepared her for sexual blackmail. She wondered if it would be different if she found him attractive. She could not imagine it. If she could have, it might have been easier to lead him on, letting him kiss her and telling him to come back in a week.

Anna's voice brought her back to reality. She was standing at the top of the steps and started in again, "This is all your fault, locking me up in this room. The concentration camp would be better than this. At least I would have someone to talk to. And you can bet that I am telling my brother about you. He will do something. And, you are right! If I get caught, there's going to be more people involved than just me. You can count on that!"

Maria was in no position to debate the situation with Anna, who was completely out of control. She turned and walked slowly back to the school room.

Sunday, Maria attended church as she had done for years. After the services, she strolled to the rear of the church, entered the parish house and talked with Father Andre, revealing the entire story. He was sympathetic, but offered no solution. He suggested that she try to stall Miso as long as she could without committing a sin.

Anna went into the village against Maria's orders to see Dr. Klein. "It's my heart," Anna told him in his office. "I can't take it anymore. A year in a cellar and now this. That horrible girl."

Dr. Klein removed his stethoscope, "You have been here three times, it is very dangerous. All three times I found nothing wrong with you. You are as strong as an ox. If you need to talk to someone, talk to me; but don't waste my time with your stories."

Anna vented her frustration, "Ach! What can I do? It hurts, it really hurts, here (pointing to her chest). You don't know what it's like to be ordered around by an adolescent, a *shikse*. I lived under the ground for a year. Here smell my hair. It still smells of mold and dampness. And now that my brother isn't in danger; now that I have papers, official government documents for all the world to see, I still can't go out to shop, to get some air. Maria can't shop, the merchants cheat her. She gets the worst vegetables, stale bread and she pays too much. I could save her money and trouble, but no! She has to buy. Forget about me, she's poisoning the boy. Food must be fresh. She says it's all she can get; so how do I somehow manage to find what she cannot? I have experience. I take the time. But she won't listen...

"Stay home! Stay in the room! My jailer, with the eye of a hawk. She slips her cot out of the room the very first night and sleeps in the classroom. She eats there, cooks there. We're not good enough for her. What kind of company is that for a woman who spent a year in a hole in the ground? What kind of consideration? You tell me, doctor." She burst into tears and threw her heavy arms around Dr. Klein.

He patted her on the back and as she withdrew her arms he sighed, "Things are not the same as in the old days. These Nazis have made the world different. When this is all over, you will have your own house and you'll do as you please. Go back to the school now. Maria is young and probably doesn't understand. Remember that she is risking her life to take care of you and your son."

Dr. Klein helped her with her coat and walked her to the back door. He cautioned, "Be careful when coming here. You are welcome, but it's not altogether safe for either of us; watch out for Sopko when he makes his rounds."

Anna patted Dr. Klein on the cheek, "You're so kind, doctor, but if you only knew how I suffer. You just wouldn't believe..."

When Maria returned from church, Anna and her son were gone. Had Anna been arrested as promised by Miso or had she gone for a walk? Maria sat and waited until after dark. Finally, Anna arrived with David.

"Where did you go?" Maria demanded.

"I went to see Dr. Klein," Anna snapped. "What difference does it make? Miso knows all about me anyway."

"I told you repeatedly, it's not only your life, but the lives of those who are trying to help you. They will be dragged off to a concentration camp, too. Doesn't that matter to you?" Maria asked.

"No, it doesn't." Anna continued lying, "Dr. Klein thinks that you are a terrible person. He told me all about you, and, believe me, there was plenty to tell."

The next week was almost unbearable. The school year was ending and Maria expected Miso to show up anytime. The friendly relationship that Maria had with the Puchys deteriorated rapidly. With Anna, the picture was bleak. She would barely speak to Maria, then would leave with no explanation, always winding up in Dr. Klein's office.

Jan Puchy returned from the butcher shop, placed his bundles on the kitchen table and hurried over to Maria's classroom. He frantically threw open the door, and stammered. "I was just at the butcher shop and the butcher asked me why Anna was so friendly with Dr. Klein."

"What can I do, Jan? I can't lock her up in her room."

Mr. Puchy urged Maria, "You better get rid of her as soon as you can, I have to think of my family."

"I'll talk with her again, tonight," Maria promised.

"Talk with her? That stupid ass doesn't understand the possible consequences!" Puchy shouted.

Maria apologized, "I am so sorry, Jan. If there were something I could do, I would do it immediately. All I can do is try again. I guess what my old philosophy professor said is true: Women act on emotions. I try to help someone and look what happens."

Maria lectured Anna that everybody was involved now, not just her. All of them were in danger. Anna was never, never to go to see Dr. Klein again.

Maria remembered Father Andre's words: avoid sin! It seemed she could do nothing but sin. Protecting Anna put the Puchys in danger. That was sinful. She could undo that by yielding to Miso's advances, but that would be a sin—and unthinkable. The only way for her to avoid sin was to get help from Julius and Olga. What if their help did not come in time? How could the morality of her actions depend on what someone else did? If she sent Anna away, she would place some new, unknown persons in danger.

Was that a sin? These were all large sins. What if the large sins got out of hand? What if God determined the course of the large sins by the small sins that we commit, the ones in our control? What if she refused to lie to Miso and appealed to the better part of his nature? She resolved to try it, knowing there was no other choice.

With all hope exhausted and despair setting in, Maria's troubles grew the following morning when Miso, again, appeared at her door.

"Go for a walk?" Miso suggested, as he stood in the doorway, leaning against the frame. His leather holster and boots were obviously freshly polished. His pants were perfectly creased. Maria concealed a laugh. She felt her life coming to and end, but this, this was humorous, if not ridiculous. She shook her head as she stared at Miso.

"Can we talk here, Maria, or should we walk a little?" Miso wanted to know.

Maria was firm, "Here, Miso. What do you want, now?"

"You need to relax." He swung his arm around her shoulders and embraced her. She turned her head to avoid his lips, as usual.

Miso was surprised, "You're crazy. Didn't you listen to me the other day?"

Maria addressed him sternly, "Miso, I want to talk to you. Why don't you listen to what I have to say?"

"Afterwards," Miso dismissed her formality.

Maria confronted him, "I can't do what you want. It's impossible. Look, can't we just talk like friends?"

Incredulous, Miso asked, "Friends? You're joking. I meant what I said."

Maria begged, "Please, forget that. Are you really going to have all of us killed over this? It's madness."

"It's not me," Miso rationalized. "It's your trouble. I'm just offering a way out." Miso side-stepped any responsibility for such a decision.

"Do you realize they will send for the Puchys, too? If I'm not your friend, they are. You're going to hurt them because I won't have anything to do with you?" Maria asked.

"Why don't you like me?" Miso attempted innocence.

"That's what I am trying to tell you, I do like you, just not in that way. It can't be," Maria explained.

Miso narrowed his eyes and spoke just above a whisper, "I'm sorry you feel that way." He turned and left.

The next day, Maria received a reply from the letter she sent Olga asking her for help. Olga had not found a place. She asked Maria to keep Anna at the school while Julius inquired among the few remaining friends he had to see if they could help. All attempts so far had been unsuccessful.

For some strange reason, Maria no longer felt afraid. She assumed the worst was about to occur and waited for it. She hoped in the back of her mind Miso had not sent in his report, but she knew he had.

Maria took greater precautions and avoided gossips, families of German descent and government sympathizers. She had relayed Puchy's anger to Anna in terms so strong that Anna apologized and stopped her visits to town.

Weeks passed. Maria heard nothing from her sister. The end of the school year was approaching and she wondered who would arrest her. It was hard to tell with the Nazi bureaucracies, they were so intertwined. Would she be held by the police, the Slovaks or the Germans?

Her answer appeared late one afternoon while she was sitting in Helena's classroom grading students' papers. The door opened, displaying the silhouette of a man. The sun, shining from behind, caused Maria to squint as the man walked closer. She noticed he had a high forehead and thinning hair. The short and stocky man opened his eyes wide when he asked, "Are you Maria Zima?"

"Yes," she admitted. "Is there something I can help you with?"

He introduced himself, "I am Colonel Polack, Chief of Internal Security Forces."

Maria's heart sank. She looked toward the door, expecting more secret police in trench coats to enter and drag her off.

"May I be seated?" he courteously asked.

"Of course, please." Maria folded her hands together to keep them from trembling. The colonel sat on one of the students' benches.

The official continued, "I think you know what brings me here. A report has come across my desk that you are harboring a Jewish widow and her son in your room, here."

Maria started to speak, but could not. She looked at him from the corner of her eye and shook her head.

"No?" Polack looked surprised and tried to decipher her gesture.

Maria lied, "The woman staying here with her son is my aunt."

"No, they're not," the colonel corrected her. "I know who they are. I know all about them."

Maria interrupted him, "The stories you've heard aren't true. People always gossip in this town."

Polack stared at her with disapproval. "Where are my men?"

"What?" Maria sheepishly inquired.

"My men, that is what you are thinking, isn't it? You think I'm going to arrest you. Where are the soldiers? I assure you, if I wanted you arrested, you never would have seen me. If I wanted to interrogate you, I would have had you brought to my headquarters. I came here for a different purpose."

Maria looked at him without speaking.

Polack went on, "I can take care of your problems. Everyone will remain safe. But you must do something in return."

Maria thought of Miso and his offer.

"I would like you to work for the Resistance," Polack explained.

"Oh?" Maria stammered, "Why is that?"

"You should not be shocked. Your sympathies are quite clear. I happen to share them."

Maria declined, "I can't join. I'm no soldier. I'm not sure if I should even take you seriously. Anyhow, if I agree to join you, you could arrest me on two counts: harboring Jews and working for the Underground."

"You can believe what you like; but you flatter yourself. I'm not going to pack you off to the mountains with a song in your heart and a machine gun strapped to your back." Polack thought Maria looked disappointed. He continued, "I had something more pedestrian in mind. We need couriers to carry messages from one sector to another. We seem to have a shortage of innocent faces left among the Partisans. Yours is perfect. You would live in Banska Bystrica. I'd take care of your expenses, find you a room and arrange your cover."

Maria protested, "But . . ."

Polack interrupted, ". . . and take care of Anna and the boy."

"I have to go home this summer," Maria pleaded. "My father is a priest and the village men are gone. He can't tend his harvest by himself. We have to help."

Polack refused her plea, "They'll have to manage without you. You need my help and I need a courier."

"I guess I don't have much of a choice, do I?" Maria admitted.

"No, you really don't."

"So, what do I do first," Maria inquired.

"Let's not waste any more time chatting. Tell the Puchys not to worry about Anna. Don't tell them about me or what you will be doing, but let them know everything will be taken care of." Polack continued, "Use your imagination. Anna should stay here over the summer; it will be safer than moving her."

"What about in the fall? Can I tell the Puchys I'll be back in the fall?"

Polack responded, "Yes, if you like. I hope it's true. By the way, can you do anything besides teach?"

"I've done some dressmaking."

"Fine. Be in Banska Bystrica a week from Saturday," Polack ordered. "I'll meet your train. Take the one that arrives at ten, but don't bring luggage. It will just be for the day so you can get oriented. Please save your questions until then. I must go."

Maria stood at the door and watched as his car turned, stirring up a veil of dust that engulfed the car. He was on his way back to the city.

Maria returned to her desk, plopped herself down in her chair and thought the die has been cast.

How did all of this come about? One day she was sunning her face and the next she was in the midst of chaos. She had the burden of Anna's situation lifted from her shoulders. For that alone, she was grateful.

Her mood changed from relief to loathing when she thought of Miso. That traitor to the nation and to his people—spy, gossip, the dregs of humanity. That bastard! She now relished the fact that he would be getting his, and none too soon.

Maria awoke early the day of her appointment with the colonel. It was cold, still dark, but the wind was gentle. She had not been out of Hrinova since Anna's arrival, so she felt adventurous, unworried. She dressed, returned the cot to the store room, washed her face, then cut some bread and sausage to take with her. She tried to be silent, but was only quiet. The sounds of water running, rustling cloth and crackling paper were all particular. She wondered how Anna and David could sleep. They must have heard her intrusions into the silence.

She thought, as she began to place the food into her bag, it was foolish to believe she could keep secrets when everything that one did spoke so clearly.

As she stepped outside, Maria could hear the bus rattling far off in the distance. She thought, too, that she could almost smell it. She knew it was too far away, but the air had changed. She would miss the mountains, where machines did not change the way things smelled or sounded.

The old red bus was there when Maria reached the stop. There were only a dozen or so passengers so she got a seat by herself next to the window. The driver's door was still open; Maria felt the cold air fill the bus as the motor idled. The driver was busy trying to take down a bicycle from the luggage rack. Maria warmed her hands with her breath. The stars had all but disappeared when the bus finally got underway. A glow outlined the mountains to the east.

Maria looked around at the other passengers. There were three old women sitting together, like three heads on one body, protruding from a mass of clothing. A thin peasant man with his rough hands on his knees held a cigarette stub in the corner of his mouth. A fat mother slept, her arms draped around her wide-awake children.

She wondered what their lives were like. Did they have great disturbing secrets? Had their lives been disrupted like hers? Yes, she thought, looking out the window at the sunrise and its reflection on their faces, everybody had been touched by poverty and war. For the first time in months, she did not feel alone.

By the time the bus reached the train depot at Zvolin, the sky was bright and clear, the air was warm. As the train departed, Maria searched the cars for an open seat by a window. In the last car, she found an empty compartment, made herself comfortable and unwrapped her sausage and bread.

She wished she could ride the train forever, forgetting, for the moment, Anna and David behind her and Polack before her. She thought of getting off the train before it reached Banska Bystrica. Maybe she could run off to the mountains and join the Partisans "with a song in her heart and a machine gun on her back," leaving the others to fend for themselves.

Who was Polack anyway? Was he infiltrating the Resistance? Would he have her pass phony messages, only to dispose of her when she was no longer useful? She shook her head, took a bite of her sausage and went back to reading the book she carried.

When the train pulled into the station, Polack, as promised, was waiting on the platform. "It is good to see you, Maria. Lovely day, isn't it?"

"Yes it is." She greeted him, "How are you, colonel?"

"Fine, thank you. Can I carry anything?" he asked.

"No, your orders were to bring nothing on this trip," Maria responded.

"Ah, you are right. You'll be staying—turn left here—you'll be staying with a couple named Cherny. They live close by, on the other end of the railroad yard. It's a good location. You're less likely to arouse suspicion with so many people coming and going.

"By the way, if anyone recognizes me, I'll introduce you as my cousin, in from the country for a day. They won't believe it. They'll be sure that you are my lover; exactly what we want them to think. You always have to have a story ready. The story won't be necessary for the Chernys or Madame Zolkoff, however."

"Maria recognized that name and asked, "Madame Zolkoff, who is she?"

"Your new employer." Polack explained, "She's the proprietress of an exclusive dress shop on Dolna Street. You'll be an unpaid apprentice. I hope you're good."

"Will she know what I'm doing for you?" Maria inquired.

"No, both she and the Chernys know only that they are helping in some way. They don't want to know any more than that."

Maria had trouble keeping up with Colonel Polack's stride, though she was taller. He walked with his hands in his pockets and had the air of a man who was in no particular hurry. His pace was deceptive. He seemed relaxed, but his eyes never rested.

"You have beautiful hair, Maria," Polack complimented her. "You mustn't wear it like that on the streets. You will attract too much attention. See how the men turn around to look at you."

Maria gave him a dark look.

"You are uncomfortable with compliments," he surmised.

Maria qualified her look, "It depends on how they're given, and by whom."

"You're quite right, I apologize. It's the War. Isn't that what everyone says when they make a mistake: it's the War? I'm not a normal man anymore, not even on a day like this," Polack admitted.

Maria smiled at him. He surprised her by returning her smile. "How am I to live," she asked, "if I'm an unpaid apprentice?"

"I'll cover you. You can have 2,000 Korkunas, now." He handed her the money, "Let me know when you need more. Here we are."

Mrs. Cherny answered the door. She greeted Polack affectionately. To Maria, she presented a mixture of goodwill and apprehension. She was about fifty-five and stocky, with thick, red hands that pulled on a dish towel as she spoke.

The interior of the house was simple and clean. Maria noticed white lace cloths and doilies of different sizes and shapes covered most of the furniture.

Jan Cherny, resting the newspaper in his lap, seemed a part of the furnishings, as if his wife had run out of lace to cover his chair. He was a railroad signalman, about sixty, with close-cropped gray hair and a stubby moustache. He was an arthritic, Maria observed, as he rose slowly to greet Polack. He seemed honored to have the colonel in his home.

The Chernys were sympathetic toward the Resistance, but were not directly involved in it. Maria was shown to the pleasant guest room, separated from the rest of the house. It was a corner room with a southern exposure and windows that opened onto the street. Maria immediately liked it. She thought it might be difficult to get used to the noise of the street and the constant arrivals and departures of the trains. But the room was larger than the one Maria had at the school and she would be alone, so she was delighted.

After a short visit, Maria and Colonel Polack left the Chernys' home. They crossed the bridge over the Hron River and headed to the center of town. Banska Bystrica was an old mining city, originally settled in the twelfth century by German colonists. Its buildings reflected the mixture of Western and Slavic influences. Hlavna street, facing the town square, was the town's main commercial street and its proudest, with wrought iron balconies and tiled walks. A flower box hung in nearly every second story window. The street was crowded with passers-by. They were just window shoppers. There was little money and few goods to buy.

Polack warned Maria about Madame Zolkoff as they approached her shop. "Now, listen, she is not simple or humble like the Chernys. She is a White Russian noblewoman. Came here after the Revolution. She's a superb dressmaker and decent, but sometimes given to theatrics."

The mannequins in Madame Zolkoff's showroom window were dressed better than any woman Maria had ever seen. Cafe curtains behind the window display hid the parlor from the street. When they went in, Maria found herself in a gorgeous drawing room. There were wingback chairs and hassocks resting on Persian rugs. A crystal chandelier hung low over the center of the room, and in the far corner stood a massive mahogany table, crowned by a copper samovar. Madame Zolkoff might be given to theatrics, but she had taste.

Chapter Two

DRESSMAKER COURIER

Madame Zolkoff marched out from the back room when she heard the tinkle of the bell over the entrance door. She was elegantly clothed, her gray blouse adorned with pearls and a tailor's tape draped around her neck. Her face was heavily rouged, her eyebrows plucked, her nails, lips and hair painted in colors not found in nature. She seemed delighted to see Polack and offered him her cheek. She looked up at Maria solemnly through her glasses, put a hand on Maria's shoulder and asked in a voice that combined velvet and gravel, "Can you work hard, girl?"

"Yes . . . and I've had some experience," Maria responded humbly.

"Have you, really? I am sorry to hear that. That means I will have to spend most of my time undoing what the incompetents taught you." Madame rolled her eyes in dismay. She added, "Those people who think they know what they are doing are particularly annoying to those of us who do. Don't stand there. Come have some tea. Sometimes, I feel English must be in my blood. I just love tea, day or night, it makes no difference. Do you enjoy tea, Maria?"

She answered quickly. "Why, yes, but I haven't had tea in a long while. It is difficult to obtain coffee, let alone tea."

"How true," Madame Zolkoff agreed.

Maria was curious and wanted to stay for tea, but Polack made excuses. They exchanged good-byes and headed for the train station. When they reached the bridge, Polack checked his watch. They had enough time for a walk along the river. Maria had more questions, but he seemed too preoccupied so she did not disturb him.

"We should not be walking together like this," Polack said. "It's odd what one takes risks for. I haven't had spring fever since the War began. Thank God it's ending."

Maria was curious, "Which: your spring fever or the War?"

Polack caught Maria's inquisitive look. "They're losing badly in the west; it's only a matter of time until the Russians reach us from the east. We're not very well organized yet, but we're getting there.

"Who is getting there?" Maria asked.

"The Slovak National Council. It's what used to be called a popular front in the days when we had politics. The Council consists of the Partisans in the hills, the Communists and much of the army. The senior officers are German, but the junior officers are chomping at the bit for a rebellion. It's a question of when, rather than if. Everything has to be coordinated properly or we'll only make matters worse."

He paused for a moment. "Did I tell you that I have a Jewish grandmother?" Polack continued, "Isn't it curious. I'll bet there isn't a single person walking along this river without Jewish, Hungarian, Polish or German blood in them. No one used to care about a Slovak race or nation, especially not the Catholics—they're the ones that stirred up this nationalist business. Now, the Slovaks have their sovereign nation and they're more enslaved than ever. The Germans are smart. Much more intelligent than our old rulers. The Hungarians and Czechs sent their own men to keep us in line and collect the taxes; the Germans got us to do it for them. They only stick around for the mountain air; it's just one big resort with two million sub-humans to wait on them." He looked disgusted and was soon silent.

"How will I know when I'm supposed to deliver a message?" Maria got the courage to ask.

Polack instructed, "I will send for you. Otherwise, just go about your normal routine. You're a dressmaking student in Banska Bystrica. The journeys you take will be job-hunting trips for the fall. If you think of it like that, it should be easy for you."

Maria was tired on the trip back. The sun gave way to clouds. On the train, she tried to compose a letter to her parents, but failed. She could not invent a believable reason for her "decision" to attend dressmaking school. She knew what their response would be.

Maria spent the next few days preparing for her move. School was out. Anna and the Puchys were puzzled by both her plans and her assurances that the danger had passed; but it made them more comfortable to believe her than not.

There was a midsummer festival in Hrinova the night before she left, with a bonfire and circle dancing. The peasants wore their finest embroidered clothes. The warm evening brought out almost everyone in the village.

Maria was standing by the fire listening to the music when Miso came up to her, drunk and obnoxious. "Hey, schoolteacher, let's have some fun."

Maria smiled and turned away, whirling her dress. As she walked toward the Puchys she heard Miso shout, "Hey, Hanka, let's have a dance," as he grabbed Hanka and started to twirl him in all directions, both drunk as jackasses on a Friday night.

Maria placed the worry with Miso in the back of her mind. With her new-found friend, the colonel, she felt protected from Miso; he was no longer a threat.

That night, lying in her cot, Maria thought how beautiful the evening was—the dancing, music and the laughter of the people of the village. Soon the melodies of the songs turned to dreams and she was asleep. In the morning, she woke to timid knocking on the school door. She folded her cot and tried to make herself presentable before opening the door. She held her nightgown tightly at the collar as she cautiously peeped out the door. It was Miso. "My God, Miso. What is it now? I am surprised that you can walk this morning."

He apologized, "I just wanted to let you know that everything will be all right for you and your aunt and her wonderful young son. It seems, after all, that she is your aunt and the boy will be starting school when the new term begins. I just wanted to tell you how sorry I am about this misunderstanding. It is all straightened out, so there won't be any more trouble from me."

Maria nonchalantly replied, "See, Miso, I told you she was my aunt, but you just wouldn't listen." With that, she closed the door as leisurely as she had opened it. A feeling of exultation ran through her body. Polack had kept his word.

Maria packed her things, then went to the room to see Anna. She told her that she would be away for awhile, but not to worry. There would be more room with her gone and more to eat. Jan was going to look after her.

As Maria closed the door, Anna babbled on about seeing Dr. Klein again. Her back and shoulders were killing her and she had developed a severe pain in her right foot.

Maria raised her eyebrows and thought, "Yeah, probably from sticking her foot in her mouth."

The train rolled into Banska Bystrica. This time, Maria recognized her surroundings and went directly to the Chernys' house. They were delighted to see her. The three of them had coffee and chatted about her trip. Nothing else. Neither Maria nor the Chernys wanted to offer any more information than necessary.

Mrs. Cherny terminated the conversation. "We have kept you long enough. I'm sure you want to go and say hello to Madame Zolkoff."

Maria agreed, "I was just about to suggest that myself."

Maria stood, patted Mrs. Cherny on the back and thanked them both for being so kind. Leaving the house, she walked leisurely down the street, remembering Polack's words, "Do not bring attention to yourself." She enjoyed the people and the hustle and bustle that she had not known in her own town.

She turned the corner and saw the emporium. Before entering, she paused at the show window to admire the design and beauty of Madame Zolkoff's creations. Maria wondered where all the material came from. She had never seen anything like it—certainly not during wartime.

The tinkle of the petite brass bell above the door announced Maria's arrival. Seeing her, Madame Zolkoff walked toward her, displaying an insignificant smile. "Ah, Maria, how nice to see you again. This time I can take you on a short tour of the boutique."

She walked directly in front of Maria, pointing out the different styles, stitching and designs of her work.

Maria remarked, "Madame Zolkoff, these are gorgeous! How do you obtain this material in wartime?"

"You will learn . . . all in good time." She led Maria to the sewing area located in the rear of the shop, "Here is where you will work. I have no time for nonsense, so please let's have none of it."

Maria consoled her, "I am only here to learn and to help you in any way that I can. I have no intention of causing you any grief."

Madame ignored her response. She continued, "The first thing you will notice, Maria, is all of the apparel is of the highest quality. Don't go anywhere near these garments."

Maria held back a smile, thinking to herself, "Christ, I am going from the frying pan into the fire."

Madame gave Maria more instructions. "Now, the first thing that you will do tomorrow is to bring in a couple of your old dresses for practice. I will teach you the correct and proper way to launch your new career."

Then she left, waving her arms about as though she were giving a final performance before making a grand exit from a stage. Maria found it very amusing. Madame returned as suddenly as she had departed and said, "What are you waiting for? There is nothing for you to do now. You will begin tomorrow. Be on time. I do not tolerate tardiness. People who do not pay attention to punctuality will never pay attention to anything else."

Madame gracefully pointed toward the door. Maria took this gesture as her cue to exit and close the door behind her. Outside, she walked a few steps, stopped, turned and looked back at the showroom window again. An enormous smile spread across her face. She giggled. She lost control of her emotions like a dam giving way during a flood. Finally, she gave way completely and began to roar with laughter. She was masquerading as a seamstress.

In the morning, Maria reported with an old, blue coat. Madame tore the garment to shreds, throwing the large pieces to the top of the table and the smaller ones to the bottom. Maria watched as her coat was dismantled. If Madame knew that Maria had only two, she might have suggested an apron or an old hat. Coats, dresses, hats, or aprons, it didn't matter one way or the other. Since the War started, Maria had nothing.

When the slaughter of the coat stopped, Madame Zolkoff stepped back and said, "There now, I want you to turn all of the material inside-out, the lining, too, then follow this pattern. Begin by stitching these two. When you finish that, I want you to learn a more difficult stitch. Only a few people know how and when to use it. I, however, do know. I will leave you to your work."

The directions she gave to Maria were more like orders: stitch this; move this over here; tear this out; I never told you to do anything like this, make this round, not square; where is your common sense? This procedure continued for days. It didn't bother Maria. She knew Madame Zolkoff was exactly what she said she was, a true artist.

The day Maria finished the coat, Madame Zolkoff demanded to watch Maria sew the last few stitches. Then, Madame ordered her to help straighten up the store. Maria did as requested, but every time she started cleaning, Madame reappeared and impatiently prodded, "Well, try on the coat, we don't have all day, you know."

Maria brushed away the threads that still clung to the material, but was told, "Hurry up, Maria, you can take care of all that later."

Maria walked over to the huge mirror hanging on the back wall with Madame right behind her. As she placed her arm into the sleeve and lifted the coat to her shoulders, Madame pulled at the bottom of the coat. Then she pulled at the shoulders, running her arms down the sleeves.

Maria stared at her reflection in the mirror and mumbled to herself, "My God, I really am beautiful."

The coat was a masterpiece. She had never owned nor seen anything so heavenly in all her life. It was breathtaking. She looked repeatedly, whispering in disbelief, "Did I really make this? I can't believe it, I just can't believe it."

Madame Zolkoff stood to her right when Maria glanced once more into the mirror. Maria noticed a delicate smile on her face. Immediately realizing she had been exposed, Madame gave Maria a stern look, "Never mind helping clean today, we can do it tomorrow. You can leave now, but be sure you are here first thing tomorrow."

Maria started to remove the coat when Madame snapped, "What are you doing? I said you could go now. And don't leave that awful-looking coat here. Some of my customers might see it. I have a reputation, you know."

Maria yanked her coat back on again. She felt the sleeves and moved her shoulders back and forth; it was a perfect fit. She hurried to the door, stopped and turned again, catching Madame's glance, "Go, now. There is more to life than working in this dress shop," followed by one of her famous lines, "Oh! that I had my youth."

Maria gave her a mammoth smile and departed, "I'll be in first thing. Don't you worry, Madame."

She could hardly wait to walk down the street so everyone in Banska Bystrica could see her new coat. At each store, she stopped and looked at her reflection in the window. Most of the time, others stared at her. She realized Polack prohibited such behavior, but today Maria just didn't care. Today was her day.

That evening, feeling like the most beautiful girl in the city, she returned home. When she reached into the mail box, there it was: the white slip of paper, the signal to contact Polack as soon as possible. Maria followed her instructions. Instead of going home, she went directly to Polack's apartment, located a few blocks from the military headquarters office. The light in the window was there—the signal that all was clear. Maria tapped lightly on the door.

Polack opened it without delay and commented, "You look scared."

"I am scared." Maria told the truth.

"Why? You haven't done anything yet."

"Who cares. I am still scared. Another thing: I am not used to being in a man's apartment. That alone scares me."

"The reason I signaled you to come here, Maria, is to give us an alibi. We can always say that we are lovers. First, I want to instill in you the rule that if you are ever caught, always stick as close as possible to the truth."

"Just what does that mean?"

"I don't mean that we are going to be lovers. My God, I am trying to fight a war. I consider you one of the nation's soldiers that I give orders to, that's all. Remember, stay as close to the truth as you can. That way, it will be easier for you to recall the same story if you are ever questioned."

He shook his head, hoping that would put Maria's mind at ease over the meeting. Then, with a slight smile, he continued, "I want you to go to the city of Martin, sixty miles north. Go to the museum, stand in front of the display on the first floor marked number twelve at 1300 hours tomorrow. Your code name will be Gita. A man will ask you if that is your name. He will give you an oral message. Return and repeat it to me.

"I must tell you this, Maria. We have lost many couriers. You must look like the situation that you are in. Dress accordingly. If you are detained, remember what I told you about sticking close to the truth. Don't shun the Germans. You are a beautiful girl and they will want to talk with you. I understand that your German is flawless. Regardless, don't back off and don't overplay your hand. Go home and get some sleep. You must leave first thing in the morning. And now you may leave this den of sin." They both laughed as Polack walked Maria to the front door.

Maria was on the first train to Martin. The car threw her from side to side, as the steel wheels screeched at every turn. She pondered how intelligent Polack must be. All of the thought he put into the logistics of recruiting her. From her house, she need only cross the tracks and enter the rear of the train station, ducking the German guards at the checkpoint. Madame's dress shop; arrangements to take care of Anna; silencing that stupid Miso. All these events had to be carefully planned for her to become a courier. Maria thought: They must be losing a lot of people if they had to go to such extremes to recruit her.

When she left the train, she noticed a young girl selling flowers on the platform of the station. For a minute, she was going to ask her directions to the museum but reeled in her enthusiasm, realizing the Germans may have placed someone in a strategic position to procure information from arriving passengers. Maria turned and passed through the checkpoint without incident. On the street, she noticed an elderly carriage driver feeding a small turnip to his horse. She was sure he was safe, knowing that anyone loving animals couldn't possibly harm others. He pointed out the museum. Maria walked toward the museum with an even stride, trying not to call attention to herself. She arrived early and decided to view the exhibits on the second floor.

She loved art. The trip gave her an opportunity to see a few rare sculptures. Most of the art had been hidden to avoid damage from the bombing raids. The rumor was the Germans carted off most of the valuable art to Berlin. However, they always left some, knowing it would keep the people tranquil.

Maria glanced at her watch, it was 1300 hours. She walked as though she were examining several bronze sculptures, continuing to blend in with the visitors, down the stairs to the first floor. She moved slowly, almost loitering, as she approached exhibit number twelve. She glanced gently from side to side, but saw no one. Then she looked at exhibit twelve. It was a huge bronze figure of a Slovak soldier. Beneath the statute read the title, *Hero of the Republic.* She stood for a second and thought, "How can this be? The Germans would never allow such a bronze figure on display." Something was wrong or else the Underground had taken over the museum during the night.

A man asked, "Pardon me, is your name, by chance, Gita?"

"Why, yes, it is," Maria answered naively.

A little old man with a balding head and brilliant green eyes, smiled, "I knew your mother from my school days in Banska Bystrica. But, oh, that was so many years ago. You look so much like her. How is she?"

"She is doing just fine. I saw her only last week."

Maria's contact continued, "When you see her next, would you give her a message from me? Tell her that some of her old school chums are coming to see her. All of them are making their arrangements in the next two weeks. Tell her that Mr. Obcheck will not be able to attend. Will you remember to tell her that?"

"Yes, I will remember, there is no need to repeat it," Maria answered.

The unnamed man asked, "Are you enjoying the exhibits?"

"Yes, it is so seldom that I get out these days, but I love to view the exhibits."

"What do you think of twelve here?"

"I can't believe it." Maria responded softly.

"Neither can anyone else. If the Germans notice it, it will be the curator's last day here . . . and on earth." He grasped Maria's hands and said, "Do what you can and may God watch over you." He quickly disappeared.

Maria mixed into a small group leaving the building. She soon found herself on the street. On her way, she stopped at the small four-seat restaurant and ordered coffee. Making sure that she wasn't followed, she waited for a half hour before she returned to the train depot.

The return trip was much different. German troops traveled with their weapons. This meant the Germans were reinforcing their garrisons. Their occupation became more pervasive. That meant trouble. It was common to see troop trains rolling through the country. But when troops traveled with civilians, they were being assigned to reinforce an area where trouble was expected.

After her return, Maria reported to Polack at once. He had the light in the window so she hurried up the stairs to his apartment. She knocked, but there was no answer; she turned to leave when the door opened.

Polack greeted her, "Maria, come in, come in. Have some wine. You're from the mountains, and everyone knows mountain people love wine."

As soon as Polack closed the door, Maria delivered her message. Then she relaxed and enjoyed some heavy red wine, swirling it around the glass and inhaling its bouquet.

She went over the trip step by step while Polack encouraged her to have several glasses of wine. He reasoned, if the apartment were watched, it would be better if she stayed for an hour or so. Maria agreed. It gave her an opportunity to get to know Polack better. She found he was difficult to talk to. He was always closed-mouthed, not wanting Maria to know anything about the Underground. She told him about the dress shop and how hard Madame Zolkoff was on the outside while, inside, she had a heart of gold, a heart that she never wanted anyone to see. Neither Maria nor Polack could figure out why. Apparently, she was just that way. Polack offered his standard analysis, "It's the War."

Maria walked into the kitchen and left her wine glass on the counter. When she returned to the living room, Polack said, "It is nice having you here for a visit. Don't worry, you must bear in mind that if we are suspected as lovers, we must spend some time together."

For the next half hour, Maria carried the conversation. Polack tried to act interested, but when Maria noticed his interest ebbing, she looked at her watch and realized it was time for her to go. She rose and thanked him, "Thank you for a lovely evening and the wine; it was perfect. The evening and the wine."

Polack opened the door for her. He kept an eye on her from the window until she turned, looked up at him and gave a dainty wave, then disappeared from under the streetlight.

Maria continued with her dress making. Madame never mentioned her absence, nor did Maria offer an explanation as to her whereabouts. Seeing that Maria was capable, Madame allowed her to put hems in some of her finest creations. Maria grinned and thought, "I have finally graduated."

It was the weekend, Maria was always happy when she could return to the school. To her, it was a place of security. On this weekend, she was surprised to find Olga waiting. Maria thought that something must be wrong. Olga quickly assured her that all was well. She had only come to bring Anna some food and clothes and to spend a little time with Maria.

They attended church together Sunday. Father Andre, seeing Maria, asked where she had been. Maria explained to him that she was attending a sewing school in Banska Bystrica. He rolled his eyes toward heaven, shrugged his shoulders and walked off.

Maria enjoyed her visit with Olga. They packed a lunch and walked through the woods that surrounded the school. Those woods were always magnificent, no matter what season. Olga repeatedly asked Maria why she began a sewing apprenticeship in Banska Bystrica. Wasn't there anyone in the village that could help her? Maria would always change the subject.

Pressed once too often, she fabricated on explanation, "I met a young man who lives there. I see him quite often, so I decided it would be easier if I moved to the city. I thought I would learn sewing at the same time, you know, you have to have an excuse. I couldn't say, 'let me follow you.' Now, he has a place to come and see me."

Olga warned, "This just isn't the time for becoming involved with anyone, Maria. There are rumors that the Germans are pulling back from the Russian Front. We may find ourselves in the next battlefield of the War. Wait until all of this is over before you start thinking about a man."

Maria promised, "I will, Olga. It is only for the summer, anyway. Afterwards, I'll return here to teach."

That afternoon, Maria took the train to Banska Bystrica. Olga stood on the platform waving as the train rolled off in the distance. Looking down the rails, Olga saw the two tracks become one. Soon the train appeared as nothing more than a dot.

At Madame's the next afternoon, Maria met Polack for lunch at their arranged meeting place along the river. Polack had a worried look. He told Maria that couriers were being picked up one after another. He felt that someone inside the Underground was leaking information to the Germans. Consequently, he needed to increase her courier activities. She would now travel twice a week, instead of once.

For the next few weeks, Maria shuffled back and forth between outlying cities, repeating messages to Polack. She felt her services were routine and that there was no danger involved. However, her thoughts were dispelled near the end of July 1944.

Polack told her to take the train to Bratislava, the capital of Slovkia. She was to go to the Department of Commerce and contact Mr. Slavik, a high-ranking official with the department. He would give her a radio. Usually, Maria had no idea what was in the packages. But this time, Polack, realizing that if she were caught she would face a death sentence, thought it best to tell her what she would be carrying. Maria already knew that carrying a short wave radio was the same as committing treason and was dealt with as seriously.

Maria's contact, Mr. Slavik was a former Nazi sympathizer who had switched sides, knowing the War was going against the Germans. He tried to impress Maria by telling her that he was one of the most important individuals in the Resistance. She knew that he was worse than a neutral; he was an opportunist who, like the chameleon, changed colors to adapt to his current surroundings. Neutrals always presented themselves as better than others. Yet, if they were not for the country, Maria concluded, they must be against it. She viewed them with contempt.

Maria took the heavy package from Mr. Slavik and was glad to be rid of him. Before leaving his office, she hid the heavy, cumbersome shortwave radio in her suitcase. She lifted it without assistance, pretending it was easy to manage, and left. Outside, she couldn't believe how difficult it was to handle; the weight was almost too much for her. She wrestled with it for a few steps, then noticed a horse-drawn carriage. She signaled the driver and let him lift her suitcase into the carriage.

The driver noted, "You won't be able to carry this suitcase very far, miss, you are going to need help."

Maria responded, "Please don't concern yourself. It's only some old books I am borrowing from the Commerce Department. I am on my way back to Banska Bystrica. Would you please take me to the train station."

He was eager to comply, "Certainly, sit back and enjoy the city, it's a nice drive to the station."

Maria was anxious. She knew she should not be riding in the open carriage, someone could easily recognize her. Although, her thoughts were on the radio. How was she going to maneuver this heavy, massive object?

The driver attempted to point out some of the elegance of the city, but Maria couldn't concentrate and failed to notice any of the sights. The closer they got to the train station, the more anxious she became. How was she going to get past the checkpoint at the entrance? How was she going to carry the bulky suitcase without showing her distress from its weight? Usually, she could conceive a clever scheme, but this time, nothing. Her pulse was rapid, her breathing increased and her mouth was dry. They finally reached the station. The old driver helped her down from the carriage and offered, "Would you like me to carry that suitcase of yours into the station?"

Maria approved, "Yes, I already have my return ticket, so we could go directly to the departing platform, but who will watch your horse?"

"Don't worry about her, miss. She knows every stop in the city and, if need be, can find her own way home. This case is really heavy, is someone meeting you at your destination, someone that will be able to help you with this?"

Maria wished, "I hope so."

He pushed other passengers aside, swinging the suitcase and telling them to get out of the way, using the suitcase as a weapon. He was upset because he was aging. His youth had faded, his strength was gone, but he was still a man, and he was going to prove it by carrying this heavy bag all the way to the platform, which he did.

Maria thanked him for his efforts and gave him extra money, suggesting he could feed his horse well tonight. He bowed his head and touched the rim of his stovepipe hat with two fingers as a salute to her kindness. He left with a smile, knowing on this day he was still a man, and a damn good one at that.

Fear overtook Maria. The old man, her last bit of security, had gone. She was alone. What now? How was she to get through the checkpoint? She stood next to her suitcase, tapping her foot, trying to relieve some of her tension. She had to get on that train, and soon. The only thing in her favor was the terminal was disorderly. Troops were everywhere: enlisted men, officers, civilians, nuns and German pilots, going on leave from the Russian Front.

Time ran out. The second boarding call sounded, Maria had to make her move. She reached down and took the suitcase by the sturdy handle, lifted it, took three steps, and heard, "Here, allow me to help you with that. It looks as though it is much too heavy for you."

Maria stepped back as a young officer in the SS raised her suitcase over his head as though it was nothing more than a weapon he was slinging over his shoulder. He extended his free hand and grasped Maria's right hand, "I am Sturmbann Fuhrer Armbrust."

Maria nervously introduced herself, "I am Maria, Maria Zima. I am a teacher from a village north of here and I have been asked to bring these books back to our school. I am sure that the director had no idea that there were so heavy, or he would have sent a man. Thank God you are here."

As they approached the checkpoint, the four military personnel manning it snapped to attention. The three men in civilian clothes, also inspectors, stood rigid as Maria and the sturmbann fuhrer passed. Maria's fears dissipated as the two of them boarded the train. Once in the compartment, the sturmbann fuhrer slung the suitcase into the overhead rack. Immediately, Maria thought of Polack's words, "Use your beauty to your advantage." Removing the dull and unattractive scarf from her head, she brushed her hair free from her collar with her hand, opened her coat and sat directly across from the sturmbann fuhrer. She thanked him, "I don't know what I would have done if you hadn't come along—and just in time."

Maria generated a conversation with the young officer. She told him that she was taking classes in sewing in Banska Bystrica and all about her teaching in the little school that she loved. He interrupted her by asking if she were German. She spoke fluent German, she was tall, blond and had blue eyes.

For a moment the officer thought she might be making sport of him, that she really was German. She finally convinced him when she made the remark that she hoped the occupation would not last too much longer. She wanted to return to the university and complete her doctorate in history.

She found the sturmbann fuhrer handsome and charming. He was well educated and possessed manners that would charm the devil. She could not help but find him attractive, but never forgot he was the enemy. If she were caught, he probably would execute her right there on the train. Regardless, she had to keep up her ruse by flirting, subtly, including glancing at him seductively, making sure he observed her. Their conversations covered history, the War, politics, and the reported collapse of the Russian Front.

Armbrust was taken with Maria, he enjoyed every topic, becoming completely relaxed as they conversed. He told Maria about his military career. When she asked him why he volunteered for the SS, he told her he would find himself politically at the top of the ladder, holding one of the highly-sought-after positions, should Germany win the War.

Several times, Maria stared at him, thinking, "How could this young, innocent man do any wrong? Maybe he never did, but he was SS." Her thoughts were interrupted when the conductor standing at the door announced, "Baggage inspection, baggage inspection!" Then he saw the sturmbann fuhrer and clicked to attention. He glanced at Maria, then over her head to the luggage rack. She leaned toward Armbrust and whispered, "Do you think anyone on the train has coffee, I am dying for some."

The conductor looked at the sturmbann fuhrer again and withdrew from the compartment. Once he left, Maria laughed, "I was only joking, sturmbann fuhrer. I know there isn't any coffee on board. I hope there will be some in Banska Bystrica."

This left an opening for the sturmbann fuhrer; he swiftly took advantage of the timely opportunity, "Would you like to go for coffee when we reach the city?" Maria agreed unequivocally.

Passengers poured from the train when it stopped in Banska Bystrica. Lines formed at the inspection desks. Armbrust had the suitcase on his shoulder and guided Maria with his free arm through the concourse. Without pausing, the sturmbann fuhrer nudged Maria through the inspection point as though it didn't exist. Several guards glanced at Maria and grinned. They were certain she was the mistress of this handsome sturmbann fuhrer. Who would dare question him?

His confidence building with this attractive Czech, Armbrust probed further, "I am not leaving you until we have coffee. On second thought, what about dinner, will you have dinner with me?"

"I would love to have dinner with you." For a second, Maria faced a dilemma: If only there were not a war, if only he were not the enemy. She snapped back to reality and said, "I'll meet you at the Narodny Dom."

"Ahaa, the best restaurant in the city. What time shall we meet?" the SS officer asked.

"Would seven be all right with you, sturmbann fuhrer?"

"Please call me Karl. You can't call me sturmbann fuhrer all the time, it will give everyone the impression you are my driver or secretary."

"Very well, Karl it is. I shall see you around seven," Maria promised.

He beamed, "Seven will be perfect. I am looking forward to a very enjoyable evening."

The encouragement continued, "I'm sure it will be, Karl."

They parted, but each stopped, turned and looked back. After smiling at each other, they continued their separate ways. Maria managed to carry the suitcase to the Chernys' house. She tried to walk like the case was lighter. She didn't want to attract attention. All she needed now was another Nazi officer to offer help and discover the radio.

She was on her way to her room when Mrs. Cherny called to her from the bottom of the stairs, "Maria, a young man came by and said that he would be here at six to see you."

"Thank you, Mrs. Cherny," Maria answered.

Maria had no idea who called for her or what he wanted. Polack was the only one who knew where she lived. Even Madame didn't know, nor did any of the ladies that worked with her. It had to be a messenger sent by Polack. She pushed the short wave radio under her bed and immediately went to freshen up.

Mrs. Cherny kept calling to her, "Maria, come and have something to eat, you must be starving."

Maria was in the kitchen eating fresh bread when she heard the screech of auto brakes in front of the house. Looking out the window, she saw a small gray truck. The driver ran to the front door and knocked. When Maria answered the door, he asked her to come with him and to bring the package with her. Maria hurried up stairs and retrieved the wireless from under the bed, then lugged it down the stairs to the driver. He quickly relieved her of the heavy burden. The two of them buried the radio under the manure piled in the back of the truck and then they sped off.

As the sun set, Maria remembered it was 7 P.M., the time she was supposed to meet Sturmbann Fuhrer Armbrust. She knew he would be in the restaurant listening to music—they would, she thought, never enjoy each other's company.

The messenger drove for an hour to Donovaly, a mountain resort town located in the lower Tatra Mountains. The young man turned off the engine and they sat. They waited for almost an hour. Maria frequently asked the driver how long he intended to wait, but he didn't answer. She then changed the subject, asking him if he were unaccustomed to driving in the area.

He admitted, "I am new at this."

Maria questioned him no further. She was pulling up the collar of her sweater when two men approached from the back of the truck. One stayed slightly to the rear, training a British Sten-gun on the truck, while the other walked directly up to Maria, smiled and said in English, "Do you have something for us?"

Maria kept an eye on the man with the machine gun while she opened her door, "We have it here in the back. It is very heavy. You will have to lift it."

Maria watched as the man dragged the radio out from the pile of manure. She noticed that he was dressed in a combination of civilian clothes and British uniform.

He placed the radio on the ground, asking, "Is this home grown?"

Maria joked, "No, but it's fresh."

He walked over and placed the radio in front of the man waiting for him, then returned to Maria, "I thank you and the people of England thank you."

"On behalf of the Slovak government, you are welcome," Maria said facetiously.

Maria stood for a few seconds while the two men disappeared into the dark, carrying with them the heavy radio. She was happy to be rid of it. She knew that the wireless was going to a British agent. This made her feel useful. It wasn't like passing messages; it was exciting, yet dangerous. She did it for Czechoslovakia, her nation. She loved her country.

When she returned home, Mrs. Cherny handed her an envelope. Maria opened it, the only thing written on the page was, "0700."

Polack wanted to see her at seven in the morning. She rose at six, dressed and had breakfast with Mrs. Cherny. Maria walked with confidence along the river toward the meeting place. Polack was already there when she arrived. He asked her if everything went well the previous evening. She assured him that they had no problems and that the delivery went without incident. He appeared nervous—unusual for him.

"Maria, I want you to go by train to Trechin." He impressed upon her the message she would deliver was vital. More importantly, she was not to return until she delivered it. He repeated the message to her several times.

Finally, Maria had to stop him. "Polack, I understand. You don't need to repeat yourself. What is the trouble? You are uneasy. Is there anything I can do to help?"

"Nothing, Maria. Everything is in order." Polack calmed down and continued, "Please go and deliver the message, and be careful."

Not wanting to probe any deeper, Maria assured him that she would follow his orders. She went directly to the train station and purchased her ticket to Trenchin. Maria didn't waste any time. She felt something was not quite right. Following the directions Polack gave her, she rushed to the home of Milos Havlik, the head master of the local school. When she knocked on the door she was met by a beautiful young girl. Maria asked, "Is Mr. Havlik home?"

The girl responded coldly, "No, he isn't."

"Do you expect him soon?" Maria asked.

"Why do you want to see my husband?" The girl was perturbed and questioned Maria, "What do you want with him?"

Maria made an excuse, "I am a teacher in Banska Bystrica. I heard that there may be an opening for an instructor at his school, and I would like to apply for the position."

"Shouldn't you take care of that sort of thing at the school and not here at our home?" Havlik's wife asked.

"I wasn't really sure where the school was and someone directed me here," Maria explained. "I am sorry if I am causing you any trouble, it's just that I didn't know what else to do. I have to take this evening's train back to the city. I don't want to spend most of my time looking for him because I might miss my train. Do you mind if I wait?"

Mrs. Havlik objected, "Yes, I do mind. I don't know what he is up to, but he is always gone, never here. I have no idea what he is doing. I know that he isn't at the school. I thought he was drinking, now I am not even sure of that. If you want to see him, just sit right out there on the street until he comes, you are not staying in this house."

Maria lingered in front of the house as instructed, then she walked up and down the streets, through the tiny alleys looking into the shops. There was nothing else to do. Feeling conspicuous and no longer wanting to remain on the streets, she moved through the trees to the back of the house.

The sun was going down and the mountain air was creating a chill. Maria pulled the collar of her light trench coat up around her neck, trying to keep warm. Hours passed, she waited. Fatigued from the trip, she stood and stretched her back. Pulling up the sleeve of her coat, she peered at her watch, it was two in the morning. She decided to walk to increase her circulation and to try to keep warm.

As she walked to the front of the house, a man appeared out of nowhere and demanded, "Who are you, and what do you want?"

"Never mind that, are you Milos?" Maria asked.

Milos acknowledged, "Yes, are you looking for me?"

"That's right. I have a message for you: 'The dam is ready to break, four and two are six and three makes nine.' Now, can you tell me where I can find a place to sleep? And please don't say in your house. Your wife is ready to kill you and me. The poor girl thinks that you are with other women."

"I know that," Milos said. "It is one of my biggest problems and I am not really sure how to solve it. But it is my problem not yours. Yours seems to be finding a place to sleep at this hour."

He walked over to the side of the house and opened two large storm doors that lead to the cellar, "Sleep down there and try to be as quiet as you can. There are some blankets in the corner, right next to the entrance on your right."

Maria didn't argue. She was happy to be out of the cold mountain air.

In the morning, Maria quietly latched the doors leading to the cellar and walked to the train station. She waited for what seemed like hours. Finally, the platform filled with early morning travelers. They talked to one another almost in whispers. They discussed the latest news: Tracks were blown up, troops were deserting and the nation was restless. Once on the train, Maria picked up the newspaper on the seat next to her and read that Monsignor Tiso, President of Slovakia, had been called hurriedly to Berlin to meet with the Fuhrer. He was a puppet of the Nazi regime in Slovakia and the people hated him. However, he was still being received by the Pope. The Slovak people never understood why.

Two men sitting directly behind her discussed the latest news from the BBC: Slovakian Partisans were engaged in a battle with the government forces near Parnica, in the northern part of the country.

Her thoughts were interrupted when a voice called her name, "Maria!"

It was Marsha, her former classmate from the school in Presov. It had been two years since their last meeting. As they sat and chatted, Maria learned Marsha was married to a captain in the Slovak Army. They lived in Banska Bystrica and he was stationed at the headquarters building there. They talked mostly about the old days in school, the other girls, the teachers and their vacations. Marsha glanced out the window and noticed they had arrived in Banska Bystrica. She invited Maria to visit her the following evening at her home.

The next morning, Maria reported her successful delivery to Polack. Afterward, she decided to rest and not go to work.

In the evening, she dressed and walked to Marsha's home for dinner. She was introduced to Captain Vesta, Marsha's husband. He was tall and slender, with straight black hair that kept falling down on his forehead. There was a gap between his front teeth, causing him to whistle when he said a word with an s in it. He had a pleasant manner, but seemed slightly arrogant.

They were enjoying an after-dinner wine, when Captain Vesta mentioned, "When the communists take over, it will be a blessing for the Slovak people."

Maria was horrified. She listened in disbelief. She assumed that the liberation forces were all one group.

The captain continued, "The Red Army is forming in the mountains. Soon they will sweep the country, freeing us all."

"What of our liberation forces?" Maria asked.

"Russia will be the liberating force," was the captain's authoritative response.

Maria declared, "Colonel Polack told me that we would govern ourselves under a constitution when the fighting ends."

"Colonel Polack is a dreamer," responded Captain Vesta. "He believes we can side with the West, but you have seen what the West has done to us in Munich. Our future is safe only if we side with Mother Russia."

"There is no way I could ever embrace the communist philosophy. I hate dictators, whether they are German or Russian," Maria argued.

The captain offered his final words, "It doesn't matter if you embrace it or not, that is how it is going to be."

Maria stood, hugged Marsha and shook hands with Captain Vesta. "I have many things I must attend to tomorrow, so I should return home now and get some sleep."

"Yes, I hear that you are doing an excellent job," Captain Vesta commented.

"What do you mean, 'doing an excellent job?' Where did you hear that?" Maria demanded.

Captain Vesta said slyly, "We have our ways of knowing things, Maria."

"By excellent work, do you mean that I am still alive?" She smiled and thanked them again for the dinner.

On returning home, Maria was surprised to find Polack waiting for her. He never did this and she knew it must be important. "Maria, I have been receiving reports about Anna. She is still seeing Dr. Klein and having frequent conversations with people in the area."

"Maria furiously replied, I can't believe that bitch. I'm telling you she is going to get everyone killed: Julius, Olga, the Puchys and that fat slob, Miso. But who would miss him?"

Polack began, "Here is the plan . . ."

"The plan?" Maria interrupted. "I should just go and put her ass on a bus to anywhere. Who would care? The bus driver? She would have him crazy before he drove her a mile. . . . I'm sorry. What is the plan?"

"Here is the plan: I am moving my grandmother to Rysovo, an isolated mountain village. She will be safe there and I want to take Anna and her son along. Early tomorrow morning, I will send an army staff car to pick you up. My grandmother will be in the car. The driver will take you to Hrinova. You put Anna and her son in there with her. They will all go to the same resort. That way I will be rid of my problem, and you won't be bothered with Anna any longer."

In the morning, the staff car arrived. Maria hurried out of the house as the driver opened the door of the car for her and introduced the passenger, "Madame Polevka this is Miss Zima."

Madame acknowledged the introduction by dropping her head slightly. Nina Polevka was a woman in her late sixties with mop-like hair. Her nose was so small, one had to look twice to make sure that she wasn't breathing through a wart. She was a senile, old, neglected woman.

The trip took several hours. During the ride, Maria and Nina Polevka talked about the Nazis. The old lady cracked jokes and laughed until she could hardly breathe. Maria thought several times the lady was going to have a heart attack.

The chauffeur started driving faster, fearing that if he were stopped, the old woman would make one of her remarks about Hitler and they would all be put to death on the spot.

They arrived at Hrinova at 1800 hours. Maria hurried up the steps to her old room, knocked on the door and quickly explained to Anna that the staff car was waiting and she must pack and leave at once.

Anna started yelling that it was a German staff car and that Maria had betrayed her. From previous experience, Maria did nothing, she allowed Anna to continue. The protests became so loud that the Puchys came out to see what the trouble was. Seeing the German staff car, they hid by the corner of the school.

David put his book down and packed his things in his travel bag. Maria offered him a hand, assuring him that all would be safe and not to worry.

Anna and David carried their belongings to the waiting car and the driver put the baggage in the trunk. Maria hugged David tightly, then helped him into the back seat. Anna slammed herself down, demanding to know who the old woman was and where they were going.

Nina Polevka put her arm around David's shoulder and said, "Did I ever tell you the one about the SS general?"

The car moved slowly forward. As it pulled away, Maria could hear Anna, "If we are going higher into the mountains, I will need more blankets. David, did you bring your mittens? That Maria is nothing more than a damn Nazi herself, doing all of this to me when she knows how sick I am. Who is this old woman back here?"

When the car was out of sight, the Chernys cautiously moved from the side of the school. Jan inquired, "What was that all about?"

Maria explained, "Anna is gone, gone forever. I am not a hateful person, but if I had a gun, I swear to God that I would have emptied nine rounds into her myself."

Jan offered, "Come, Maria. It is time for some wine, and God knows we can all use a drink after this."

It was several hours before the car returned. The driver stayed and had several glasses of wine, then warned Maria that they must be getting back. It was a government car and someone had to account for it. The driver, not wanting to know what was happening, drove speedily back to Banska Bystrica with Maria. He stopped in front of Maria's house, nodded his head in a farewell and drove off.

In the morning, Maria tried to resume her normal duties at the dress shop. She arrived and smiled at her boss, "Good morning, Madame."

"Child, where have you been?" Madame Zolkoff inquired.

Maria lied, "I haven't been feeling well, I decided to stay home for a few days."

"It is nice to have you back to work," Madame said casually. "There is so much to do."

Chapter Three

THE UPRISING

As she started sorting material, Maria saw Polack through the window. He motioned with facial expressions, indicating she should leave the shop at once. Madame Zolkoff also noticed Colonel Polack motioning to Maria.

Maria apologized, "Madame, I'm sorry, but I think that I am going to be sick again."

Madame excused her, "I can't have you sick around the customers. You should take off until you feel better."

"I think you are right," Maria agreed. "I'll go home and lie down for the rest of the day and come back in the morning. Is that all right with you?"

"Certainly. If you are not better tomorrow, take a few days off. You know we have many cases of pneumonia this time of year. You must be careful," Madame cautioned.

Once outside, Maria looked for Polack. He was standing at the corner. She rushed over to him and said, "What is it? What's the matter?"

He nervously shared his concerns, "I think they are on to us! I have reports on my desk asking who you are and why you are in the city."

"What should I do?" Maria asked.

"It isn't a problem now, but I am sure they will follow you," Polack reported.

"And you say that isn't a problem? What do you call it?" Maria demanded.

Polack explained, "They suspect you; they aren't sure of anything, yet. If they were sure, you wouldn't be standing here, I can tell you that."

Maria didn't understand. "Why can't you do something? After all, you are the head of the security."

"Yes, but this bunch of officials isn't known to anyone. I think they came from Berlin," Polack reasoned.

"Great, just great. What do I do now?" Maria wanted to know.

"We can't do anything about it now. You must go to Budca," Polack instructed. "I will arrange transportation—the old truck again. The driver will know where to take you. A Czechoslovakian officer will parachute in. You will take him to the large barn on the right as you leave town. It sits about three hundred yards from the main house. It's isolated and close to trees that he can use for cover, should anything go wrong. The officer's name is Pavlovich and his safety is crucial to the Partisans."

By nightfall, Maria and the driver of the old truck were on their way to Budca. The driver complained about the risk: The truck had government license plates so the Partisans, who were fighting nearby, might mistake them for Nazis. They could never convince the Partisans they were not attached to the Nazi government forces.

Maria and her driver arrived at the designated clearing without incident. Within minutes of their arrival, a Russian bomber made one pass over the clearing. Seconds later, they saw the outline of a parachute against the full moon. As it fell, its outline became larger and more defined.

The officer hit the ground in front of them with an enormous thud, falling backwards. Maria and the driver ran to assist him. They gathered his chute, dug a hole and buried it in the newly-plowed field. All three of them hurried along the path leading to the farm house. As Polack promised, the barn was approximately three hundred yards behind the house and it was isolated—an ideal hiding place.

Following her orders, Maria told Pavlovich he was to remain hidden until she contacted him. He was prohibited from seeing anyone. Once they settled him in the barn with his gear, Maria

The Uprising

explained she could do nothing more then; when she received additional orders, she would return.

Pavlovich offered his broad smile and replied, "I guess it is all up to you."

Feeling that Pavlovich wanted to talk to someone—anyone—Maria sat on the corner of an old tub used as an animal feeder and continued the conversation. The driver didn't care about Pavlovich and wanted to leave immediately, but Maria felt she should listen to the officer, if only for a minute.

Pavlovich willingly described his past, "I was an army officer when the Nazis came. I escaped to Russia and found communism is the only way of life. How are things here in Slovakia?"

Maria thought to herself, "I've just met this man and he is already trying to pry information out of me; another comrade has landed."

"Are things better or worse?" He persisted.

Maria asked, "Better or worse than what? Things are as they are in every occupied country. We are short of fuel, food, medicine, clothes, and, naturally, you can't trust anyone. I really must go now. I have to be at work early in the morning."

The driver peeped through a crack in the barn door, then delicately opened it. He peered out into the darkness, as though he expected an army waiting to capture him.

Pavlovich stood by the door and said, "Thank you again, Maria. I appreciate all that you have done for me."

"Good night, Pavlovich. I will come as soon as I hear anything or receive orders," Maria promised.

For the next week, Maria received no communication from Polack. The usual white piece of paper he left in the mailbox signaling he wanted to see her did not appear. She hesitated to visit his apartment, fearing she may bring suspicion upon him.

Coming from the market one afternoon, Maria noticed the courier driver that had taken her to the meeting with Pavlovich. She hurried and crossed the street to meet him, inquiring, "Pavel, what has happened to Polack? I haven't seen nor heard from him in over a week."

"Didn't they tell you? You are being followed. I don't think they will ever use you again. It's too dangerous, besides Polack is out of the city. Military occupation is increasing all over Slovakia."

"Well that's just peachy. What do I do in the meantime? I knew that I was being followed, but Polack said not to worry, so I didn't. What am I supposed to do now? I get followed and Polack deserts me. I can't go back to my family and I no longer have my job."

"Just be glad you are still alive. Other than that, I have no answers."

Depressed, Maria strolled leisurely toward her living quarters. Once in her bedroom, she sat and stared at the floor. She felt alone and abandoned. What about Pavlovich? For all she knew, he was still alone in the barn.

Pavlovich, who had heard nothing from Maria, was lying in the sun in the heavily-wooded area behind the barn. Here he spent most of his days in the sun, undetected by the Germans or passers-by. Returning to his hiding place in the barn from one of his usual days in the sun, he recognized the dreaded sound of screeching tires and excited voices coming from the main house. He stayed hidden in the underbrush and watched as German troops rapidly surrounded the home. After several gunshots, three men marched out at bayonet point and were thrown into the back of a German Army truck.

Pavlovich hurried back to the barn, buried his equipment in the mud by the pig pens, then quickly washed. He donned a dress shirt and a jacket and a worn Slovak mountain cap. That evening, he made his way into the city. By morning, he was standing on the train platform among the many workers waiting for trains.

After breakfast, Maria decided to find Polack. She hurried through the rear of the station, then stopped abruptly. She couldn't believe her eyes. Standing on the station platform in front of her was Pavlovich. She eventually maneuvered her way through the sea of passengers until she stood next to him. She directed him, "Follow me."

Pavlovich explained that he was going home to see his family in Nitra, sixty miles to the south. Maria begged him not to go.

The Uprising

Pavlovich insisted. Maria tried again to convince him to stay, at least until she could contact Polack. Pavlovich refused to have anything more to do with Colonel Polack and suspected him of being a traitor.

"Why do you suspect him of that?" Maria asked.

"Someone betrayed me because the Nazis raided my hiding place yesterday."

Maria was distressed. "My God. They must be closing in on us. Who did it?"

"How should I know? I just got here, remember?" He continued his protests. "It had to be you or Polack. You were the only ones who knew I was coming."

In disbelief, Maria tried not to raise her voice, "Me? You are out of your mind. I assure you I was not the one who turned you in."

She escorted Pavlovich to the coffee room so they could talk while he waited for the train to Nitra. Maria listened to a repeat of the story she heard from Masha's husband. This Slovak officer trained in Russia for the past five years with the sole purpose of helping the Russians liberate Slovakia. The story was identical: When Slovakia was under Russian control, the nation would finally be free.

He sensed Maria did not share his sentiments so he changed the subject and talked about his family. They weren't that far away, and if his days were numbered, he wanted to be with them, if only for awhile. He tried to convince Maria that she was not safe, either. He concluded Polack left or was taken into custody, abandoning Maria. She had to admit he made sense. Pavlovich suggested she take the train with him to Nitra. She agreed. Traveling as a couple seemed wiser than going alone. So, off they went.

They slept most of the way. On their arrival, Maria stayed on the platform and wished Pavlovich well. She crossed the tracks to wait for the train back to Banska Bystrica.

On the return trip, Maria wondered what to do. There was no place to go, she had no contacts. Should she involve her family in her situation? Pavlovich told her that if he were not caught he would return to her apartment in Banska Bystrica.

There was only one thing to do now: stay out of sight and hide in her room.

Four days later, a man arrived at the Chernys' house. He was shown in by Mr. Cherny. "Maria, there is a man here to see you."

The visitor was a tall, unassuming man who could have been an artist. He seemed bored with life. Even his speech was lethargic. He looked anemic; he was ghostly white.

He delivered his message, "Pavlovich is back and wants to speak with you."

Maria was surprised. "Pavlovich, my God where is he?"

"He wants you to come with me."

"Just a minute." Maria hurried back to her room and grabbed her lightweight jacket, then returned. They left the house and walked through the streets of the city. Maria, out of habit, frequently glanced over her shoulder to make sure that they were not followed. They walked two miles out of town to a wooded area that surrounded the city. Leaving the main road, they entered the heavy underbrush, toward the foot of the mountains.

Suddenly, the bushes moved and Pavlovich appeared, "Ta daaa ... Maria, I'm glad you are still alive."

"So am I," she confirmed.

"Conditions are too hazardous in the city. You can no longer stay there," Pavlovich warned.

Maria was curious. "Why? What have you heard?"

He reported, "Plenty. An uprising is about to occur. I am sure you have figured that out with all of the military activity."

Maria wondered, "What do you want me to do?"

"I want you to leave right away for the mountains," Pavlovich ordered.

Maria hesitated, "I can't. I don't have any clothes with me."

"It isn't a good idea for you to return, but if you have to, I guess there isn't much we can do about it, is there?" Pavlovich reasoned.

Maria wanted to return home not only to gather some clothes to take to the mountains, but to explain to the Chernys that she might not return. She hoped they would understand.

She threw handfuls of heavy winter clothes into her knapsack and hurried back to Pavlovich.

He briefed her, "Maria, the reason I am asking you to go into the mountains is that it is essential you find two officers: Major Oleg Maslov and Captain Igor Yeagorof. Both are setting up units in the mountains north of Terchova. When you find them, tell them to set up communications with my unit. We will use Terchova as the center for all communications, for now. You are the only one who can do it because you speak Russian, German, Czechoslovakian, English and God knows what else. I'll have one of my drivers take you to Terchova. From there you will have to find your own way into the mountains. I wish I could tell you where the two of them are, but, unfortunately, I have no idea. That is why the communication network is so important."

Maria asserted, "I'll do my best to find them, but I want you to understand as soon as I convey your message to them, I am going to join the Slovak Liberation Forces. You can play footsies with the Russians, but not me. I want nothing to do with them or their communist doctrine."

The driver took Maria to Terchova, as promised. She was on her own, now. She stood at the edge of town looking over the breathtaking sights—the low, rolling mountains and the leaves caught in the first breeze of winter. She watched as the sky filled with color. In the stratosphere, thin clouds blew in all directions.

Maria remained motionless thinking, "How beautiful God's earth is. Man, well, he is a cancer eating away at all that is holy, bent on destroying himself and his world."

A voice surprised Maria, "Hello, beautiful lady."

Maria spun around and looked into the face of a little, white-haired mountain man. Sticks were piled high on his shoulder, all wrapped neatly in small bundles. He was collecting his firewood early. He added, "I know everyone in the mountains, and you are not from here."

"No, I am not," Maria admitted. "But, maybe you could help me. I am looking for two Russian officers forming units in the mountains near here. Have you seen any soldiers in your travels?"

"Oh, yes," he pointed off in the distance, "Way over there, in those hills, you know, between Brezno and Donovaly. They are all in that area. I haven't seen any Russians, though, only our own men. If you are going there, miss, you should watch out for the Germans. What I have seen of these Partisan groups, you should watch out for them, too."

"Thank you. I'll be careful," Maria promised.

The old man walked away, then turned and said, "Come to think of it, anyone as pretty as you should watch out for everybody."

Maria meandered toward Brezno. She traveled one path, then another. She had to take cover several times when a German reconnaissance plane passed overhead. She walked for hours until nightfall, then gathered branches and leaves to make a bed. She covered herself with several sweaters and a jacket and slept just off the side of the mountain road.

In the morning, she brushed herself off, fixed her hair and came out onto the road. She had only walked a few hundred yards when she heard the grinding of gears behind her. It sounded like the driver was having difficulty shifting. As he approached, she flagged him down. He pulled to the side of the road, reached over and opened the door on her side of the truck, "Get in, lovely, get in."

They had driven less than a mile when Maria realized he was drunk. The truck swerved to the edge of the road, then the driver jerked the steering wheel back in the opposite direction. These actions caused the truck to repeatedly veer and scrape the brush along the ridge of the mountain.

Maria sat close to her door and observed the man. He looked like a sausage in a uniform chewing tobacco. He had dried snuff caked around his nose. He wore a military cap from a Slovak artillery officer, a jacket from an enlisted man in the infantry and pants from a soldier in an armored division. He hadn't washed in a week and smelled of wine and liquor. Several times, he tried to reach over and pull Maria toward him, but she lifted his arm away.

He asked her, "What are you doing up here in the mountains?"

Before Maria could answer, he started singing and spitting tobacco. She looked out of her window into the side view mirror. Seeing herself, she thought if anyone saw her, they would think that she was suffering from the black plague. Her face was dotted with tobacco juice, from her chin to the top of her head.

The disgusting driver continued his monologue, "I stole this damn truck from the Slovak government, those Nazi-lovin' fuckers . . . this uniform, too. I took it from their barracks." Then he broke into song again and acted as though Maria wasn't there. He repeated his question, "What are you doing up here in the mountains?"

Maria answered, "I am looking for two Russian officers. Have you seen any in this area?"

He replied, "No, I ain't seen no fucking Russians. Those bastards are worse than the Nazis. Come here, little one."

Maria pushed his arm away and tried to engage him in conversation, "Have you seen any of the Partisan groups in this area?"

"Yeah, there are Partisan groups up the road here, but there ain't any of them fuckin' Russians with them. What do you want with those commie bastards, anyway?"

Maria admitted, "I have to see them on business for the liberation forces."

The driver continued, "Well, lovely, I have nothing better to do, so I'll take you right to the camp myself. Come here sit next to me."

"No, I don't feel well," Maria responded. She rolled down her window and took a deep breath, trying to clear her head. She was inhaling fresh air when she again felt tobacco being sprayed on the back of her neck.

They were both startled as they saw soldiers; the sausageman shouted, "These fuckin' Russians! What are they doing here? Say, lovely, you aren't one of them damn Bolsheviks, are you?"

Maria denied the accusation, "No, I am not, but one would never know it. I seem to be doing much of their work."

"Well fuck 'em and quit doing it," he suggested. "They are no damn good."

At last, they passed small units of Partisans. Most of them were cooking, washing or hanging clothes on bushes to dry. Small fires were everywhere. The truck crawled along as Maria looked for the largest encampment.

Maria loved music. She listened intently as she heard the sound of a mandolin's delicate strings and the almost-angelic voices of Partisan women echo through the mountains. As the truck bumped its way around the mountain, the melody faded into the distance.

Suddenly, sausageface jammed on the brakes. Maria's head hit the windshield then she bounced back against the seat. She grabbed the door handle, flung the door open and jumped out. Simultaneously, the driver opened his door and fell head first onto the ground and rolled several feet. He mumbled something about assholes from the Kremlin trying to take over the country, then passed out. They had arrived at the main camp.

Maria glanced around. The troops were not much better off than the driver, they were drunk, and so were the women who had joined them. In the distance, she noticed a large lean-to and headed toward it. Hands grabbed at her from all directions. She pushed them back; it wasn't difficult, the soldiers were so drunk they quickly lost their balance.

All at once, she was overwhelmed by an enormous man. He put both of his arms around her and squeezed tightly. She could barely breathe, but managed to shout, "I am here on government business, you jackass, put me down."

Next, he kissed her on the neck and said, "Now, I am going to make a woman out of you." He threw Maria over his shoulder as the others laughed and cheered.

Then, before Maria knew what happened, she was on the ground. The colossal molester was laying next to her. She was able to sit up and look behind her. There stood another huge man, rubbing his right fist with his left hand. Dressed in a sheepskin jacket, his blonde hair made him stand out. He had to be a Russian. He walked over to the soldier still lying on the ground massaging his jaw and said, "Go find one of your whores. Can't you see this girl is different?"

He offered his bulky arm to Maria. She grabbed it as he pulled her to her feet. He asked, "Are you all right?"

Maria gulped, "Yes, I am fine. A little beat up, but not too bad."

He was curious, "Why are you here? You are certainly no Partisan."

Maria explained, "I am here on official business, trying to find a Major Maslov."

The strongman responded, "The major is higher up in the mountains, but I won't be able to find a guide for you until morning. For now, you can stay in my shack. It will be better if we keep you out of the sight of the others. Forgive me, I am Lieutenant Michkovich."

Michkovich was an athletic man, slender but very muscular—the kind of man that possessed much physical strength, but looked like a long-distance runner. His movements were all deliberate. He had substantial self-confidence. He directed Maria; he didn't converse with her. She was to eat with him, stay in his quarters and be ready to leave in the morning, when the high-mountain couriers returned. The lieutenant built a small fire for her, scrounged some food and handed her a military blanket.

"It is best that I sleep close to you, right outside the shack," he cautioned. "These troops are untrained and nothing more than animals. They are armed and dangerous, so be very careful what you do or say."

Maria slept no more than an hour all night. How could she, with men drinking, women screaming and weapons being discharged indiscriminately? Several times during the night, she got up and stood at the door of the lean-to. She watched an orgy, begun at dawn, continue until the women, most of whom looked like men, were dragged off one-by-one into the surrounding forest.

The few times that Maria appeared, Lieutenant Michkovich, sitting by one of the small fires, raised his hand and waved her back to her quarters. In the morning, the lieutenant handed Maria a strong cup of coffee, made from the bark of the black walnut tree. Notwithstanding its horrible taste, Maria drank it down. It was warm, if nothing else.

Michkovich toasted bread on a stick over his fire. When it was almost burned, he handed a smoldering piece to Maria. Then he pointed off in the distance, "Here comes your guide."

A young Slovak peasant boy arrived and the lieutenant spoke with him for several minutes. The boy looked up to the mountains several times during the conversation. The lieutenant removed a map from a small leather case hanging from a branch in front of the lean-to and showed Maria where they would be going. The young soldier agreed with him as the lieutenant pointed directly north.

"He will take you as soon as you finish your coffee," Michkovich told Maria then returned to his small fire and toasted more bread.

Maria got up from the large stone where she had been sitting and slipped her knapsack over her shoulder. She looked over at the lieutenant, who all but ignored her, then raised her tin coffee cup suggesting a farewell salute and drank the dark residue.

Maria and the guide were off. They traveled one small mountain road after another, winding and twisting higher and higher into the Tatras. The young Slovak boy was used to climbing, but realized that Maria was not. He would stop every now and then, allowing her to catch her breath. She was not used to strenuous activity and carrying a pack.

Not wanting Maria to be self-conscious, the young guide would stop, look back and say, "There, way down there, is where we have come from. Tell me if you get tired and we will stop, unless it is vital that you reach the major as quickly as possible."

Maria rationalized, "I don't believe it is necessary to kill myself getting there. Apparently, there will be plenty of time for that later. Unless you plan to run me to death."

For the next few hours, they traveled what seemed to be vertically. Maria developed dyspnea from the thin mountain air. Fatigue caused her to slow almost to a stumble.

"If you are not accustomed to the high altitude, it will take you about twenty days to get used to the lack of oxygen. Like anything else in life, one gets used to it," the guide said.

"I don't intend to be up here that long, and I doubt that I would ever get used to it. I feel as if I could lie down and fall asleep for a week."

"Don't fall asleep yet. The major's camp is right over this crest."

Maria was relieved. "That is the best news I have heard all day." Once inside the campgrounds, the young soldier led Maria through the troops forming small companies. Some were training on machine guns, others on mortars. In the distance, she noticed snipers firing at targets that were almost out of sight. Maria realized the Russians were organizing a huge operation. The troops were well disciplined, unlike those she had seen at the camp down the mountain.

The young guide stopped in front of a large field tent, so well camouflaged that Maria barely noticed it until she was standing next to it. He pulled back the flap of the tent and entered while Maria watched the training activities. A man emerged from the tent and in a soft but deep voice said, "I am Major Maslov, you are looking for me?"

Maria promptly responded, "Yes. I am Maria Zima, sent here by Pavlovich. He wants me to relay this coded message and instructions."

The major took the message from Maria, then said, "You had instructions, did you say?"

"Yes. You are to set up communications as soon as possible in Terchova. Pavlovich suggested that you use the last house on your right as you leave the village," Maria dutifully reported. "Apparently, the occupants are aware of his intentions and have agreed to let you set up a radio station there."

The major entered the tent, leaving Maria standing outside. She walked over to one of the tables that surrounded the tent and picked up one of the tin cups that were always available in such camps. Then she walked to a small fire and poured herself a cup of coffee from a pot resting on an iron tripod.

The major reappeared, looking for Maria. She saw him but paid no attention. She was tired and had delivered her messages. She could care less about the major.

He walked over to the fire, sloshed coffee into his cup and said, "Your information was important. Thank you for bringing it all this way. I know it wasn't easy, comrade." The major's aid appeared with a bottle of vodka, poured some into his cup, then overfilled Maria's coffee with vodka. The major continued, "Things will be moving fast now, comrade."

Maria corrected him, "Maybe it would be better if you didn't call me 'comrade.' I am a member of the Czechoslovakian Liberation Forces."

Maslov stared at her for a moment, then said, "I am, above all else, a loyal Communist Party member."

Maria was still dissatisfied with the intentions of the Russians, but tried to acknowledge the major's position. She forced a patronizing remark, "It is wonderful, major, how you are helping our cause for liberation."

He laughed and raised his coffee cup high asking, "What liberation?"

"Why are you here with your forces, if not to help us?" Maria asked.

The major responded formally, "A pretty little thing like you should not bother your head with such matters. Everything will be decided by Stalin. The future of this country is in the hands of Russia. The guide will take you on to Captain Yeagorof. If you don't mind, I would like you to take him a coded message."

Maria wondered, "Should I stay here tonight and leave in the morning?"

The major gladly answered, "I wish you would stay the night in my tent."

Maria refused, "Major, I must have traveled over a hundred miles today, all uphill. If you want someone to do a tambourine dance with you in your tent, I suggest you get one of the local females. You seem to have an ample supply in this camp."

He roared with laughter, "You are right. We don't see many like you around here. When we do, we try a little vodka and some love—it doesn't hurt to try."

The major still suggested that Maria sleep in his quarters. He had several blankets and assured her he was used to sleeping outside. "You will be perfectly safe, I will be just outside the tent entrance."

Maria acquiesced, "That really makes me feel safe, major. I guess I will have to take your word as a Russian officer." Maria quickly found when she referred to a man's honor, she was successful in averting an otherwise explosive situation.

Unlike the camp below, this encampment was orderly, quiet and military in appearance. An officer walked through the area and ordered the men to turn in. That was the last sound Maria heard before she fell into a profound sleep.

It was still dark when the guide smacked the side of the tent with his hand and called to Maria. It was time for them to move out and head for Yeagorof's encampment. She pulled the flap of the tent back and dragged her knapsack behind her. The guide handed her a cup of the pungent black liquid the soldiers called coffee. This time it tasted good. The young man spoke quietly, "I didn't want to wake the others, but we must be going. Yeagorof could move any time."

It was still dark as they moved along a narrow foot path, winding in all directions. The guide stayed close to Maria, fearing she might lose her footing and fall down the mountain.

As the sun peeped over the crest of the mountains, it threw gigantic shadows in all directions, giving an eerie appearance in the valleys below. For hours, Maria kept pace with the young courier. By noon, she was exhausted, and did not appreciate his whistling and brisk pace. He tossed pebbles at the trees while he waited for her to catch up. Maria, at her wit's end, caught up to him and was about to suggest that they stop for the day when he said, "There it is, Yeagorof's camp."

Seconds later, a Partisan soldier stepped from behind a tree and challenged the two of them. The guide quickly gave the password so the sentry lowered his weapon and let them pass.

Moving through the camp, the young guide explained that these troops were the best in the area, "If you noticed, this is the only group that has a sentry."

Yeagorof was setting up communications gear when Maria and the guide approached. He appeared very military: his hair, cropped close to his head, his square jaw, and neck, thick as a bull. As he rose to greet the two, Maria noticed he stood straight, without an ounce of fat on his body. She sensed he was an educated man. He looked polite and had that air of authority about him. At the same time, he showed signs of fatigue; there was a weariness to his life. The War, for him, had lasted too long. Wherever he had come from, the fighting must have been intense.

He introduced himself, "Hello, I am Captain Yeagorof." Looking at the guide, he said, "Corporal, report to the mess area and tell them that I said you are to have something to eat." The corporal saluted, then vanished.

Maria returned the introduction, "I am Maria Zima. I have a coded message for you from Major Maslov, also one from Colonel Pavlovich." Maria then delivered her messages, as instructed.

He smiled, "It has been a long, long time since I have seen a girl as beautiful as you, if you don't mind a compliment."

Maria removed pieces of sticker bushes from her hair, saying, "Not at all, but I have—and not too long ago—looked much better."

Yeagorof laughed, then signaled his sergeant to bring food to his table. The captain tried to speak Slovak, but Maria answered him in flawless Russian. He straightened up, his eyes brightened and the conversation quickened. It was as though he found someone he could confide in, as a man will speak only with a woman. He explained to Maria that his son and wife were killed in Russia by the Germans. He had been fighting since the beginning of Russia's entry into the War. Most of his fighting had been in and around Stalingrad. Several times during the conversation, he remarked that this would be his final campaign, then the military would send him back to Russia for a long-needed rest.

He was a kind and sincere man and Maria trusted him. She kept in mind, though, he, too, was a Russian. To her surprise, he mentioned several times he was not a communist; he had refused to join the Communist Party. He was strictly military. As he continued, Maria sensed he was releasing his feelings and listened intensely.

Suddenly, he stopped and apologized, "I can see you're tired. Take my blanket and sleep here. You will be safe. In the morning, I'll send you with a member of my staff to contact Pavlovich."

"Pavlovich, do you mean to tell me you know where he is?" Maria asked in disbelief.

"Yes," he confirmed. "Now that we have communications set up, we are contacting our other units."

"Have I come all this way for nothing?" Maria sighed.

"Not at all," Yeagorof confirmed. "Your mission was very important. We cannot send coded messages over the radio, nor could we send your other message over the wireless. Where he wants us to put central communications, that, too, must remain secret."

"That's good. If I thought for a minute that I came all of this way for nothing . . . riding with a drunken sausageman and climbing every damn mountain in the country, I would join the Germans," Maria jokingly threatened.

"What the hell is a sausageman?" Yeagorof wanted to know.

"Believe me, you don't want to know," Maria laughed.

Yeagorof smiled and looked inquisitively at Maria, almost like an adolescent, then repeated, "Tell me, who is this sausageman?"

Maria started laughing, trying to restrain herself.

Yeagorof was persistent, "No, really, who is he?"

"I don't know, but I could just picture Madame Zolkoff riding in the truck next to him," Maria said facetiously.

Now, she was obligated to tell Yeagorof the entire story of the sausageman and why, if Madame Zolkoff were riding with him, the story would have been even more humorous.

Yeagorof chuckled when he heard about the incident. After the story, he poured Maria some vodka coffee and replied with a huge grin, "Maybe you should call him tobaccoman instead of sausageman?"

The two of them roared, while the soldiers looked at Yeagorof in amazement. They had never seen him so unreserved and friendly. To them, he was the leader, an authority figure, a hero and a man among men. This night, their hearts were filled with joy, knowing that their captain was, after all, a warm and gentle man.

The return trip was easy for Maria. Yeagerof provided an excellent guide who took shortcuts through the mountains.

In a little over two days, Maria was in Banska Bystrica. Pavlovich had gone with members of his staff. He heard rumors that heavy fighting broke out in several places and was trying to confirm the reports.

Small units had attacked the Germans in several sectors. They had few radios, and their organization was poor. The only direct communication between the groups scattered throughout Slovakia were runners, trying to carry memorized messages between factions.

The Slovak government controlled radio transmissions, so they kept telling the people that the Germans were on their side, and not to worry. They reported it would remain peaceful throughout the nation. Any uprising was pictured as caused by radical dissidents trying to embarrass President Tiso.

Pavlovich returned after several days. He was dressed in a major's uniform bearing Czechoslovakia emblems on the collar. His staff was with him. Maria watched from the old barn, where it all began—the place where Pavlovich originally landed in his parachute. Here she was in the same place with the roles reversed. Now, she was receiving her orders from him. He hurried to Maria, "Did you contact Maslov and Yeagorof?"

She explained that she delivered both messages and that Yeagorof provided her with a guide to see her safely through the mountains to their meeting place at the barn.

Pavlovich sat on the old feeding tub and looked around the barn. He recalled, "How I remember this place. I thought it was all over for me before it began."

Maria reassured, "You are here and you are safe. Now, you can get on with your mission."

"That is exactly what I want to talk to you about, my mission. First, I want to thank you for helping. Next, I am going to ask you to continue to help us."

Maria hesitated, "By us, do you mean the Slovak people, or do you mean the Russians?"

Pavlovich reaffirmed, "I mean the Russians. Remember, they are fighting with us, not against us."

"I hope you are right. I guess time will tell," Maria added.

Pavlovich continued, "Regardless, it is the here and now that we must be concerned with. Not what is going to happen way off in the future."

Maria disagreed, "I'm not looking at the here and now, I am looking at the future."

"If we don't finish off the Germans, we won't have any future," Pavlovich emphasized.

Maria gave in, "Oh, all right, what is it that you want me to do, comrade major?"

Pavlovich gave her a barbed glance; he did not appreciate her remark. He went on, "I want you to translate for Major Studenko, the liaison officer between our groups and the Red Army."

Maria objected, "I have told you, repeatedly, I am not a communist. I think the Red Army should have their own interpreters."

"Maria, this is for Slovakia, not for the Red Army," Pavlovich pleaded. "You, of all people, should realize that there will be many languages spoken during this campaign. Someone has to interpret the incoming information and translate it into Russian. That someone is you. I am sure that your translations for Studenko will be accurate—though they will be going directly to the Red Army."

"Since we understand each other," Maria insisted, "I'll work hard for you. But I want you to tell Major Studenko how I feel."

Pavlovich agreed, "Well, it is all settled. I have to leave you now, but I'll send the driver for you in the morning. That is, if you don't mind spending the night here." Pavlovich and his staff then drove off to the south.

Maria, still tired from her trip, laid her sweater over the hay and tried to rest. She couldn't fall asleep, because she heard the cracking of small arms fire. Then she heard a large explosion, then another. Maria got up and pushed back the old barn door. She looked toward the mountains. No, firing was coming from the other direction, toward Banska Bystrica. Black smoke rose and floated over the hills that surrounded the city. The earth shook her feet, repeatedly, as charges detonated. She heard none of the usual sounds that accompanied artillery—the distant bang, the whistling projectile, the impact percussion.

Maria concluded the explosions were not from artillery, but the result of a detonated device, the ones used by the Partisans. At last: the Uprising.

Darkness slowly drifted in from the east. The sky was sporadically lit with one flash after another. Tracer rounds illuminated the blackness as they crisscrossed the city.

The Partisans were attacking in force. The firing lasted all night. Before sunrise, silence fell on the city. The air, thick with black powder, drifted as far as the barn. It was so thick that it blocked the sun, making the dawn look like twilight. It ended as quickly as it had begun; the War had come to Czechoslovakia.

Maria sat and looked for the staff car that was to take her to Major Studenko and her new assignment. She was surprised to see Pavlovich in the car. He quickly directed her, "Hurry, get in."

Maria grabbed her things and was out of the cold barn in an instant. She knew he would tell her about last night's battle. "What has happened?" she asked.

He told her, "The Revolt has started."

"Do we have control of Slovakia, yet?"

"No, we only have control of Banska Bystrica and an area surrounding it forty miles long and ten miles wide," Pavlovich reported. "Battles are raging all around—Vrutky and God only knows where else."

Maria wanted to know more, "What about Bratislava, Nitra, Zilina and the other cities?"

Pavlovich shook his head, "Nobody knows. Our communications are terrible. The Germans were tipped off and crushed the attempts in most places. However, Banska Bystrica is now the headquarters for the Czechoslovakian Liberation Army and the Central Command Partisan."

"Where do you want me to go now?" Maria asked.

"It looks as though we are meeting in Banska Bystrica. You won't have to go far, just up the road. I'll move you back in with the Chernys, if their house is still intact," Pavlovich told her.

"Maria," Mrs. Cherny called as she saw her stepping from the car. "I guess it is safe for you, the Underground has taken control of the city. I am delighted to see that you are still alive. You wouldn't believe it, the secret police were here, not once, but several times. Come in, come in. Tell me what is happening and what are you doing here?"

The Uprising

"There isn't any place that I can go. I have been forced to stay in the city and help our liberation forces. Not only that, but they keep pushing me off on these damn Russians," Maria complained.

"It's the War." Mrs. Cherny offered the standard explanation. Back in familiar surroundings, Maria slept well that night. Mrs. Cherny had breakfast ready in the morning. She gave a faint call, then tapped on the door, "Maria get up. There is a government staff car waiting. I have some breakfast for you, not much, but it is hot."

Maria hurriedly dressed, while hollering to Mrs. Cherny from the top of the stairs that she couldn't stop to eat. On her way out, Mrs. Cherny handed her a piece of black bread with a few berries scattered on top.

The driver of the staff car opened the door. Before she entered, Maria placed her hand on the door and stood for a moment. There was nothing but silence as she looked at the driver. He lifted his shoulders, squinted and said, "I guess the Germans have gone."

"For good?" Maria wondered.

He guessed, "I seriously doubt it. They aren't ones to give up, don't ya know." The driver headed for the center of the city. All sorts of people wandered through the city. Most all of them were armed. Maria spotted every kind of weapon produced: German, French, American and Russian. How this new army was going to supply its troops with different types of ammunition was a mystery.

The driver pulled up to the military headquarters, turned to Maria and said, "This is your duty station, second floor."

Maria opened the door, got out and the driver sped off. She stood for a second and watched as military personnel rushed in and out of the headquarters building. Pavlovich was right, Banska Bystrica was now the nucleus, the command center, for all that was about to take place.

On the second floor, Maria met with Pavlovich. He introduced her to Major Studenko and his staff. There was a Lieutenant Tamara, possibly the most beautiful girl Maria had ever seen. She was tall, flaming copper hair and eyes—the eyes were unique, the color of emeralds—and that smile, the kind that stopped men dead in their tracks and melted them where they stood. She was the Russian decoding officer, responsible for all decoding between the Russian Partisans and the main Russian Army marching on Czechoslovakia.

Maria was then introduced to Nickolai Popov, the political commissar. She greeted him politely, but in the back of her mind, she knew that this man represented evil. He even looked the part, with his pointed face and greasy, black hair. He always stood hunched over and could never quite manage a smile. He had that way of looking not at you, but through you. Maria had an icy feeling about the man and wanted nothing to do with him.

The others were all lieutenants with the sole purpose of carrying out Studenko's orders. Studenko looked anything but Russian. He reminded Maria of a German from the aristocracy. The major was tall, slender and blond. He even had an old saber scar across his forehead. Maria noticed it went through his right eyebrow and down to the center of his face. She watched him as he gave orders to his men: His eyes were forever glancing, his head moved like a deer, always raised and listening as though at any moment something was about to happen.

As he spoke with his men, Maria turned to Pavlovich and said, "Is that a saber scar?"

Pavlovich answered, "No, he was in hand to hand combat in Stalingrad and was slashed with a bayonet." Studenko began his training in the Russian cavalry and he still wore his riding britches and, apparently, polished his boots daily.

Studenko asked Maria to begin work at once. The messages from the battle areas came in regularly. Most of them were written in Slovak. Maria translated them into Russian. Once Maria output the messages in Russian, she gave them to Lieutenant Tamara, who coded them and sent them by radio to the Russian Army.

With the Partisans gaining ground and fighting increasing all over Czechoslovakia, Hitler ordered a counterattack. He ordered SS Obersturmbann Fuhrer Friedreich Beyersdorff, a young intelligence officer, to mobilize all non-committed forces into one fighting division. Beyersdorff drew troops from the SS training school in Moravia and Bohemia. He mobilized the 18th *Horst Wessel* Division, ordering them into Slovakia. For the base of his fighting corps, he used the 29th SS Division, already under his command.

Hitler surveyed his armies to see which ones he could move to put down the Czechoslovakian revolt. He flew into a rage when he was informed that the 14th SS Galician Division had not been in combat for almost a year. This dreaded division was composed of Ukrainian soldiers. They hated the Russians with a passion and were violent anti-communists. At the same time, they viewed the Germans as inferior, even though they were serving in the Nazi Army.

Hitler sent written orders to Beyersdorff, instructing him to disarm the Galician Division the moment they suppressed the uprising. Beyersdorff made an excellent choice by throwing the Galician Division against the Partisans. He had convinced them the Partisans were communists. His massive army moved from the west to the east to engage the revolt. It was well equipped with armor units, artillery and automatic weapons.

The Slovak Army Partisans put up stiff resistance, but with only a few artillery pieces and light machine guns, they fell back. Repeated requests for help from the Russians went unanswered. The Red Army stayed in the mountains and refused to aid the Czechs. With all hope of reinforcement from the Russians exhausted, the Slovaks retreated to Banska Bystrica.

The revolt continued and the need for Maria's translation services increased. Studenko put a cot in a room so Maria could move her things into the headquarters. It made no difference whether she was sleeping, someone would always wake her to translate written and wireless messages. When there was a lull, Nicolai Popov asked Maria to translate Slovak newspapers. He wanted to know who was organizing the Slovakian Liberation Partisans. When Maria asked him why he wanted to know, he calmly replied, "If they can organize people against the Germans, they could just as easily organize people against Russia."

Chapter Four

THE AMERICANS

Maria would usually deny Popov's requests, telling him there was nothing in the newspapers. Sometimes, she would make up stories about medical units and transportation companies, nothing of any use to him. She would try to find an article ending with his favorite, ". . . and the Red Army is advancing on all fronts."

Her editorializing seemed to satisfy him; he would always retire to write his report. She knew her first impression of him was correct: He was a bastard, a man who lived off the misery of others—misery he created.

Several times, on her off-duty hours, Maria spoke with Studenko, always on a friendly basis, never mentioning politics. Pavlovich probably told him of Maria's feeling toward communism. Maria liked Studenko—even felt sorry for him. He told her he had not seen his wife or children in over two years. The only letter he received from her was when he was in the Ukraine. It was obvious he was homesick for his family.

When Maria talked with Tamara, it was nearly the same story, the last time she heard from her husband, a lieutenant in the Red Army, was from a field hospital in eastern Poland. She described his circumstances with a longing face; he suffered a severe stomach wound, that was all she knew.

Tamara told Maria she had strict orders not to talk to her. Maria was surprised to hear that. Tamara's orders prohibited her from going into the city; she was to talk to no one. All day and half the night, she was locked in the decoding room doing her job.

The military headquarters soon became engulfed with people. More Slovak officers, those trained in Russia, arrived daily. It was obvious if the West didn't get involved, Czechoslovakia, once freed from the Germans, would fall into Russian hands.

In Algiers, North Africa, 1944, Captain William McGregor, wounded in the right leg at Salareno, was recovering from surgery. A man of substantial physical ability, a former lacrosse all-American at the University of Delaware, he was impatient and restless. During his rehabilitation, he finished an advanced course in demolition. Tall and handsome with wavy brown hair and over-size brown eyes, he had that "don't I know you, or didn't we serve together somewhere?" look. He was quickly given the name *Pretty Boy* by his men. His outgoing personality, even to new acquaintances, made him immediate friends. Everybody called him Mac.

For weeks, he had been training in the unbearable heat of the North African desert. There were times he wished he were back with his old outfit in Italy. Disgruntled over the conditions in North Africa, he requested reassignment to a combat unit. By the end of August, Mac was disgusted. He mentioned his predicament to Major Nash, USMC, with whom he was training.

Nash suggested McGregor place his name with the Office of Strategic Services (OSS) to see action. Mac took Major Nash's suggestion and put his request through channels. On August fifteenth, orders arrived, Mac was to report to OSS Headquarters, Bari, Italy. He was excited at the news. His euphoria was compounded when he discovered his friend Lieutenant Kenneth Lain also was assigned to the OSS and would go with Mac to Italy.

On August twenty-eighth, the two men boarded a military transport plane. Both were filled with excitement, more from leaving North Africa than for their new assignment. Upon their arrival, they were taken to OSS Headquarters in Bari. The central command was located in a beautiful villa, the former home of an Italian general, on the shore of the Adriatic Sea.

As the two men settled in, they felt they had arrived at a vacation resort instead of a military installation. The vacation was over the following day. The men were not permitted to leave the area. Training continued all day and into the night. Some evenings, when they had a few free moments, the new OSS officers spent their time removing all identification from their belongings, including: matches, notes, ID cards, tags—even the labels on their clothes. Everything they removed was destroyed.

Their classroom curriculum focused on procedures to follow upon capture. They were told to tell the enemy they were in the Air Corps and were shot down. Repeatedly, they were told to trust no one, absolutely no one. Mac and Lain saw the hand writing on the wall. This type of mission sounded exciting, but it didn't sound safe.

One morning, as reveille sounded over speakers, Mac and Lain headed to the showers. Half way down the hall, they were approached by a smiling young man. He whipped off his towel and cracked Mac on the ass. "Hey, I'm Fred Mayer. I can't wait to kick ass and take names. How about you two?"

Mac and Lain looked at each other for a second, then broke out laughing. Lain said, "We're ready to kick ass, too, only it's going to be yours if you try that again! What is this, some kind of test to see if we fraternize with low-class people?"

"Low-class people, my ass! I'm from Brooklyn. There are no low-class people in Brooklyn. I mean, how can you say that when I worked in the Ford plant?"

All three of the men laughed. To Lain and Mac, he was a shot in the arm to their boring life. Mayer looked at McGregor and told him the first chance he had, he was going to arm wrestle him. Mac gave him a grin, then flexed his biceps. Mayer shook his head, telling Mac there was no way he would ever take him. Mayer glanced over to Lain and started a conversation in Spanish. Lain could not respond. Then to show them that he had class, he continued, speaking in German, French and Italian. Mac looked at Lain, then turned and said to Mayer, "O.K., you have class. But there ain't no way you are ever going to take me in arm wrestling."

Mac and Lain loved the guy from the beginning. They were not sure if he was intentionally trying to get them into trouble, or whether he was just as he seemed. He was bored and wild, more wild than bored. Anyway, he disregarded his orders by fraternizing with Lain and Mac. Since he was on another mission team, he was prohibited from speaking with other trainees. It didn't bother Mac or Lain, and it sure didn't bother Mayer.

That afternoon in the dining room, Mayer recognized Mac and Lain, this, too, was against regulations. He waved so everyone would notice. Mac and Lain were more embarrassed than anything else. They knew that it was against the rules to discuss their job or even contact anyone on another mission. Mayer enjoyed the whole thing, even when he embarrassed them. One of the men permanently stationed at Bari, not assigned to any mission, leaned over to Mac and Lain and said, "I see you two met Mayer."

Mac inquired, "I know we aren't supposed to say anything, but who is he?"

The staff officer responded, "Look at him. He looks more like an Arab than he does a Jew. Wavy black hair, olive skin, gleaming teeth and a constant smile. That comes from his constant grab-assing all day."

"What is he doing? Teaching or going on a mission?" Mac asked.

"A mission . . . and if he doesn't go soon, he probably will walk to Germany." The staff officer surmised, "That guy's fear nerve was removed at birth."

Mac wanted more information, "What do you mean?"

The officer explained, "There is nothing that man is afraid of. I have been here for a long time, let me tell you, he is one in a million."

Mayer was ready to undertake any assignment against the Nazis. The funny thing was he had no hatred for them. Unlike his demeanor of power and energy, he was a calm and tolerant man, with compassion for all men. Even more surprising, he was recruited out of the ranks of the US Rangers. They were not known for being gentle and tough; they were known for just being tough. Mayer was training to operate behind German lines. He had already trained for over a year and was still not assigned. A staff member at Bari placed him in a new unit, the German-Austrian section.

Lieutenant Colonel Chapin was in charge of the German-Austrian section. He teamed Mayer with a Dutch Jew, Hans Wynberg. The two were opposites. Mayer was unsophisticated, but clearly cunning. Wynberg was tall, shy, scholarly and looked naively innocent.

During a class, Mayer was asked if he could kill, face-to-face, using a knife. Without hesitation, he answered yes. Wynberg responded to the identical question with a no. The instructor continued, "Do you understand what will happen if the Germans get you?"

Mayer answered, "It's more our war than yours. I think we should take a heavily-armed team and drop them into the concentration camp at Dachau, to lead an uprising."

When he finished, the instructor replied, "Why don't you jump out of the window? It would be more practical."

Wynberg was convinced that Mayer was nothing more than a medal hunter. The old adage, *opposites attract*, certainly applied; the two men became very close during their training.

As they were completing the final phase of their instruction, the Air Corps requested information from the OSS on enemy movement through the Brenner Pass. The pass was the supply trunk line for German Field Marshal Albert Kesselring's force in Italy.

Innsbruck was less than twenty miles from the Brenner Pass. If a few agents could make it there, they could observe the pass. Central Command decided Mayer and Wynberg would parachute in somewhere near Innsbruck. From there, they could report movements through the pass. Hans Wynberg would serve as the radio operator for Mayer. The only element lacking was someone who knew that section of the country and was acquainted with local people.

OSS Bari searched the POW camps of Europe for a candidate. In December, they found one: a German POW held outside Naples, Franz Weber. He was a lieutenant in the Wehrmacht's 45th Infantry Division of the regular German Army. Weber was from the old German school—excellent manners, well educated, polite and military. Unlike many men in the German army, he was a man with much foresight and reasoning.

He was chosen by the OSS mainly because he was a Catholic. Several times during his internment interview, he stated if Hitler controlled Europe, it would mean an end to his religion. When one of his interviewers asked him why he was willing to help the Allies, he replied, "To remain silent in the presence of evil is worse than committing the evil."

Mayer and Wynberg liked him as soon as they met him. He was exactly what they had been looking for—a mountain man. He resembled a woodcutter on the front of a travel poster: tall, slender, with a constant smile. He had thick, wavy blond hair and the most powerful legs seen on a human. With the mountain man, the team consisted of two Jews and one German soldier.

The team remained in strict isolation while preparing for their mission. Everyday, they studied maps, trails, houses, stores, the highlands, the lakes and rivers. Everything seemed against them: snow, winds, poor visibility and the lack of current information on German troops in the area.

Mayer suggested a clever daring scheme, to turn winter to their advantage. Since the flat lands were occupied by the enemy, it was impossible for them to parachute there. On detailed examination of the maps, he noticed two lakes, hemmed in by the mountains, just north of their target, Innsbruck. The lakes would be a perfect landing zone. They were frozen and no civilians or military personnel would be nearby. Mayer's plan was to parachute on to the lake. Once they landed, they would hide their parachutes and ski down the slope to the town of Oberperfuss, where Weber had relatives.

When the team was ready to leave, the OSS contacted the 334th Wing of the RAF to request the air drop. They received a prompt reply from Squadron Leader H.F. Brown: "Negative." Brown thought it would be too difficult to locate the landing zone in such bad weather. The aircraft would have to fly at sixteen thousand feet without ground navigation. He thought the entire mission sounded unsafe.

Mayer's mission then sought help from the US Army Air Corps. Colonel MacCloskey of the 88th Heavy Bomber Squadron had just the man they needed—Captain Billings, a red-headed wildman. When asked to volunteer, his only reply was, "If those fuckers are crazy enough to jump into that area, and at night, who else but me could fly them?"

Before departing Bari, the men were told about the fate of the agents who preceded them. Most of them had been executed, some had not been heard from, but were presumed dead.

McGregor and Lain watched from the window of their room at the Bari Headquarters, as Mayer, Wynberg and Weber loaded their equipment into the back of the staff truck. They wanted to throw open the window and holler, "Good luck and God bless you." It was forbidden. They could only stand and watch as their friends looked at them and smiled.

The takeoff went without incident. The four-hour ride was too long for Wynberg. He was on edge because he hated to fly. He would never show his anxiety, though, it wasn't proper.

On their first approach, they found the mountains blocked with clouds. They couldn't find the drop zone. Mayer was in the cockpit of the bomber trying to shout above the roar of the engines. Billings was trying to listen to him and fly at the same time.

"What now?" Mayer asked.

Billings confidently replied, "I find a break in this soup and we drive this baby right through it."

Wynberg, listening to the conversation, became even more apprehensive. He didn't want to hear the rest.

Billings continued, "The hard part is going to be locating the lake. It's like looking for fly shit in pepper. Only here, it's more like looking for a marshmallow in a snow storm."

Weber kept winding his watch; Wynberg peeked out the gun mount, watching the wind turn the snow into a blizzard. Suddenly, his heart stopped. The engines vibrated as Billings rolled the plane into a steep dive to the left. Wet snow turned to ice on the windshield.

Billings yelled for them to get ready. Then he whipped the plane to the right, slamming them against the side of the aircraft. He suddenly flicked on the wing-tip lights to see if the wings were about to hit the mountains. Weber pissed himself.

An airman pulled off the cover of the jump hole and told the men to standby. On command, each would plunge forward and down into the darkness. Mayer sat on the edge of the jump opening. The icy wind blew into his face. There was no visibility, only the snow whirling up into the jump hole.

Weber and Wynberg lined up behind Mayer. Billings hit the green jump light and Mayer, with his equipment strapped to his feet, pushed himself into the ugly blackness below. Weber stood fast, frozen on the edge of the jump hole.

Wynberg screamed, "For Christ's sake, jump! Jump!"

Weber wouldn't move, so with all the strength he could muster, Wynberg pushed him through the hole. There wasn't enough time left for Wynberg to sit. He simply took one step from his standing position directly into the opening and disappeared.

Billings rammed the throttles forward and pulled the plane into a near-vertical climb. Seconds later, the propwash from his engines blew snow off a mountain peak. God spared Billing's life—again.

Back at OSS Headquarters, Mac and Lain continued training, chomping at the bit for an assignment. Mission after mission departed for unknown destinations while they sat and waited, feeling their time would never come.

They were up early one day and ran through driving rain to the conference room. As they entered the room, they noticed Lieutenant J. Holt Green, the Navy officer, and Sgt. Horvath and Pvt. Brown missing, meaning they had been assigned. Mac, perturbed over not being assigned, asked an instructor sitting across from him, "How much longer do they expect us to wait? This is really starting to be a pain in the ass."

The instructor answered, "As soon as Green and his bunch get settled in, we'll see what we can do for you two."

"Are you bullshitting us or are you serious?" Mac demanded.

"Hey, I'm serious. I shouldn't tell you this, but it won't be much longer," he admitted.

Mac pushed him, "Just what does 'much longer' mean?"

"Quiet . . . not more than three weeks, O.K.?" the instructor replied.

"I hope we have your word on that," Mac remarked.

The instructor added, "You do, but if it is three weeks and one day, don't come bitching to me."

Their spirits picked up at once. Now, they had a specific deadline, a goal, something to look forward to. Life was livable again. Each night, they passed the radio room and asked if there was any word from Mayer. Every evening they were told the same thing by the operator, "Just as soon as I hear something, I'll let you guys know."

Holt Green landed at Tri Duby Airfield in Czechoslovakia. Two American flying fortresses were on the ground unloading medical and military supplies, while American fighter planes flew cover overhead. Once the supplies were off, the planes were reloaded with British and American flyers that had recently escaped from German POW camps. With Green was another mission team composed of a radioman, Charles Heller, and John Schwartz. Green was not sure what their mission was, but for the time being they were to remain with him and his group, known as the Dawes Team.

Lt. Green's orders were to attach his mission to the Czechoslovakian Forces of the Interior (CFI) at Banska Bystrica. They were to transmit enemy intelligence and situation reports on the progress of the campaign to Bari. They were to estimate arms, ammunition and demolition requirements for further resupply of the CFI. The Czechoslovakian people welcomed the Americans at Tri Duby Airfield. They escorted them from the airfield, blowing car horns and firing rounds in the air. The Americans quickly settled into the headquarters building in Banska Bystrica, next to the Russian mission.

Maria was still translating day and night. The Americans' arrival didn't change her thinking—she was in the Russian Army. The Red guards watched Tamara constantly and never permitted her near the Americans.

Desperate messages came from all fronts. The CFI withdrew its forces. The Liberation Partisans and the Communist Partisans sent the same negative messages. The typical message read, "We are falling back to Banska Bystrica; ammunition running low; under heavy artillery fire; we are out numbered."

The city filled with retreating troops. The hospitals overflowed with wounded. Retreating troops wandered the streets. Maria watched from her window in the headquarters building and saw troops come into the city then walk from one end of town to the other. Clear lines of authority were lacking. Maria witnessed no more than orderly confusion. The enemy's noose tightened around Banska Bystrica. Tents were set up in every open area and along both sides of the river.

Two weeks after Lt. Green's team arrived, the Germans sent in the Luftwaffe to cause panic. Stuka fighter planes strafed and bombed the city sporadically.

Hope for a victory vanished; the Uprising had failed. The first week of October, Major Studenko called his staff together. He told them the situation was uncertain. They would soon evacuate. The essence of his speech was to stand by to leave.

Daily, Maria heard the sound of enemy artillery closing in on the city. In the evenings, the flashes of their explosions seemed closer.

The communication center was in turmoil. The Russians would contact the Red Army, then Moscow. Tamara could not decode the overwhelming volume of messages. This deficiency put Studenko on edge. He shouted orders in all directions.

On October 7th, the CFI requested an explosives expert from Lt. Green. If a retreat were necessary, the CFI was not about to leave the Germans any bridges or military equipment. Lt. Green forwarded the request to Bari. The OSS responded at once. McGregor and Lain, plus partially-trained Gaul, Perry, Dunlevy and Parris, were ordered to leave at 0500 hours the following day.

They stumbled out of the villa in the darkness of the early morning and threw their gear into the back of the troop carrier. Lain was first in, he stood at the rear and pulled in each man as they extended their hand. Once they were in, the driver slammed the tailgate shut, jumped back in the cab and they were off.

To their surprise, there was a figure sitting in the dark in the forward part of the truck on one of the benches that lined both sides of the vehicle. He introduced himself, "Hi, I'm Joe Morton, St. Joseph, Missouri, you know, about ninety miles north of Kansas City."

The others sat stunned for a second, then Lain introduced the men one by one. Mac, with a little hesitation, asked, "Are you part of this mission?"

Morton explained, "Not really, I'm a correspondent for the Associated Press. I thought there might be a story here, so the brass is letting me tag along."

Joe Morton looked like a Catholic priest. His face was round, he had large brown eyes and was in control of himself. Mac took one look at him and was satisfied that he was an asset, not a liability.

The truck came to an abrupt stop at the edge of the airfield. The men filed off with their gear and started toward the waiting bomber. The door of the truck slammed shut and two men hurried to join Mac's group.

"This is Catlos and I'm Tibor Keszthelye. We will be joining you for awhile, if that's O.K.? We are the Hungarian mission."

McGregor looked at Lain, smiled and said, "This damn thing is turning into a circus. How can all these people come with us?"

"Well, you are a good looking man, McGregor, and don't think these guys haven't noticed," Lain wisecracked.

Mac shook his head, "You bastard."

The pilot of the bomber was clever; on his arrival, he followed a formation of fortresses on their way to bomb Berlin. As the planes passed over Tri Duby Airfield, he peeled off from the formation and landed. Mac and the group from Bari quickly departed the plane. When the plane was empty, it was loaded with wounded and downed American and British pilots. The pilot never cut his engines. He taxied to the end of the runway and was soon airborne again.

McGregor and the rest of the Americans were taken by truck to the headquarters building in Banska Bystrica. When they arrived, Lt. Green explained the situation was now critical. He questioned the sanity of Bari headquarters for sending in eight more agents and a reporter.

The Germans could not risk the continued sabotage behind their front lines, so they began a powerful drive to wipe out the Czechoslovakian resistance.

The end was near for Lt. Green's group. He sent continuous messages to Bari requesting evacuation by air as soon as possible. While they waited, they continued with their assignment, sending Bari enemy battle order and target information.

The CFI headquarters in Banska Bystrica was a zoo. The Czechoslovakians faced the fate of Warsaw. They thought the Russians and Americans had stabbed Poland in the back and now it was Czechoslovakia's turn. Most of the Czech officers felt the Russians thought the country was getting too close to democracy. The Russians, apparently, decided not to help defend Czechoslovakia. There were three Slovak brigades trained in Russia. These forces were promised at the time of the Uprising, but were never sent.

Downed American and British pilots, waited in the headquarters building for word on the evacuation. The Russians were no better off. Confusion approached panic. The formerly sedate Partisan groups who roamed the streets were now plundering. All evidence of discipline vanished. The Czechoslovakian Army units were without leaders, and the few officers who tried to maintain order could not prevent the looting.

The Partisans consisted of mostly young undisciplined men. With them were POWs from France, Poland and Russia. The only orderly group in the entire lot was the French. The Russian officers quickly moved to gain control of the Partisans, many of whom were veterans from the Russian Front. They tried to organize whatever groups they could.

An American, Captain Tibor Keszthelyi, US Army, approached Maria as she was sitting at her desk transcribing messages. He startled her when he spoke to her in Hungarian, "I would like to speak with the Russian commander."

Maria replied, "Need I tell you he is very busy? Shall I interrupt him?"

"No, don't do that," Tibor said. "When he is free, tell him I would like to see him for a few minutes."

"Captain, do you speak Russian?" Maria asked.

"No, I don't," he admitted.

Maria suggested, "Would you like to tell me what this is regarding, so I can tell him. The Russians are a strange lot. I think we will do better if you tell me, first. Then, I will be able to explain it to him in Russian."

"Aren't you Russian?" the captain inquired.

"No, I have been ordered by the CFI to translate for them. Now that you are here, captain, may I ask you a question."

He agreed, "Yes, of course, what is it?"

Maria began, "Who in the world is running your organization? I can't believe they would deliberately send in all these men and not one of them speaks Slovak. It is beyond my comprehension."

Tibor told her, "I was born in Hungary, so let me tell you nothing that they do ever makes sense. To most of them, life is just one big giggle."

Maria, noticing Major Studenko walking toward his desk, hurried over to him and submitted Tibor's request. Studenko looked up and motioned him over. Tibor spoke English, causing Studenko to throw down his pen and look at Maria. She told Tibor, "I will translate."

Tibor continued, "I am not officially with this group. My orders are to enter Hungary at the first opportunity. Can you help me gain entry?"

Studenko, picked up the field telephone on his desk, cranked the handle and screamed into the phone. Maria looked at Tibor, smiled, then said facetiously in English, "I think your audience with the Pope has ended."

Tibor glanced down at Studenko, snapped to attention, turned and left the room with Maria. When they reached Maria's desk, he said, "You know these Russians. What does he mean when he says he will look into it?"

Maria said honestly, "If I translate directly from the Russian to English it means, 'Go screw yourself.'"

With no way of entering Hungary, Captain Tibor Keszthelyis' mission ended. He waited for orders for evacuation.

Sergeant Steve Catlos, US Army, was the radioman sent in to assist Tibor. His mission, too, was terminated. If Tibor couldn't get the two of them into Hungary, they had failed.

From time to time, Tibor would speak with Maria, but only when she was free and when Studenko was not around. Maria was curious about the Americans and asked Tibor who the Navy lieutenant was, pointing to James Gaul.

Generally, Maria did not care for Gaul. He was a Harvard graduate in archeology who had spent time in the Middle East before the War. He was arrogant, and acted as though he was one station above everyone. His motto was, ". . . first comes me, then Christ, then the masses."

Lt. Green was the opposite. He was from a well-to-do family in Charleston, South Carolina. Maria liked him very much. He had wonderful manners, was soft spoken and assumed an unmilitary stature, unless the situation warranted otherwise, then he would spring into action, raising his voice and shouting commands.

Maria was talking to Tibor when they were interrupted and called to an emergency meeting. General Viest, commander of the Slovak Army, reported to the Americans and Russians that all was lost. He said he would pull what is left of his army back to Donovaly, at the foot of the Tatra Mountains, ten miles from Banska Bystrica. There they would try to make another stand against the Germans. General Viest looked tired and drawn. He welcomed the Russian and American missions to join the retreat, or to find their own way out. He thanked them for trying to help and wished them God's protection.

Maria, watching General Viest, knew he was a beaten man. The right lens of his glasses was cracked, his face was thin and there were dark circles under his eyes from worry. He spoke with a soft voice. It was clear he was depressed.

Maria's nerves contracted, forcing her into a rigid position when she heard him say, "Gentlemen, the Russians will attempt to fly out their high-ranking officers and civilian personnel tomorrow. Tomorrow will be the last day our forces can defend the airstrip at Tri Duby. It will be your last chance to leave."

Lt. Gaul yelled to the General, "Is there any way we can get out on a Russian bomber?"

Maria translated. General Viest looked over at Major Studenko. Studenko looked back with a blank stare and shrugged his shoulders. General Viest was embarrassed.

Lt. Green tried to bail him out, "I think we better wait for our planes. My last communique stated our planes will arrive before noon."

The Americans and British cheered. Then, to their surprise, General Viest added, "Yes, I think you are better off relying on your own people, rather than the Russians."

Another cheer went up for the general. He waved to all those in the room, then walked among them, shaking hands as he left.

Lt. Green finally received the message he had been waiting for, "Five bombers returning from raid over western Poland will break away from formation and land at Tri Duby. Have all personnel ready to evacuate before 1200 hours tomorrow." He notified the Americans and British to be ready in the morning. It was welcome news to the pilots, most of whom were in poor health. They had been in prisoner-of-war camps since the beginning of the War. They did not understand the situation, nor did they care. They just wanted to leave as soon as possible.

Lt. Green replied to the message, saying he would try to get all of the pilots out, even if his command had to remain. The OSS trained them to live off the land, to kill in hand-to-hand combat and, if need be, to live and fight as a guerrilla.

The staff set fire to all correspondence. Nothing was left to the enemy. Green arranged for the morning transportation: The pilots were to be sent on the first transport.

With all of their plans formed, the group relaxed. The conversations were about getting home, eating good food, finding women, and getting a few cold beers. At last, the tension faded, along with the enormous responsibility.

Maria was worried. She had received no new orders from the CFI. Several times she attempted to talk with Tibor to get his advice on the situation, but she was always interrupted by Studenko who gave her messages to translate. In the afternoon, Tamara asked Maria if she knew where to get a pair of good boots. If she had to return to Moscow, she didn't want to freeze when she arrived.

Maria asked Studenko if she could return to the Chernys' house to grab some of her winter clothes. Studenko begrudgingly consented. The temperature continued to drop every hour.

When Maria was ready to leave, Studenko walked over to her and pointed to a Russian guard, "He will see you safely to your destination and return."

Maria protested, "That won't be necessary. I have to go to several places, and it may take me awhile."

Studenko shouted, "I said, he will see you safely there and back!"

Maria immediately understood she was being guarded, not protected.

In the street, Maria asked the guard where he was from, how long had he been in the Army and what he intended to do when the War was over. He answered her questions. She had him thinking she was a high-ranking Russian officer in no time.

Maria knew the shoemaker in the shop next to Madame Zolkoff's business. She stopped in and asked if he had any boots. She opened her hand and showed him several gold pieces that Polack had given her.

The old man said, "Could you stop back, say in a half hour?"

She agreed, "Yes, there are several other things that I have to do. I'll be back."

Maria returned to the street and looked at Madame Zolkoff's dress shop. She was nauseated. The shop was destroyed; all of the windows were broken; the charm and grace were gone, along with Madame's magnificent creations. There was nothing left but a burned pitted shell. What a tragedy, Maria thought.

Maria crossed the railroad tracks to the Chernys' house. She walked through the door with the guard behind her. Then she suddenly stopped. The wounded were everywhere—in the living room, dining room, and the bedrooms. All were full, with several men in each bed.

Mrs. Cherny, changing a dressing on a chest wound, turned and saw Maria, "Maria, thank God you are all right. Can you believe all of this? My husband is ill and is with a neighbor. I don't know how, but the wounded started coming here and I didn't have the heart to turn them away. I don't suppose you could stay and give me a hand?"

Maria took a chance that the guard did not speak Slovak and said, "I am here with a Russian guard. If anything happens to me, please tell my family I was with the Russians against my will when you last saw me."

Mrs. Cherny quickly looked over at the guard who stood silent. He offered no help to the wounded; he was either shocked at what he saw, or he just didn't care.

Then Mrs. Cherny apologized, "Maria, I am afraid I have given all of your clothes to the wounded men. I hope you don't mind. They needed them to keep warm."

"That's all right, Mrs. Cherny. I only wish I could stay and help, but I have been ordered to return at once." Maria added, "Please remember what I told you about the Russians."

"I will, dear, and be careful," Mrs. Cherny warned. "If you see anyone we know, please ask them to give me a hand. I am all alone here."

Maria motioned the guard out and she followed. She headed back to the old shoemaker. Crossing the tracks, she noticed the train station was full of dead and dying soldiers. She stood and looked around. All the homes were filled with wounded and the roar of the artillery continued.

They made their way through the crowds of soldiers pouring into the city. The rumors were that the Czechs were going to thrust one last counterattack at the Germans before withdrawing at Donovaly. Soldiers broke into stores as Maria and the guard hurried to the shoemaker.

She banged on the shoemaker's door while the guard stood at the entrance. The old man peered through the window, then slowly opened the door, allowing Maria to enter. He apologized, "I have two wonderful pairs of boots for you. I only hope they fit. If they don't, there isn't anything I can do."

Maria handed the old man the gold pieces. He wrapped the boots in rags, then tied them with string and walked with her to the door. Maria asked, "What about the people you made these boots for. Won't they wonder where they are?"

He sadly replied, "Don't worry. After today, no one will pick up anything. Tomorrow, we will have no country."

Maria, touched him on the shoulder. She said nothing and left the store.

Returning to headquarters, Maria went directly to the editing room. She tapped quietly on the door, Tamara opened it and Maria passed the boots in to her.

Studenko saw Maria trying on her boots and remarked, "If we make it out of here, you'll certainly need those."

Messages were coming in as fast as they were going out, only no one was paying attention to them. Books were destroyed, maps burned and files packed for shipment to Moscow.

Maria took advantage of the confusion and sought out Tibor. She asked him what he and the Americans were going to do. He assured her that their planes were coming and that there would be no further problems. Indirectly, Maria was trying to find some way to break loose from the Russians. She hoped Tibor would offer some help. He didn't.

Tibor asked Maria what she had been doing, since he had not seen her in a couple of days.

She replied, "I was trying to round up some warm clothes. If you think it is cold now, let me tell you I have seen it drop to forty below in an hour."

"Did you find any warm clothes?" Tibor asked.

"Yes and no. I found these boots, I just love them. Other than that, I have a light sweater and an even lighter jacket."

Tibor laughed and told her, "Wait here."

He walked back into the American supply room and returned carrying a large military parka with a fur hood. On the back, stenciled in large black letters was: *US Navy*. Maria looked at the back of the jacket and laughed, "This will go over big in Moscow."

Tibor asked her what would she do if she couldn't make it out in the morning? Maria responded, "If that happens, I can assure you we will all be in the same unfortunate situation."

That night, the Slovak Army launched their counterattack, pushing the Germans back nine miles from the Tri Duby Airfield. German artillery kept up a steady barrage. From the sound, they pulled their light guns a few miles back.

Everyone slept in the offices, hallways and supply rooms. Many, filled with anticipation of evacuation, stayed awake and drank coffee, watching the German guns flash in the mountains, and the city of Banska Bystrica die before their eyes.

Maria translated messages all night. Several times, Tamara came out to thank her for the boots. Studenko ordered Tamara to remain at her decoding desk, but told Maria to stop the translations and get some sleep. It was welcome news to Maria. She was exhausted. The last thing she remembered was sitting on the side of her cot. The next instant, she was shaken by a Russian guard. It was morning.

Tamara burned the last of her papers in the trash can. The men destroyed anything that could be used by the enemy. Without warning, Studenko shouted, "Forget the rest. It is time for us to leave. Get into the trucks and staff car in front of the building." He pointed to Maria and yelled, "You, stay close to Lieutenant Tamara."

Almost at a run, everyone left. The building was empty. As Maria and Tamara hurried down the long marble stairway, Maria asked, "Have you seen the Americans?"

Tamara answered, "Yes, they left while it was still dark." Tamara paused for a second, then said, "There, Maria, is the staff car."

They were helped into the back by the driver. Studenko appeared, looking for the automobile, and hurried over and jumped in the front seat with the driver. The driver honked his horn twice and the column of vehicles rolled toward the airfield.

The traffic was horrendous: Cars, trucks, wounded soldiers and artillery jammed the roads. The driver blew his horn and yelled for the troops to move out of the way. The trip, which usually took twenty minutes, took over an hour and a half. As they approached the airfield, a Slovak soldier stopped them. From the way he walked—slowly—Maria could tell he was a veteran, the kind of soldier that nothing could shake. The soldier told them, "This is as far as you can go. The airfield is expected to be under heavy attack soon."

Major Studenko got out of the car and looked forward to the air base. The Germans concentrated a heavy bombardment just north of the field. Their guns were silent for a minute, then the Czechs opened up on the Germans' positions with cannon fire.

There was much small arms fire, but it seemed to be getting faint.

The Slovak soldier addressed Studenko, "If you are going to go, major, now is the time. It may be your last chance."

Studenko ordered the driver forward, barking orders for him to slam the accelerator to the floor. Studenko's face beamed as he spotted a Russian bomber landing on the airfield. He motioned the driver to pull over to the side of the runway. When the plane pulled up, he ordered everyone on the plane. The staff jumped off the truck, unloaded their cargo and carried it on the plane.

Tamara looked at Maria. She knew Maria wanted to be anywhere but on this plane. Maria had translated too many messages; she knew too much about the Russian Army. This fact alone made her a security risk, which would never be tolerated by Moscow. Tamara wanted to help Maria, but knew it was impossible. Maria, only partly aware of her predicament, was a prisoner.

Chapter Five

INTO THE MOUNTAINS

The staff scrambled aboard the plane. The pilot kept the engines turning while the Germans lobbed shells on the field.

Tamara and Maria sat together and gripped their seat tightly as the pilot revved the engines to taxi. Suddenly, the pilot idled the engines. The plane stopped. Studenko ran forward to the cockpit. The pilot pointed to the window and raised the palms of his hands, indicating confusion. In seconds, the crew opened the side hatch. A colonel in the Russian Army shouted through the open hatch for the staff to get off the plane.

Studenko protested, "We have orders to return to Moscow at once."

"You are not going ahead of these wounded soldiers. Get your people off at once—that's an order. There are several more bombers behind this one. You can get on one of them, but you can't stay on this one!" he ordered.

Studenko complied and directed his people off the plane, telling them to leave their equipment on board. They stood watching as the bomber roared down the runway and went into a steep climb to the left.

The next bomber was on its final approach. The wheels were down, the flaps were at seventy-five percent and the pilot prepared to land.

Maria frantically grabbed Tamara's arm as the entire airstrip went up in six gigantic explosions. German artillery laid down a pattern, walking their shells right up the runway.

One mighty detonation after another. The artillery soldiers had the target and the range pinpointed; they continued firing.

The bomber pilot slammed the throttle forward and pulled up. He veered to the left and headed over friendly territory. Maria and Tamara, along with the rest of the staff, were spread flat on the ground. The explosions continued around them. Studenko got up, brushed himself off and announced, "That's it for us. Everyone head for that truck over there."

The driver did not have to be reminded to accelerate. The truck, loaded with the Russian staff, roared back to town. It seemed like the Germans used it for a target. Rounds hit all around the truck. The staff gathered in the forward part of the truck, trying to protect themselves.

Soon they were out of range of the artillery; they joined the doomed caravan headed back to Banska Bystrica. Blood-soaked troops marched along side the truck. Burning vehicles were everywhere. Maria lifted her head and looked back at the airfield. It was one enormous explosion. Black smoke billowed into the air, and the thunder of explosions echoed throughout the mountains.

The driver proceeded slowly toward the headquarters building, weaving his way through retreating troops. When the truck stopped, Studenko jumped from the cab and ran around to the back, "Maria, Maria, I want you to get out here and go back to the office. See if you can salvage anything we can use. Most of our stuff is still on the bomber that left for Moscow. I guess our only chance is to head to Donovaly with the Slovak troops. See what you can find. I'll be back for you in about an hour."

Tamara gave Maria a tight hug. You could tell that she knew they would never return. Maria waved farewell as the truck again inched its way through the mass of troops leaving the city.

Standing on the sidewalk, Maria wondered what was happening. First, the Russians watched her like a bird of prey. Next, she felt they had dumped her on the street.

Maria walked up the stairs of their old quarters and assembled parts of a discarded field phone in a box. Considering the Russians' erratic behavior, they might return. She was distracted by loud voices down the hall. Not sure of the situation, she proceeded with caution. Hiding herself, she peeked around the corner: It was the Americans.

They noticed her and yelled, "Maria, what in hell are you doing back?"

She answered, "I couldn't get out on the Russian bomber. The Germans blew the place to bits."

Schwartz hollered, "Tell us! Our asses nearly bit the dust."

"What does that mean?" Maria wondered aloud.

Tibor looked at her, grinned and replied, "It's just another American expression, Maria. It isn't English."

Maria continued, "I thought that your planes were supposed to come early, what happened?"

Joe Morton, the reporter, told her "Lt. Green was instructed to fire three green flares—the signal for the bombers to breakaway from the formation and land. Green fired the three flares as the planes passed overhead, but not one of those bastards broke formation." He went on, "They never made the slightest attempt. As you see, here we are. I feel sorry for the pilots with us. Most of them are weak and sick. I wish they could have made it out."

McGregor interrupted, "Maria, do you have any ideas? We have no transportation; we don't know the area; and none of us speaks the language. The biggest problem is transportation. There just isn't any."

McGregor had an idea. He jumped off the desk that he was sitting on and said, "Listen, I want everyone who is able to go and look for a car, truck or anything we can travel in. If we all split up and look, maybe one of us will find something. Meet back here, say, in two hours. That should give us enough time."

McGregor, before leaving, turned to Maria and said, "You should come with us. It will be sure death if you remain here."

Reluctantly, Maria agreed.

The Americans, except a few sick pilots, scurried off in search of a vehicle.

Looking out the window, Maria watched as the army, once the pride of Czechoslovakia, turned into a horde of animals, roaming the streets, smashing, looting, fighting and drinking. History was unfolding right before her eyes. The horrible sight she witnessed had the impact of the French Revolution, the fall of the Roman Empire and the collapse of Spain under the Moors. If this was the end of her life, so be it, but first she was going to act.

While she stood watching, she casually zipped up her Navy foul weather jacket. Against McGregor's orders, she walked out of the door—and into the embryo of her nation's death. It was the beginning of the end. The temporary government had collapsed. There was no law or order, no leadership. The mask of humanity was removed, exposing man as the brutal animal that he was.

Soldiers broke into wine cellars and wandered the streets. Waving their bottles and singing, they grabbed any woman they saw. Store windows were shattered, looting was commonplace. Civilians and military personnel carried lamps, statues, clothes, chairs and a million other useless articles. The homes not abandoned were broken into. Things not carried off were destroyed in fits of whirling frenzy.

Maria walked with her hands in her pockets and the fur hood of her coat turned up around her head. One drunken soldier then another grabbed at her. She had no trouble shoving them away. She looked at the hospital, knowing that the wounded, too sick and weak to travel, would be left in the care of medical personnel. They would have to take their chances with the Germans. There was no way they could make the trip to Donovaly.

Horses, thin and weak, were forced onward. Their drivers beat them without mercy until their backs were soaked in their own blood, forcing them to pull overloaded wagons filled with wounded or military equipment. Troops, obviously fatigued, hung onto the sides of the wagons, knowing, if they stopped, there would be no way to resume the march to Donovaly.

Maria had seen enough of the disaster. She trudged back through the ragtag humanity, pushing and shoving back the men who made advances. She knew not what her fate was going to be, but she was sure of one thing: There was no way that she was going to become part of the rabble.

As Maria turned the corner, the soldier guarding the entrance to the headquarters building was a welcome sight.

When she reached the office, Tibor said, "Maria, those Russians aren't coming back. I think you should get ready to move out with us."

Maria snapped, "What do you mean 'get ready?' This is it! And don't you say, 'join the crowd.' You Americans use that expression far too often."

"How about this for a good old American expression: If we don't get our asses in gear, we won't be going anywhere, except to a German prison."

Maria laughed, "What kind of expression is that?"

The Americans returned one at a time. Mac asked Lain if the men found any transportation. Lieutenant Green felt McGregor was gaining the confidence of the men and that he was gradually losing his authority. Attempting to bolster his command, Green walked over to Mac and said, "If no one finds anything, let me know, as soon as the last man returns. If worse comes to worse, I found something. First, let's see what the others find."

All the men returned within the two-hour period. Their stories were always the same: no luck. One man said he spent an hour trying to speak Slovak to a man who only spoke French, and he was really pissed.

When he finished telling his story to McGregor, Maria leaned over to Mac and asked, "What did he mean when he said, '. . . really pissed?' "

Mac explained, "It's an American expression."

Maria soon surmised the phrase "It's an American expression" meant don't pursue the meaning.

Mac notified Lt. Green that everyone returned and there was no transportation. Green banged on the table with the butt of his .45 caliber pistol and yelled, "Listen up! I want everyone to stay in this room until I return. When I do, I want you all to be ready to haul ass. Is that understood?"

The men acknowledged his order. He walked over to Mac and said, "If anything happens to me, you better take command. If I am not back here in fifteen minutes . . . well, you get the picture."

With that, he turned and hurried off, as though he only had a few minutes to complete what he was doing.

The men waited, wondering what he was going to do. Time rapidly passed. Mac, not quite sure what was happening, became concerned when Green didn't return. He called to the pilots that were sitting in the hallway. Just as he was about to speak, an artillery shell slammed through the rear of the building. All of them hit the deck. Plaster fell from overhead. As the men brushed themselves off, Green finally returned.

He shouted his order, "Everybody's ass out of here, now!"

Maria ran behind the men, helping the weaker pilots. Mac ran along with her. She guessed, "Don't tell me, another American expression?"

He acknowledged, "Right."

Once out front, the sixteen downed pilots and eighteen members of Green's mission stared at a beat-to-death school bus.

As they gawked, Maria parroted, "Everybody's ass on board."

Mac, Lain and the pilots laughed out loud. Lt. Green yelled for them to get in. Something caught Lain's attention, "Jesus Christ, look there, it's the fuckin' Nazis."

Green got a quick look at the German infantry as they moved from house to house down the street. In minutes, they fired at the bus.

Lain and Mac were the last to dive on board as Green floored the bus and drove down a side street.

Green gasped, "Maria! For Christ's sake, where am I going?"

"When you come to the end of this street, turn left," Maria instructed.

As they passed another alley, two German soldiers fired several rounds through the rear window of the bus. One round went through Lt. Gaul's cap. He responded, at the top of his lungs, by shouting several harsh *American* expressions.

Once on the road to Donovaly, the tension eased and the men returned to bitching about the planes not arriving. Maria felt uneasy. She was the only woman in the group and the constant swearing and yelling was foreign to her.

As they approached the mountains, the road was cluttered. They were engulfed in human and vehicle traffic jams. Thousands of people fled the beautiful city, trying to escape the German onslaught. There were wounded on top of cars. Dead horses lined the road. Children screamed. The elderly, with a futile gaze, scanned the passers-by, looking for relatives.

The farther into the mountains they went, the worse the conditions. All the soldiers, Partisans and civilians made it impossible to move faster than a crawl. Drivers blew horns. Occasionally, a military MP would try to control the situation by pushing stalled trucks and cars to the side of the road. Soldiers blew up heavy artillery so it would not fall into the hands of the Germans.

The lines of people reminded Maria of a giant boa constrictor, winding its way through the mountain pass. There was, however, a sense of order about it. Military units tried to remain together. A few units still had officers leading their columns. Maria sat dazed on the bus, staring at the appalling sight. She was torn between fear and depression.

Not wanting to see the misery any longer, Maria looked through the window to the snow-covered mountain tops. Fear raced into her heart as she noticed six dark spots, outlined by the snow, racing toward them. Maria called out, "Mac, I think we are going to be hit. German fighters are coming in on us."

Lt. Green jammed on the brakes and swung the door open as he yelled, "Out! Everybody out! Jesus Christ, this is all we need."

The men scrambled to the side of the road, finding cover anywhere they could—behind boulders or flat on their stomachs in the open. Maria helped two of the weak pilots to a ditch at the side of the road. As the planes turned and lined up with the column, she heard the familiar but terrifying sound of sputtering machine guns. She lifted her head to watch as the planes attacked the forward part of the column. Thousands scattered as the fighters strafed back and forth over the retreating mass.

Light bombs caused more panic than damage. Slovak soldiers returned the fire, using only rifles and small automatic weapons. They hit nothing. As quickly as it started, it was over. The moment the planes disappeared, people filled the road again. The bodies of their countrymen lay strewn on either side of the road. The moans and cries increased as people had to leave their loved ones lying in the road. There would be no Christian burials, the Germans were too close.

Standing on the side of the first mountain, Joe Morton watched as the Czechoslovakian rear guard held the advancing German patrols.

Mac was now driving the bus; driving meant stopping and starting every few minutes. Darkness crept through the mountain passes. Firing near the rear of the column faded, and a feeling of temporary security spread through the group.

Adding chaos to the confusion, cars and trucks piled up at the base of the second mountain. It was steeper than the first, causing more vehicles to fail. Now, the refugees had to wind their way through the debris. The old bus billowed steam from its radiator. The engine, under too heavy a load, finally died.

Mac tried to restart it repeatedly. Finally, in disgust, he hit the steering wheel with his fist, turned to the men and said facetiously, "End of the line men. Make sure you have your transfers for the next bus, which should be along at any moment."

The group filed off the bus into the cold blackness of the night. As Lt. Green passed by Mac, still sitting in the driver seat, he said, "Remember, I'm still in charge and I will give the orders."

Mac, who had an enormous amount of combat experience, replied, "What other order could you give in this situation?"

Green warned, "Look, don't start. I'll give the orders and that's all there is to it."

"Fine by me," Mac remarked.

As the group trudged through the night, they occasionally stopped to look through the discarded articles, on the side of the road. A burden to their owners, personal belongings were scattered everywhere. The men looked back down the mountain into the valley and saw the rear guards jam gas-soaked rags into the gas tanks of cars and trucks, then ignite them. They did their best to see that nothing would get into the hands of the enemy.

The group halted for a minute to watch the explosions illuminate the walls of the valley. The trees threw dancing shadows back and forth across the snow. Then there was one enormous detonation. A ball of fire shot up into the blackness. Finally, silence and nothing but the wind.

The refugees pressed on higher into the mountains. Civilians and military personnel departed the main route, following tributaries to unknown destinations.

Cold and covered with mud, Green's group moved slowly, but continued all night. As they approached a fork in the road, they saw a Czech colonel with several armed guards. It was his job to direct stragglers to their units and to periodically check papers, looking for deserters. He motioned the group to come close to him and questioned them in Slovak, "Are you the Americans?"

Maria answered for them, "They are."

"Tell them my orders are for them to report to the hotel at the top of the mountain. It is now headquarters for the CFI."

This was welcome news for the team and their pace picked up. Lain and Mac, along with Green, worried about the pilots' condition. They suffered more with each mile they covered.

Military units set up camps throughout the mountains. Soon small flickers of light emerged as the men started fires to keep warm. First one, then another, until thousands of glimmering lights stretched to infinity.

Rounding a bend in the road, Green's group stopped. There, constructed of highly polished logs, was a resort hotel. With all of its majesty, it resembled a temple to God, reaching from the mountain into the heavens.

Cold and hungry, Maria and the Americans filed into the hotel. It was extraordinary. The former ski resort was spacious and rugged, yet filled with dignity—a dignity that was deteriorating rapidly. The Slovak Army, while establishing their headquarters, tore out walls, dragged communication wire between rooms and set up gun positions from every opening in the building.

The Slovak commanding officer called the men over and told them, "Your group can sleep on the third floor. We saved rooms there for the foreign missions."

A CFI corporal lead the way and the men, fatigued from the debacle that began with the bombing of the airfield, retired to their rooms.

Maria stayed in the lobby, trying to get information from the Slovak commander. She explained that General Viest ordered her to help the Russians and now she was with the Americans. He listened sincerely. When she finished, he suggested she remain with the Americans: None of them spoke the language, they didn't know the area, they had no connections in the country and they had only two radios, one of which frequently failed.

Having nowhere to go, Maria decided to stay with the Americans and share their fate. She was up early and ventured out into the hallway. There was much activity already. Rumors flew: The Germans were forming for an attack on their position. There was no contact with the rear guard. The main command under General Viest could not be found.

As she approached the Americans' rooms, she heard Mac arguing with Lt. Green, "We should break into small groups. That way, at least some of us will stand a chance of getting out."

"We are not going to separate, and that's final," Green maintained.

Outside, the Slovak Army dug in, setting up what artillery they had left and placing their machine guns in a cross-fire position, overlooking the roads and valley.

Maria strolled through the hotel, observing everything. Walking along the hall on the second floor, she heard, "Maria!" She turned to see Tamara running down the hallway toward her.

"Tamara, thank God, you are all right," Maria responded.

"We were caught up in the evacuation and couldn't return," Tamara explained.

Then Studenko came out of his room. He immediately took Maria's hand and apologized for not returning to pick her up at headquarters. Maria accepted his apology and reported that she destroyed what she could at the old headquarters. She was not totally convinced that he was telling her the truth about coming back, but decided his explanation would do for now.

Maria turned back to Tamara, asking, "What are you going to do now?"

"We don't really know. We are trying to contact Moscow, but we aren't having much success."

Showing his concern for Tamara, Studenko announced, "I only hope that I can get Lieutenant Tamara out of here. Do you realize what would happen to her if the Germans got her?"

Maria wasn't impressed. "I'm sure they would do the same thing to me, but they are never going to get the chance."

Studenko continued, "You should stay with us, Maria."

She refused, "No, I have been assigned by the CFI to aid the Americans.

Studenko looked over at Tamara. She raised her eyebrows and shrugged her shoulders. Tamara was concerned with Maria's plight. She even suggested Maria better head for the Russian lines if all else failed. She knew how Maria felt about communism and the Red Army. They hugged each other and Maria shook hands with Studenko, wishing him well with whatever he decided to do.

On her way back to the Americans, Maria recognized one of Pavlovich's friends from Nitra.

He greeted her, "Hello Maria. What do you think of this mess?"

"My God, don't mention it. What are you doing here?" Maria asked.

He explained, "I have been with Pavlovich on the front lines. When our position fell to the Germans, we were forced back to Banska Bystrica. Finally, we tried to hold them on the northern outskirts of the city. When that failed, we joined the victory parade to Donovaly."

Maria was scared. "Do you think the Germans will attack soon?"

"Any hour now, Maria, I'm almost positive," he warned.

Maria inquired, "If you can't hold them off, what do you suggest I do?"

"Are you with any group?" he wanted to know.

"Yes, I am helping the Americans," Maria told him.

He suggested, "Tell them when the attack starts to head in any direction that looks open and run like hell."

"What about Pavlovich?" Maria asked.

Pavlovich's friend told her, "He is here, down the road. He decided to fight it out with the Germans. He is tired of running."

"When and if you see him, would you tell him I said hello," Maria requested.

He promised, "I sure will. And you take care of yourself, Maria. Remember what I told you. Get the hell out of here in any direction that is open."

Maria thanked him, "Thanks again for your suggestion."

The two parted and Maria continued through the hotel. Standing in the lobby, she noticed the Americans were outside and decided to join them. Walking through the huge entrance door, Pvt. Brown, a radio operator, called to her to join the group.

Lt. Green walked over to greet her, "Maria have you heard anything, anything at all? So few people speak English, we can't find out what is going on."

Maria repeated what she heard, "Everyone expects the Germans to mount an attack any time. The Russians are here, but they are no better off than you. So far, they have been unable to contact Moscow, and they have no idea what they are doing."

Lt. Gaul chimed in, "There isn't any reason to ask you how the Czech Army is doing. We already know they're finished."

Mac gave Gaul a piercing glance, then turned to Maria and said, "Listen, you have to stay with us. If we are going to stand a chance, we need someone that speaks these languages. I will notify the commander of the CFI. He will notify General Viest, and that should end it."

Lt. Green responded, "I'll notify the CFI commander. Now, you are an official part of the group, code name: Dawes Team."

"Is that good or bad?" Maria wanted to know.

A pilot sitting on the wall remarked, "This is just great. Now we have a woman in command."

Lain, Perry, Dunlevy and the rest of the team laughed, but the pilots, who kept mostly to themselves, shook their heads in disapproval.

John Schwartz, a member of the team Maria had never spoken with, stepped forward and said, "Maria, you have been with those Russians for quite awhile, haven't you?"

Maria responded, "Yes, but I was under orders, the same as you are. At first, I thought all of the liberation forces were under one command, fighting to free my country. I found out differently later. It made no difference, since I was already under orders to help the Russians."

Schwartz continued, "You must be one hell of a naive person to believe that."

Maria admitted, "You're right. At first, I was oblivious to the situation. It didn't take me long to figure out what was going on."

"Maybe you can tell us what the real situation is." Schwartz asked.

The men listened as Maria explained that General Malar of the Slovak Army and part of his staff flew to Russia in May. He took with him the secret German plans for the defenses in the Carpathian Mountains, their main resistance against the advancing Red Army. If the Germans could hold those positions, they could keep the Russians from spreading through eastern Slovakia.

She explained, "For General Malar's help, the Russians promised to throw in two full divisions when the Slovak uprising started." Maria looked Schwartz straight in the eyes and continued, "They were the only ones who offered to help us."

Schwartz said nothing and walked over to join the pilots standing next to the entrance, smoking and drinking beer.

Joe Morton approached Maria, "Don't worry about these men. Most are on edge and all of them are uninformed."

Maria replied, "I understand, Mr. Morton."

Morton corrected her, "If we are going to be together, you have to call me Joe. Isn't that what you call all the American soldiers over here?"

Maria smiled and walked back through the lobby. On her way to her room, she stopped at the communication center and asked if any activity had been reported. She was told there was none.

New soldiers arrived every hour, crowding the hotel. Three more women were assigned to Maria's room. They questioned her, asking where she had come from, what she was doing at headquarters and who were all the Americans? She politely, and with some tact, eased herself out of the discussion and crawled into bed. She was still recovering from the ordeal of the retreat.

Mac, followed by Lain and Dunlevy, entered Green's room. The men sat on the floor and the bed as McGregor explained to Green he had walked back through the valley and was never challenged by a military guard. He suggested they not depend on the Slovak Army, they should post their own men.

The two of them hashed it out. Finally, Green agreed. He suggested they stand guard in threes. McGregor would take one post on the main road in front of the oncoming Germans. Catlos and Paris would flank him on the periphery.

Around nightfall, Mac, Catlos and Paris put on their heavy clothing: several pairs of socks, gloves and ski masks under the hoods of their parkas. After checking one another, they swung their M-1 rifles over their shoulders and left the hotel through the main entrance.

They walked three abreast down the road. The stillness was disturbing as they listened to snow crunch underfoot. Reaching the split in the main road, Mac told Catlos and Paris to return to the crossing at 0530. Mac ordered Catlos a few hundred yards down the second road. Lt. Paris was ordered to the side of the mountain, across from Mac.

Mac proceeded down the main road. He noticed the roof of a small shepherd's cabin in the trees to his right. He held his rifle at port arms as he made his way through the snow to the hut. He approached with caution, moving his weapon to the ready position. Then, with the heel of his boot, he kicked the door in. The snow flew back in his face as the door slammed against the inside wall—it was empty. He placed some of his ammunition on a shelf near the door, set his rifle in the corner and stood his post from inside, facing the valley.

Several times during the night, his chin would slowly drop until it hit his chest. On and off, he opened his eyes and snapped his head back, trying to keep awake. He stomped his feet, trying to keep warm. He slapped his arms with his hands and blew breath into his fists. During an interlude between warming exercises, a familiar sound rang in his ears—the clicking of canteens striking the legs of running German soldiers. He instinctively inserted a round into the chamber of his rifle, released the safety and stood motionless, waiting. The German patrol turned left and moved off in the opposite direction.

Wide awake, he realized his team's futile position. There was no hope, not if the Germans were sending patrols right through the rear guard, if there even was a rear guard.

Mac looked at his watch, it was 0515. He gathered his ammunition, shoving the loose rounds into the pocket of his cumbersome jacket. His M-1 rifle was so cold his gloves stuck to the stock.

It was still pitch black outside as Mac made his way up the main path toward the crossroad. Knowing German patrols were in the area, he advanced with care to the split in the road. Catlos and Paris were there waiting. Mac ran to them and asked, "Did you see anything?"

Lt. Paris answered, "The only thing I saw was that patrol. They were headed in your direction and then they turned off."

The team walked back to the hotel. Catlos, suffering from the cold, quickened the pace as he said, "If a German patrol can come this close to the hotel, you can bet your ass they are going hit this place with everything they have, and soon."

Lt. Paris, having difficulty breathing in the cold night air, replied, "You are right! If I were the Germans, I would attack soon."

The three men accelerated their jogging to a rapid trot. They made it all the way back to the hotel without being challenged by any soldiers. Mac was now disillusioned with the Slovak Army. As the three of them burst through the mammoth door of the hotel, Mac ran to the headquarters room. There was only one sergeant on duty. McGregor screamed at him to get the DO (duty officer). The sergeant, not quite understanding what Mac said, noticed the concerned look on his face, so he immediately went to the back room and woke the DO.

The Slovak officer couldn't speak English. Frustrated, Mac slammed his fist on the table and bolted up the stairs to Maria's room. He banged on her door continuously until she answered. The other women in Maria's room complained because they had been awakened so rudely. Mac shouted an explanation to Maria and she threw on her clothes and ran with him back to the DO.

As she started to relay Mac's report about the lack of posted guards and how close the German patrols were—less than a mile away—an explosion shook the hotel. Orders were shouted in French, Czech, Hungarian, Russian, English and Polish: "Get out!"

Commands echoed, "Grab the ammunition! Save the radios! Run for Christ's sake, run for it!"

Men dove out windows on the third floor, landing head first in the snow. Glass flew everywhere, as the German machine guns sprayed the hotel. The third floor suffered repeated explosions as German infantry fired rifle grenades through every window.

The CFI managed to set up two water-cooled, .30 caliber machine guns at the entrance to the lobby. As they returned fire, hotel personnel scattered. For a second, the small arms fire stopped. Then German light artillery broke the silence. Shells landed on both sides of the hotel. Another shell blasted through the roof and blew the third level to bits.

Maria was thrown to the floor with Mac. He jumped to his feet and grabbed Maria by the hair to pull her upright. She took a swipe at her face, trying to brush the debris that clouded her vision. Mac latched on to her wrist with a death grip and, at a full run, pulled her down the hallway leading from the lobby. Still moving at breakneck speed, he pulled her closer to him. As they approached the end of the hall, without the slightest hesitation, Mac, holding Maria, dove through the window head first, shattering the glass. Maria, dazed from the explosion, held on, fused to McGregor by fear.

Bodies of the dead and wounded turned the snow red as the firing continued. Maria jumped to her feet after her initial fear passed. Mac, limping slightly, led the way into the forest. Using the light from the intermittent explosions in the hotel, they zig-zagged their way through the trees. Maria stopped and covered her face when she heard an artillery shell whistle by directly in front of her. The explosion blew the bodies of several Slovak soldiers into the air, splattering blood on Maria's legs and hair. She held on to the trunk of a tree, quivering, as the barrage increased. Branches flew from the tree trunk as the blasts rained on the horrified troops. She trembled with fear. Mac took her by the arm and forced her ahead. Then the artillery abruptly changed direction to the other side of the hotel.

Just as the two of them thought that it was safe, Mac heard a distant hollow thud. He knew what it was and shouted, "Mortars!"

He threw Maria to the ground. The cycle began again, a rapid succession of explosions, followed by screams from the wounded. The German soldiers continued their deadly mortar blasts.

Maria was now lying face up. The morning sky turned black; a gust of wind swirled from the north, then from the east. Maria covered her face with her hands as a heavy mist fell on her. It ran through her fingers to her face. Mysteriously, calm settled over them. She gradually removed her hands from her face. All was quiet now, but a strange thick fog covered the mountains. It was so heavy Mac and Maria could barely see their hands in front of their faces.

Maria whispered to Mac, "My God, what is this? There must be an American expression to cover this phenomenon."

Mac answered, "There is. The man is really pissed off."

Maria shrugged, "It doesn't make any sense to me, but I'll take your word for it."

Mac gradually helped Maria to her feet. They stood side by side, listening like two deer stalked by hunters. Then a shrill scream broke the peace, "Nemci, Nemci (Germans, Germans)."

The two of them ran off again. The fog stayed about a foot above their heads. Mac tried to remember where the heavily wooded area was, but lost his sense of direction. They slowed to almost a crawl, walking as though they were barefoot in a field of broken glass. To their right, the fog illuminated small arms fire.

Again they heard the warning, "Nemci, Nemci." Now, they sensed figures darting in front of them, but they could see nothing. Machine gun fire flashed on their left, then their right. Shrapnel from a hand grenade tore through McGregor's collar and someone fired a pistol only a couple of feet from his head. Ahead and to their right, machine gun fire raked the area.

Maria fell over the bodies of several German soldiers, ran a few more feet and tripped on a dead Partisan. Then Mac threw her to the ground again when he saw the flash of gunfire directly in front of them. This time, she landed face-to-face with the Russian guard that Studenko had sent with her to the Chernys' house. She felt his pulse: none.

As they were ready to stand again, they both saw the boot of a German soldier. The bayonet that extended from his rifle was only inches from Maria's face. She closed her eyes and stopped breathing. There was a yell in Polish and a pistol shot. Then the German slumped into the fog, falling over Maria, plunging the bayonet into the ground next to her face.

Again, Mac and Maria jumped to their feet, and ran back into the fog. Maria slammed into a German soldier. He was so startled that he was unable to bring his weapon to bear. By the time he regained his senses, they changed direction, so he fired to their right.

Maria tried to stay as close as she could to Mac. When the underbrush got thicker, she knew that they made it to the wooded area. Soon the brush was so heavy they had to stop. Mac put his index finger over his lips and the two stood quietly together. Cries and moans seemed to come from every direction—distant, not close. For the moment, the two of them were safe.

Maria whispered to Mac, "Thank God for the fog."

Mac responded, "If you don't believe in God, now is the time to start."

Maria added, "We have a Slovak saying like that, only ours goes, 'If you don't drink, now is the time to start.'"

The gunfire stopped and the miraculous fog remained. It was their shield of life. To others, a blanket of death.

Mac and Maria sat on the trunk of a fallen tree still listening and trying to anticipate their next move. The fog began to lift, rising leisurely like a majestic galleon setting sail, slipping out of her harbor to the open sea. As the fog lifted, Maria thought she was losing control of her senses. She strained to see through the rising mist. A Slovak soldier approached on horseback, riding as though he was on a Sunday outing. He came closer, still riding as though nothing had happened. She squinted, trying to get a better look.

Maria recognized him, "Mac! it's Jano, Polack's driver."

As he rode up, Maria grabbed the reins of his horse. She exclaimed, "I can't believe it! How did you get here?"

Into The Mountains

"Maria Zima. I thought they captured you. Many Partisans said you were executed."

Maria asked, "You weren't at the hotel, where did you come from?"

"Yeagerof's camp." Jano reported, "I was sent here to find out what is going on. All kinds of rumors are flying around and you can't run a military operation on rumors."

Maria introduced him, "Jano, this is Captain McGregor. He is an American officer and I am helping him and his group. Now, he is helping me, but that is a long story. There was a terrible battle here. It only stopped about twenty minutes ago. At least we haven't heard any shooting for twenty minutes."

The three of them walked back to the hotel so Jano could question the survivors, if there were any, for his report to Yeagerof. Maria asked Jano, "Do you have any idea what happened to Polack?"

"No one really knows. Rumors say the Germans got him."

As they came to the edge of the woods, they noticed that the Germans had pulled out. The meadow was covered with debris, clothes, weapons, ammunition and equipment. The wounded were dragged off to temporary aid stations set up around the smoldering remains of the hotel. Staying close to the edge of the forest, they proceeded cautiously. Mac halted and looked at Maria, "Will you look at that."

They watched General Viest in the distance, with his wife and eight-year old son, stroll across the battlefield as though they were walking to church.

A group of Slovak soldiers approached from the opposite direction. Maria stopped them and asked if they had seen any Americans.

They had. "Down that way, on the other side of the hotel," the soldiers told her. The soldiers stopped and also watched General Viest. The sergeant in charge of the detachment pointed to him and said, "He is heartbroken over all of this. These forces were the remains of his command."

Reaching the opposite side of the hotel, they saw hundreds of people. Some cared for the wounded. Others moaned in pain from their wounds; many were still in shock. Maria spotted the cap of an American pilot. He was in the crowd to her right, helping a wounded Slovak soldier with his dressing. She raised her hand high and pointed in his direction so Mac could see where to head. Then she noticed Green. He, too, was aiding a wounded man. Lt. Gaul's voice could be heard above anyone else, bitching about the Slovak Army's disorganization. Catlos and Lt. Paris worked their way to Maria and Mac.

Perry greeted them, "I guess Lt. Paris was right about the attack."

Mac replied, "He was. Unfortunately, we were a little too late with our information."

Maria pulled the sleeve of Mac's jacket. When he looked at her, she motioned with her head to look in the distance. Mac raised his head to look above the crowd. There were the pilots, all huddled together at the base of a large tree. They were soaking wet from the rain that was now mixed with snow. They noticed Maria and Mac approaching and, with a burst of energy, started talking all at once.

"Where in hell have you two been?"

"You two look worse than we do."

"Welcome home."

"Sorry we can't ask you to stay. We no longer have a place of our own."

"Maria, what did you do when the fireworks started?"

Maria admitted, "I ran like hell—just like you guys."

Lt. Gaul joined the group. As he walked up, Maria said, "Hi there, Lt. Gaul."

"Hi there, my ass. Get us out of this mess," he demanded.

Maria protested, "I just got here. Give me a chance to find out what is going on, and I will see what I can do."

Maria asked Tibor and Lt. Green to join her. She was going to try to find the temporary headquarters. They were directed to the woods about a mile behind the hotel. Maria spoke with a major in the CFI. He was moving what was left of the Army to Yeagerof's camp and suggested she bring the Americans there.

The team's communications were unreliable. At least they could have the Russians relay their messages to Bari if they had trouble with their radios.

Lt. Green had Maria ask if anyone compiled a list of the missing. The officer answered and Maria translated, "He said to tell you he doesn't know where half his command is."

Lt. Green said, "Tell him we are missing four men: Mican, Schwartz, Miller and Heller."

Maria translated Green's statement. The officer replied, "You look for them. They are your troops, not mine."

Maria explained to Lt. Green that they should move as soon as possible, suggesting they go to Yeagerof's camp. Returning to the group, Lt. Green told his men that they were going to join the Russian Partisans at Yeagerof's camp to the north.

Mac asked Maria if Alexie Sevelenko, his Russian friend, was in Yeagerof's camp. She told him she had heard nothing that would confirm or deny his presence. She wanted to know where he had met the Russian. He explained he trained him in ordnance in North Africa, teaching him how to use a bazooka, an anti-tank weapon. A Russian guard in Banska Bystrica had told him Alexie was in the mountains, teaching the Russian Partisans to use bazookas.

Jano interrupted, saying he was heading back to camp with his report and that he would see Maria there. He gave her precise directions, wished the Americans well and mounted his horse.

As he rode off, the pilots joked and called after him, "Hi, ho, silver away. Who was that masked man? I don't know but his silver bullet is still in my ass."

Maria, not understanding any of this chatter, just shook her head.

Lt. Green called off the search for the four missing men. He presumed they were killed in the hotel. There was no use searching for them any longer. Green had the men organized, but they were a pitiful, tired group. Even Nelson Paris, the photographer who seldom spoke, complained. He stopped when Dunlevy started in on him, asking if he wanted to carry his radio that weighed, according to Dunlevy, over a "thousand fuckin' pounds."

Green formed them in a line, trying to maintain order. He put Maria at the head of the line so she could lead.

"O.K., which way do we go?" Green asked.

Jokingly, Maria said, "We will do like the American Indian, and follow the tracks of Jano's horse through the snow."

Maria thought her comment might lift the spirits of the men, but her attempt failed. The pitiful column trudged through the snow. Still mixing with rain, snowfall increased. The ground was churned up by the battle and turned into mud. For miles, their ankles sunk into the mud with every step. But Maria was worried more about the team's morale than their physical condition. The pilots at the end of the line constantly bitched. They wished they had stayed in the concentration camps; there they had food and a place to sleep.

The march continued slowly through the valley. When the pilots called Maria's name the column stopped. A second group of people caught up with them. The Americans yelled and whistled; Maria watched as the group came near. It was Studenko, Tamara and Popov, the evil commissar. They led the Russian mission. Maria and Tamara saw each other and ran to meet. The two girls slid in the mud and called each other names. They hugged and kissed.

Tamara pointed to her feet and said, "Thank God you got these boots for me."

A few pilots yelled, "I'm cold. Send that red-headed Russian over here to keep me warm. Tell her Joe Morton is a Catholic priest and can marry us right now."

Tamara, not understanding a word they said, did what Maria could not: raise the morale of the Americans. Maria kept the momentum going and yelled back, "She thinks that Horvath and Brown are handsome, but she only likes officers."

Horvath and Brown were both sergeants, but the pilots all cheered since they were officers.

Studenko told Tamara in Russian they must move on. Maria asked Tamara to smile and wave at the Americans. Tamara did not have to be told why. In combat since the beginning of the War, she knew what she was doing. She waved and pulled off her heavy Russian Army cap so her red hair fell to her shoulders. The pilots cheered again and she smiled. The Russians soon left. Maria, still at the head of the line, followed them.

Into The Mountains

Popov, the commissar, was last in the Russian line, just ahead of Maria. He carried a bundle that was obviously becoming a burden to him. After they traveled about a mile, he stopped and opened the package. Maria watched as he removed heavy winter underwear. He stepped over to a large puddle and dropped them into the mud. With his foot, he ground them deep into the mud.

As Maria's column caught up to him, she asked, "Why are you doing that?"

He gave her a hollow stare and condescendingly said, "They are my belongings. I will do with them what I want."

Maria pursued her inquiry, "Are all communists as selfish as you? Or are you unique?"

"Who cares what you think," he responded in disgust.

Mac asked Maria what was going on. She told him what Popov did and commented, "Half his people are freezing and he does something like that, can you believe it? What causes a man to do such a thing?"

Mac answered, "I don't know. Maybe he is just a son of a bitch from the ground up."

Tamara drifted to the rear of her column to speak with Maria. They exchanged stories of how they survived the attack and tried to figure out what was ahead. Fatigue set in, so their conversation ebbed as the march continued.

Chapter Six

SURVIVAL

By nightfall, they reached Yeagerof's camp. The night air carried a voice that rumbled and a laugh that resounded above the others. Mac slapped Lain on the back and remarked, "There is only one person with a laugh like that: Alexie."

Alexie Sevelenko, was all Russian, lived on vodka, was drunk half the time and was always ready to fight. It didn't seem to matter who Alexie fought, as long as he could fight. He was short and stocky; his rosy cheeks stood out on his oval face. He bellowed like the Russian bear he was. He brushed the snow from his oversized eyebrows and stared at the Americans.

"Gropas dupa, Mac," he exclaimed as he walked through the column as though they did not exist. He nudged Lt. Gaul and Nelson aside. Paris snapped Alexie's photo as he threw his arms around McGregor, squeezing him tightly.

"You come, we have vodka. It keeps you warm, you come," Alexie said as he shouted orders to several of his men. They helped the column into bunkers that were dug into the side of the mountain.

While Alexie, Mac and Lain renewed their friendship, Maria and the Dawes Team, along with the pilots, were guided into the warm bunkers. The bunkers had floors covered with straw—a luxury.

Maria looked at herself, covered from head to toe with mud, soaking wet, her hair matted and stuck together; even her fingers were white and numb. It took the last of Maria's strength to lie down. Before her eyes closed, she thought, "Thank God my parents cannot see me like this."

At first light, Maria, the pilots and the men from Dawes Team were up and taken to the field mess area. Here they had hot soup and coffee. To them it was like Thanksgiving, the hot potato soup tasted as good as a banquet.

Maria watched the pilots. They were ill, almost to a man. They ate slowly and tried to act interested in the group's plans. But it wasn't in them.

Maria told Alexie, in Russian, about the pilots' condition. She wanted to know how long he was going to remain here with his Partisan brigade. He wasn't sure. Maria tried to get a commitment from him, hoping that the pilots could rest, eat and regain their health before they had to move again. He explained he did what he was ordered to do, not what humanity dictated. He was, after all, a soldier.

Just as they finished eating, Maria saw Studenko, Tamara and the mouse, Popov, walking in front of them.

"Hey," Maria called. "Where are you going?"

Tamara waved and yelled, "We are off to Yeagerof's camp. It's over on the next mountain. I'll try to see you later."

Lt. Green, Mac and Lain walked to Alexie's bunker. They wanted to establish radio contact with Bari, Italy, to let headquarters know they were still intact.

Alexie the soldier became Alexie the communist. Mac was told he could not use the Russian's radio unless he got permission from Moscow. Mac and Green were stunned. Lain, personally offended, responded, "Well, kiss my frostbitten ass."

Lt. Green and Lain left the bunker. Mac stayed behind and tried to change Sevelenko's mind, but he would not budge. The subject was closed. Green and Lain relayed the conversation to the pilots and the Dawes Team. The pilots wanted to beat the hell out of the Russian staff.

Dunlevy and Catlos were on the floor trying to get their radios to work, but there was always something—static, a loose tube or a missing wire—that kept them from operating. They took parts from one radio and put them in the other, hoping they would come up with one working wireless. Dunlevy insisted someone sabotaged the radios. He knew they were fine when the team arrived in Czechoslovakia, but later, unexplained problems surfaced.

When Mac entered the bunker, all of the men turned to him and complained. McGregor, disgusted with the Russians, sat with the men and asked Lt. Green if he had any new ideas.

Green mocked, "Ya, don't trust these fuckin' Russians."

Lain looked over at Maria and asked, "Maria, you know these Russians better than any of us, do you have any ideas?"

"Ya, don't trust these fuckin' Russians," Maria parroted, breaking the tension. Everyone laughed.

The pilots started in again, letting the rest of the group know how well organized the Air Corps was and how disorganized the rest of the American military was. They brought unnecessary pressure on Lt. Green, telling him to get them out at once. He shook his head and said, "If I could get you out at once, I would get us all out at once."

Maria cut in, trying to head off a touchy situation, "Listen, I'll go through the camp and find out what I can. At least, it will give us a foundation to work from."

She walked from bunker to hut trying to gather information. There were troops from the north and the east and from other countries, escaped prisoners and regular Slovak Army soldiers.

No one was sure of anything: where the Germans were or where the Russian Army was. Rumors flew. The Americans and British were rumored to be moving through northern Italy. Some soldiers mentioned they heard American troops were in southern Austria.

Maria was returning to the bunker when two Slovak soldiers walked in front of her. They looked like they had just arrived in the camp. One looked at her and asked, "Maria?" He noticed her inquisitive look and quickly replied, "I was a guard at the headquarters building in Banska Bystrica."

"Oh yes," she remembered. "I am trying to get news, anything you can tell me?"

The soldiers hesitated, "Yes, but you might not want to hear it."

"None of the news these days is good. What is it?" Maria insisted.

"The Germans are holding mass executions. Anyone with the Underground or helping the Partisans is being shot without a trial. They posted a death list throughout the city."

He stopped for a moment as though there was more, but he didn't want to continue. Maria noticed him look at the other soldier. Maria demanded, "And, what else?"

"Not only is your name on the top of the list, but your picture has been plastered on every wall in Banska Bystrica. Apparently, they are really after you," the soldiers reported.

Back at the bunker, Maria reported what little news she had. None of it could help their situation. After discussing the situation, the only thing they could agree on was that their present position was not safe and that they should formulate a plan.

Mac and Lain tried again, as forcefully as they could, to convince Lt. Green to split the group into several sections. Alexie, he was sure, would furnish them with guides. They could disperse, making it more difficult for the enemy to find them. That also would give them a better chance to be rescued. At least some of them would survive.

Lt. Green reinforced his leadership, "This isn't a democracy, it is a military unit. I am in command and I have told you before, the subject is closed. We are staying together."

Mac quickly came up with another choice, "We can stay here with Alexie and his forces."

Lt. Green refused, "No, we will leave with the remainder of the CFI and head for the oncoming Russian Army."

There had been no change in the weather; it was still half rain, half snow.

Still uncertain what to do, Maria sat with the Americans, trying to come up with a solution, any solution, to their dilemma.

Colonel Sevelenko sent a runner to their bunker. The messenger, a private, handed Mac the note. It was brief, "Report to communications at once."

Mac showed the message to Lain and Green, then left with the private. The moment Mac entered Alexie's communication bunker, Alexie told him, "I received a report that there is a large enemy force headed in this direction. My guess is that they won't reach us until late tomorrow. You should inform your people."

With the latest intelligence data, Mac returned to the bunker. He did not tell the men. Instead, he took Green aside and shared the report with him. There was no reason to drop this bomb on everyone now.

Dunlevy, tired of trying to repair the radio, made one last effort. He wet the tip of his finger and stuck it into the rear of the set. The electrical shock knocked him back about a foot. However, the radio whistled, crackled, hummed and, to everyone's amazement, produced a faint clicking. The room went silent as Catlos and Dunlevy decoded a message.

Lt. Green inquired, "Who is it?"

Dunlevy responded, "It is another mission trying to contract Bari headquarters. They have been out of contact for some time, like us. They are requesting assistance. The message is signed: *Green Up*."

Mac and Lain leaped to their feet and told Dunlevy to stay in contact with him. The signal faded, but Dunlevy kept rotating the knobs of his radio slowly. He repeated his code name—Dawes Team—hoping Mayer would pick up his call. If Mayer was in contact with Bari, Dunlevy, using his weak radio, could have Mayer relay the Dawes Team's messages for them.

Green Up was the code name for Mayer's mission. He, Hans Wynberg and Franz Weber, did not land as planned on the frozen lake near Innsbruck. They missed their drop zone and landed on a glacier, some 11,000 feet high.

It was only an act of God that the three men found each other following the jump. If the pitch blackness wasn't enough, the snow was up to their necks. A second miracle occurred when they recovered all but one of their containers. Weber, the German, made a sled from a pair of the skis, enabling them to carry their equipment.

Conditions were so bad, Mayer had to take the sled's harness and strap the sled around his shoulders, dragging the equipment behind him, crawling on his hand and knees. Weber and Wynberg tried to help by pushing, without success.

Twelve hours later, they had only covered one mile. They were soaked in their own sweat from the struggle. When they stopped, even for a minute, their clothes would freeze to their bodies.

The next morning, the sun first appeared not over the ridges of the mountains, but at the end of a long valley. It was like a giant flash bulb, bursting into a colossal glare. The light, reflected by the snow, bounced off the sides of the valley.

Almost dead from exhaustion, Mayer looked up at the mountains and grunted, "This has got to be one of the most beautiful sights in the world."

Weber interrupted his nostalgic description of the surrounding scenery, exclaiming, "Look, look there! It's an *amberger hutte* (a ski hut)." These huts, built by local sportsman, housed them during their ski trips. Such huts would certainly be vacant. Skiers would not venture out in this weather. The snow was too deep.

Mayer burrowed into the hut. Reaching a door, he pried it open using a ski pole. The three of them stayed in the cabin a few days, recovering. Hans tried to contact OSS Headquarters, but his radio was too weak or the atmospheric conditions were not right.

On the third evening, they descended to the valley. They moved inch by inch in the darkness. The snow was so bad the Germans did not send out patrols. The team moved undetected to a small village at the entrance of the valley. Weber was wearing the uniform of a German alpine lieutenant. Mayer wanted to wear a German uniform too, but his commanding officer prohibited it.

They found their way to a small coffee shop. Weber told the owner they were German ski troops, with a few days off for recreation. This story was their explanation why Weber was in uniform and the other two were not.

The team needed transportation and asked the owner if she could help them. She directed them to the last house in the village. The man there repaired sleds, skis and shoes. She thought the only way they could travel would be by sled. No other transportation would let them move through the heavy snow.

The sled man helped them secure their equipment on a toboggan, while trying to convince them to stay put. He insisted conditions were too dangerous to travel. He explained there were too many obstacles they were unaware of. Any one of which could cost them their lives.

Weber convinced Mayer that he was the mountain man. He was used to this sort of thing. He was familiar with sleds, snow, high altitude and sudden wind changes. Mayer agreed. Weber would handle the sled; Mayer and Hans would ride, holding the equipment. Weber secured Mayer and Wynberg to the equipment, then gradually moved the sled forward, edging it over the side of the mountain.

Mayer had never known fear, but threw a death grip around Wynberg, squeezing him almost into unconsciousness. The sled ripped down the mountain, moving some seventy miles per hour, to the valley without stopping. Wynberg's eyes were locked in a fixed gaze; fear took over his body, rendering him motionless. Weber sang aloud at the top of his lungs, rocking back and forth as the sled reached suicidal speeds.

Mayer shook some of his fear and tried to break the sled's speed with one of his ski poles, but the speed and powdered snow tore it from his hand. The wild, uncontrolled ride lasted for almost two hours, without a second of calm. Finally, Weber, who actually enjoyed the ride, guided the sled to the outskirts of the town of Oberperfuss.

Mayer picked this town because Weber's fiancee lived there. Wynberg, still suffering from the downhill death ride, sat glued to the sled as Mayer and Weber approached the inn Weber's future bride's family owned.

Mayer and Weber stayed at the inn, hidden in the attic. Weber's fiancee's mother, Frau Liederkirche, not only owned the inn, but ran a farm and a bakery, she was the power of the town. Her daughter and Weber's future bride, Annie, was aghast that Franz returned to his home town. His name was on the German's list of deserters, so he faced a death sentence if he happened to be recognized.

A friend of Weber's, Peter Schatz, hid the sled and Wynberg in his farm house outside town. Wynberg rigged an antenna for his radio by stringing wire back and forth in the farm house's attic.

At the end of the first week, Mayer went to the town beer hall. He sat drinking beer and listening to the stories of the men who worked in the factory, near the town of Kamaten. He befriended some and gathered information, which he passed to Wynberg who radioed it to Bari. News from the beer hall was transformed into intelligence reports: "Messerschmitt Kematen out of production for the past three months, due to lack of supplies."

Mayer gathered and sent much information that was vital for the US Army Air Corps. He gave them important targets—targets that, if eliminated, would destroy Germany's production. His primary mission, though, was to get to Innsbruck. Weber had three sisters living there. If he could rotate his base of operations among them, the team could remain safe.

Once in Innsbruck, Weber grew weary, fearing at any moment the Germans would capture him. The hero of the sled ride was losing his edge. Weber's sister, Aloisia, who worked in a hospital, obtained papers that stated he was on medical leave. She bandaged his face, and he wore his German uniform as he moved about town.

Mayer, back to his original no-fear lifestyle, strutted about town in civilian clothes, talking with everyone he met, civilians and military alike. Weber's other two sisters, Genoveva and Margaret, also helped Mayer with his mission. Margaret worked in administration at the University of Innsbruck. Genoveva worked as a secretary in a government office. With their help, Mayer met two of their friends. One was an Austrian truck driver. He said he was a Nazi, but Austria came first. The other was a man named Leo. He didn't care what he did, if he got paid.

Mayer returned home one night from the bars to find Weber sitting in the dark. Weber had gone out to dinner with Genoveva and ended up sitting next to one of his old friends. He wasn't recognized, but the experience scared him. Now, he refused to move from the house. He was sure his time was coming to an end; he was losing his self-assurance and guts.

Aloisia, the sister that worked in the hospital, managed to get Mayer a German uniform from a lieutenant in the 106th High Alpine Regiment who died of wounds; she simply removed his uniform.

Mayer always gave the appearance of a bull ready to charge. Dressed in his uniform, he walked about town as though he *belonged* to the 106th High Alpine Regiment. Once, he was stopped and questioned by two military policemen. Without even batting an eye, Mayer looked straight at them and said, "I have no papers because our wonderful brothers in arms, the Italian Partisans, robbed me of my money and papers while I was in route to the hospital here in Innsbruck. Here, here look at this." Mayer handed the two MPs a piece of paper on which he had written, "I have lost my papers," and he had signed his name at the bottom.

The two military policemen handed him back his papers as he asked the direction to the *Offizierskasino* (officers club). He smiled, patted one of them on the shoulder and turned and gazed into a clock shop, pretending to admire a Nuremberg egg in the window. Before the MPs left, he called them over and commented, "I used to have one of those, but there is no way I could afford one now. Look at that price."

The two soldiers looked at the miniature clock, agreed with him, then strolled down the street. He felt more secure when Aloisia returned from the hospital that evening with forged papers. Hospital marks were stamped all over them. The stamps she felt, would confuse anyone examining his papers. Even Aloisia was worried when Mayer became a friend of Alois Kuen, a member of the Austrian criminal police. But Kuen was anti-Nazi. On his own, he was destroying files on his countrymen. When ordered to arrest and hold hostages for execution, he would lock up Nazis instead and have them put to death.

Mayer received and transmitted vital sources of information, including: troop movements, factory locations, headquarters buildings and supply depots. He had a chain of people who would take his messages back to Wynberg. This technique kept him from directly connecting himself to Wynberg, protecting his comrade and friend. Wynberg sent messages to Bari; they, in turn, gave targets to the Air Corps, who bombed as instructed.

In return for sending the critical information, Mayer received the following reply: "You and Wynberg promoted to sergeants."

His responding communique was, "Woop de do."

Wynberg caught the contagious Mayer no-fear syndrome. He operated back at the farm, typing his own newspaper. Making one carbon copy after another, containing information from the British Broadcasting Company (BBC) radio broadcasts, he distributed his paper to farmers in the area. They circulated it through Innsbruck.

Mayer became known. Stories about him reached the Partisans, so they sent runners to contact him for information. OSS Headquarters was stunned when they received Mayer's message, which read, "One thousand Partisans of all parties under my command. Request planeload of explosives for bridge demolition and a quantity of propaganda material be sent at once."

Mayer was ordered to stop organizing and continue only with intelligence reporting. Mayer soon reported by radio that the largest military supply train ever assembled by the Germans was forming in Innsbruck: "Twenty-six trains, forty cars each, loaded ammo, tractors, guns and gas. Leaving for Italy via Brenner Pass, 3 April at 2100 hours." The 15th Air Force destroyed the entire supply train as it rolled through the Brenner pass. The following day, Mayer was at the Offizierskasino, strolling about shirtless, sunning himself with the elite officers of the SS, gathering new information. The crazy Jew was back at it.

Back at the Russian camp, Catlos twisted the radio knobs again. Finally, his face lit up as a signal became clear. Dunlevy scribbled down the coded message. Then all went silent. Mac looked at Dunlevy and said, "What are they saying?.

Dunlevy looked at him with a saddened face and replied, "The message was 'We have had it, they are here....'"

That day, the names of Fred Mayer, American Jew; Hans Wynberg, Dutch Jew; and Franz Weber, German soldier, were struck from the list of agents at Bari headquarters in Italy.

Mac and Lain walked outside as Catlos kept trying to raise Green Up, but his message fell on silent ears. Lain looked at Mac and said, "I don't suppose that..."

Survival

Mac responded, "No, not a chance. And if we don't do something soon, Bari will be receiving an interrupted message from us."

Maria, realizing they would soon have to leave, offered to go to the Slovak Partisans and bicker with them to get supplies. Lt. Green agreed, handed her money and asked Joe Morton to go with her.

Maria always liked being around Joe. He seemed more mature than the rest, and she felt very comfortable with him. She bought bread from one group, smoked bacon from another, and was even able to find some coffee, which appeared to be more important to the Americans than food.

Lt. Green gathered the men and announced, "We are going to follow the remainder of the Slovak Army toward the Russian lines. The order to move will come at any moment. There is a large force of Germans moving in on our position. We have no other choice, we have to keep moving. If we stay behind the Slovak Army, our chances are very good. So get ready to move."

Alexie sent another runner to Mac. The message read, "The Germans have postponed their march and will not arrive until late tomorrow." This change gave the Dawes Team more time to prepare. One more night in a warm environment appealed to them.

By candlelight, they packed their gear. Catlos and Dunlevy tried to raise Bari headquarters on their newly-functioning radio. It transmitted fine, but did not receive, so they were not sure their headquarters got their message. Lt. Green ordered the men to turn in after they ate some bread and potato soup. As Green extinguished the candles, a Slovak soldier called into the bunker. Mac went out with Maria to see what he wanted.

Once outside, he yelled, "Where in the hell have you guys been?" There stood Master Sergeant Jerry Mican and the other mission's radio operator, Charles Heller with Private John Schwartz. Apparently, they returned from the dead. They had been listed as missing since the attack on the hotel at Donovaly.

Soon, all the men came out and pulled the missing men's hats off and beat them with their own caps. Everyone cheered and jumped on them. Lt. Green noticed how tired and weak they were. He told his men to stop; they, too, realized the poor condition the men were in.

Helped into the bunker, the formerly-missing team feasted on hot soup and coffee. The three of them waited, like pets in a pen, watching their master prepare their food. Then they sprang on the food like starved animals. The rest of the men looked on, thinking it might be them in the future.

A dark and chilly sky came with the morning. Green lined up his men. As usual, the pilots fell into the rear of the column. The march toward the Russian lines had not started, but the pilots were already bitching.

Lt. Green asked Maria to stand with him at the front of the line. If any trouble surfaced or orders had to be translated, Maria could translate on the spot. He wanted her near.

The Dawes Team moved out slowly and shouted farewell to the Russians. They still harbored ill feelings over the radio incident, but it was soon forgotten and they parted friends. The Liberation Army (CFI) headed toward Klacany, a small mountain town to the east. At least that was what Alexie Sevelenko's last communication reported.

The line stretched up the side of the mountain from the camp. The group consisted of some six-hundred Czech soldiers and the Dawes Team, plus the downed pilots. They pushed through snow for two straight days. They were apprehensive and knew the Germans could attack and wipe out the column on first contact. So far, they had gone undetected, but they quickly found that they had more concerns than the enemy. The mountain wind increased, the thermometer steadily dropped and snow fell continuously.

On the afternoon of the third day, their march lead to a cliff, overlooking a valley. The pack horses acted up, sensing impending doom. A Czech Army officer told Maria they had to find a way down or they would have to turn back. Maria translated for Green and Mac. The news traveled down the line through all the Americans.

Maria knew when everyone had the news because the pilots started in again: "Hey, tell those assholes to learn how to read a map. We'd be better off if one of the fuckin' horses was in charge. Are you guys sure that some German isn't leading this column. I mean no one knows what the hell they're doing up there."

Finally, the pilots moved to the front of the line, walked to the edge of the cliff and turned around to address Green and the Slovak Soldiers. "Hey, Green and you guys, watch this."

As Green and the Slovak soldiers looked on, the pilots, one after another, without hesitation, filed off the cliff, falling almost straight down. The troops on the cliff watched as the pilots rolled, tumbled, slithered and just plain fell, ass over tin cups, to the bottom. The Slovak Brigade, gathered on the ledge and stared in amazement as the rest of the Americans followed.

Maria stopped only to make the sign of the cross, then closed her eyes and stepped out into space to join the Americans.

An officer turned to his men and ordered them to follow. Boulders loosened and tumbled, striking several flyers on their arms and shoulders. Soldiers beat their horses to force them over the edge.

At the bottom, Joe Morton helped Maria to her feet. She had a cut over her right eye and suffered a bump on the right side of her jaw. Joe and Maria gazed up to watch the horses tumble headfirst, losing all of their packs and equipment. Ten horses died in the horrible descent. They were shot humanely. Their meat was cut into steaks and stored in soldiers' packs.

Ten of the Slovak soldiers were injured badly; several suffered arm and wrist fractures. They were treated after camp was set up at the foot of the mountain. The overhanging cliff offered protection from the cold night wind. The group made soup from snow and the salvaged horse meat. The food, plus the fact that they conquered the mountain together, raised the group's morale and brought them closer together. The pilots, of course, took credit for leading the heroic charge down the mountain.

Maria asked Joe Morton to go with her. She was looking for something and he joined her. She searched along the division between the mountain and its base. Finally, she said, "There, Joe! Look there."

She pointed to a large crevice in the side of the mountain. The two then returned to the group. Most of them stood in a huddle. Some pilots developed a constant, dry cough, the kind associated with pneumonia. Others ran fevers caused by influenza. After getting their attention, Joe and Maria lead the group to the huge crack in the mountain. It was like a cave. Inside, they started a fire, knowing that it could not be seen by the enemy. They were well hidden.

Maria took the pilots' caps and dried them by the fire. She pulled off their socks and arranged them on branches close to the fire. Everyone and all the equipment was soaked and freezing. Three of the pilots shivered as the fire warmed the walls of the cave-like structure. Lt. Green asked Maria and Joe to move the men who were the most ill close to the fire; the rest moved back. No one complained. Several pilots held their buddies as close to them as they could, adding their body heat to warm their suffering friends.

Maria asked Green for some more money. This time, he didn't question her, he just handed her the money. She left and returned in a half hour with horse blankets. She explained, "I knew the horses no longer needed these and the soldiers won't carry them, so I got them cheap." She covered the pilots with the blankets, then pulled her Navy jacket tight and sat with the men around the fire.

In the morning, Mac, now sharing the command with Lt. Green, sent out a few people to scout the valley. At this point, they felt they could no longer rely on the Slovak Army for protection or information, the Czechoslovakians suffered as much as the Dawes Team. Green and Mac decided to use their own intelligence and military expertise. Their group was small and could be commanded easily. Mac gathered the men, explaining they would be better off if they were responsible for themselves. They had to send out their own patrols, get their own food, obtain their own intelligence and take care of one another.

Their first objective was to send Maria with a volunteer to round up food and find out where they were. Maria and Joe Morton, the correspondent, along with Tibor and Mac decided to head southeast to search for a village.

A second group, under John Schwartz, the radio operator from the Houseboat Team, headed northeast, with five of the pilots. The general order was: head toward the Russian lines, but provide for the group as you go.

Tibor, Mac, Joe and Maria crossed the valley and looked for a village. They followed a small stream that seemed to wind forever, twisting and turning through the valley. During the next several hours, they worked their way through the cold and snow. Finally, in mid-afternoon, they staggered onto a paved road. Maria approached the area cautiously, peering from behind snow drifts, watching a small village on the mountain side of the road.

She pointed to Mac, Joe and Tibor, then motioned them down along the bank of the stream. She joined them and explained if they followed the stream, the bank would cover them and they could get closer to the village without being detected. If German patrols were present, Mac and his team could withdraw back up the stream and wait until the village was safe. They moved slowly, trying not to be seen as they closed in on the village. They frequently popped their heads up above the snow, looking like four otters who had just seen an approaching seal.

The four carefully surveyed the village. Mac started to move, but Maria grabbed him by the arm.

"What's the matter?" he asked.

Maria just stared at the houses. Her voice raspy from the freezing weather, she replied, "Don't you notice anything funny?"

"What's funny? I don't see anything," Mac replied.

"That's what's funny. Nothing is moving," Maria observed.

They waited behind the snow drift and watched. Nothing moved. No dogs, no people and a suspicious absence of smoke from chimneys.

Joe Morton came up on Maria's right and said, "If something is wrong, we should find out what it is. It's no good just standing here. At least we know there are no Germans present, otherwise, there would be trucks and motorcycles all over the place."

One by one they crossed the road, diving into the ditch on the other side. They moved closer and closer toward the village. Maria went to the back of the first house. She tapped lightly on the back door, then increased the tapping to a full knock. No response. Now, they were so cold safety was only a secondary consideration.

Maria stepped back then shoved with all her strength. The door flew open. She rushed inside, with Mac, Joe and Tibor right behind her. They walked through the house with weapons drawn, expecting to be fired on at any second. Searching the rooms, Maria called from the kitchen. She found food on the stove. The fire was out, but the food was still warm. Mac stood watch at the window. When he heard Maria's joyful report, he kept one eye on the road and the other on the kitchen.

All four of them grabbed the old pots and bowls stacked next to a cabinet. They scooped up stew, then sat on top of the old wood-burning stove, devouring one bowl after another. Tibor ate so fast he was barely able to breathe and began coughing. Joe stopped only for a second to pound Tibor on the back, then returned to his pot and gulped more stew.

The group moved from house to house, finding the same conditions. There was no sign of life anywhere. They gathered eggs, hams, bread, and even wine, shoving them into blankets to take back to the others.

Mac walked across the village to the house closest to the road, giving him a good vantage point. Tibor, Joe and Maria ran back and forth to the last house, stashing their pilfered supplies so they could take off if trouble started. They had to, above all, return to camp with the food to keep the men from starving. Mac grabbed what food he could find in the house where he was standing guard. When it was time for them to pull out, Mac crossed the village and tore down some notices and a poster left by the Germans. As he walked through the front door of the house where Maria was, he handed her the notice.

He reported, "These are up all over the village, what do they say?"

Maria looked at the poster, looked at Mac and replied, "Typhus."

"Typhus! Damn it! What in the hell? Is this food poisoned?" Mac asked.

"No," Maria explained. "Typhus comes from a mite that gets in your clothes and bites you, not from food."

Relieved, Mac said, "Thank God for that. Now we know why there aren't any people here. You don't want to see this poster, Maria. I can't read a word on it, but I sure as hell know what it says."

Maria finished tying her bundle, then reached up and took the poster from his hand. She looked at Mac and shook her head. She recognized her photo. Under it, written in several languages, was, "Reward for the known whereabouts of Maria Zima."

Joe took the poster and looked at it. Sadness crossed his face as he said, "Here you are, dragged into this war almost by force, trying to help men from a country that you don't even know, caring for sick pilots, and the Germans hunt you down. Don't worry, Maria, when all of this is over, I will write a book about what happened and we can sit back and laugh about this."

Maria smiled, "Someday, Joe, but right now there is little time for laughing. As you Americans say, we better haul ass!"

With their blankets full of food, they darted back across the road. Joe Morton was last. As he jumped over the snowbank to the stream, the first German motorcycles appeared. Without looking back, the group ran back through the valley to their encampment.

Overpowering euphoria spread through the ranks as the pilot standing guard reported Maria's return. He shouted when he noticed the scouting team carried blankets. As Maria and the others came closer, the Dawes Team watched. They charged when they saw the blankets were filled with food.

The four members of the scouting team were so tired the only thing that kept them moving was the excitement of the starving men. They handed out the captured food to the pilots and the members of the OSS teams, then stood back and watched as the men tore at it. Choking, coughing and spitting, they shoved the food down their throats.

Maria looked around and said to Joe Morton, "I guess we are the first ones back. I don't see any of the others."

Joe looked off to the north, guessing, "Maybe they had to go farther than we did. Or maybe they didn't find anything and are still looking."

The pilot, still standing guard, shouted, "Man approaching from the north."

He looked through his field glasses as Lt. Green inquired, "Is it one of our guys?"

The sentry responded, "No, it looks like a Slovak soldier. He is moving slow, I don't think he is in good shape. Better send some men out and give him a hand."

Lt. Green motioned several pilots forward. Ten minutes later, they returned with the young Slovak.

He reported to Maria and she translated to Green, "One American soldier and five pilots were captured by the Germans. They had joined part of the Slovak Brigade and were hit by Germans from two sides. The Americans fought with the Slovaks, but finally surrendered to the Germans."

Green looked at Mac and said, "There goes Schwartz."

Mac replied, "And five pilots."

Lt. Green acknowledged, "I know."

Mac began again to press Lt. Green. He still believed that separating was the only solution to surviving. This last incident proved his point. If Maria's group would have kept going, they might be behind Russian lines already. Schwartz' group no longer existed. Some pilots voiced the same opinion as Mac. They, too, wanted to separate. They reminded everyone that a concentration camp was better than their current suffering.

Lt. Green agreed if things didn't change in the next couple days, he would approve Mac's plan. He convinced Mac that, since the men were in better physical condition than they had been for the last two weeks, they should move as soon as possible. Lt. Green then ordered the group east.

Still freezing and pushing their way through snow, they reached a shepherd's shack. They piled into the only room. The pilots continued bitching. With the loss of their comrades, they were depressed and kept constant pressure on Lt. Green. He was worn down to a shell of a man from the responsibility of command and his deteriorating physical condition. Coupled with the uncertainty of the group's attitude, he was pushed slowly toward depression.

When all were settled in, Mac and Lain went on a hunting expedition. They returned in less than an hour, dragging a deer behind them. They banged on the door to the cabin and yelled, "Santa Clause is here."

A pilot from Texas whipped out his knife and dressed the deer. The men facetiously asked Maria to make wine sauce and plenty of potatoes. The group's mood was positive again. They had a fire going in minutes and gathered stones, placing them next to the fire. As soon as the stones were hot, the cook put the meat on them. The men sat and listened to the venison sizzle.

Suddenly, they stopped. Mac whispered, "Someone is out there."

He was about to take out his carbine, still propped up against the side of the shack, when he heard an unknown voice holler, "The amount of noise you Yanks make can be heard for kilometers. You should really keep it down, boys." There stood Major Sehmer, a typical British officer, stiff back, trying to maintain his uniform as though he were on the parade ground.

Standing to his right was his aid, Sergeant Davis, Royal Paratroopers, a Welshman, jokingly referred to by his men as the *Bull*. He was the epitome of the Royal Paratroopers with his powerful face that reeked of self-assurance. His large manly features were set off by his short military haircut. His huge shoulders and arms came from years of hard work and military training. All of this force and power was diminished by his large, kind eyes. Looking at his face for any length of time, one would develop an ambivalence between fear and kindness, a sort of undulating feeling of unquestioning authority and friendliness.

Major Sehmer requested to see Lt. Green when he found he was in charge of the unit. The major lifted Green's spirits by suggesting a few plans. Green left his depression and was in command again.

Sehmer and Davis had been dropped by plane into an area known only to God. They found no reference points and couldn't carry out their mission.

Sehmer did not try to force himself on Green, but suggested he and Davis remain with the Dawes Team and pilots until they decided what to do. He thought there was no need to rush. The radios were out, the missions were failures and the men were sick. Escape was the only concern now. He convinced Lt. Green that time was on their side.

Now that the British joined them and the men had a meal, morale rose. The men sat around the fire with blood stains around their mouths, dirt on their faces and their lips cracked open from the cold. They sang to Maria, knowing that it always embarrassed her, "For it was Mary, Mary, plain as any name can be . . ."

Mac threw his arm around Maria to further embarrass her. Blood rushed into her face as she tried to ignore him and pull his arm away. The men loved it, telling Maria how lucky she was to be with them, and that half the women in the United States would change places with her in a minute, just to be next to them. Maria replied, "I don't know what kind of women you have in the United States, but I am sure that none of them would want to be here with, or without, you guys."

They cheered and sang again. "We'll meet again, don't know where, don't know when, but I know we'll meet again, some sunny day . . ."

Maria felt a little depressed as she curled up in the corner of the shack, trying to sleep among the men. She reclined with her eyes open, thinking there wasn't any other place she could be. Her picture was up all over the cities and villages. With a price on her head, she could trust no one. The Russians had no intention of allowing her nation to become a republic. If she tried to return home, her parents would be imprisoned or put to death. She did not want to endanger any of her friends. She pushed the thoughts from her mind, knowing she was in the same fix as the Americans. The only difference was they had a country to return to, she did not.

Wind tore through the openings in the cabin, causing the men to gather closer together to keep warm. As Maria fell asleep, she heard a pilot mumble, "Washington and those bastards at Valley Forge had it easy."

Not knowing what the phrase meant, she pulled the horse blanket over her head and, still shivering, fell fast asleep on the shoulder of a pilot. As they slept, the snow silently continued to fall. At sunrise, Maria spoke with Green and Mac and offered to find a way out of the mess they were in. She would travel in the direction she believed would take her to the town of Dolna Lehota.

Mac helped Maria with her peasant clothes. She thought if she could make it to the road, she could hitch a ride to the town. She would have to move quickly because her clothes were light and she would freeze by nightfall without shelter. On this day, God was with her as she quickly found the road twisting through the mountain. She walked only a mile when she heard a truck coming from behind. As it approached, the driver applied the brakes, causing the truck to slide to the right. Maria looked up into the back of a German Army truck, filled with troops and was greeted with smiling faces and cheers.

The soldiers pulled her into the back of the truck and started talking all at once. When Maria answered in German, they cheered, believing she was from the Fatherland. She gave the excuse she was working in Czechoslovakia, and her aunt who lived in the village ahead was ill, so she came to help her. Maria prayed there was a village ahead. As they turned the corner, the driver blew his horn. They came to a village so he shouted back, "Is this it?"

Maria looked out from under the tarpaulin and hollered, "Yes, this is it. Thank you for the lift."

The soldiers cheered and waved as Maria took her cap and twirled it above her head in a gesture of farewell. She walked nonchalantly past several houses. She had to suppress her apprehension, not knowing anyone in the village.

A middle-aged woman shoveling snow from her porch kept an eye on Maria, watching her as she glanced from house to house. Suddenly, the woman called out, "Hello, my heavens, I didn't expect you until tomorrow!"

Maria hurried over to her. To Maria's surprise, she threw her arms around her and said loudly, "Come in you will catch your death walking in weather like this."

Once they entered the house, the woman explained, "My name is Henda. Your picture is everywhere. You must be crazy walking around in public."

Maria explained what she could to the lady without giving her cause for alarm or any information that could harm the American mission. Henda drew hot water, making a bath for

Maria, and prepared a sandwich and some wine while she waited for the hot water to fill the tub.

Henda talked constantly, telling Maria not to trust anyone. She explained, "The most dangerous people are our own. I would trust the Germans before I would trust my neighbors. What a terrible world this is! I am helping you because you are the future of the nation. If you survive, tell the people what happened during these days. How the Allies tried to throw us to the wolves, how our own people turned against each other, until no one could be trusted, not even members of one's own family."

Maria listened as she soaked in the hot bath. Since she could not make it back to the camp, she decided to spend the night. Henda gave her a large feather bed. In seconds, she was fast asleep.

Before sun up, Henda woke Maria, promising to ask several people in the village for help for the Americans. If they refused, she told Maria, she would threaten them by promising to tell the Germans they helped the Americans, even if they didn't. Maria figured it was better to trust someone rather than allow the men to continue suffering. Henda wrapped food in newspaper and instructed Maria to return after sundown. Henda's house sat up against the mountain, so Maria could descend the mountain and enter through the back of the house without being seen.

Maria trudged through the snow back down the highway to her path and the Americans. She handed out the food and explained the situation to the British and the Americans. She wanted to return that evening to make sure everything was all right.

When she was sure it was safe, her plan was to move the men down the mountain four at a time, so they could wash, eat and warm themselves. Then they would be ready to move toward the Russian lines. On her return, Maria walked down the road in her peasant clothes. She had on every stitch that she owned, trying to keep warm. Joe Morton guarded her pride and joy, the US Navy jacket. If she happened to be captured wearing it, she would face death on the spot.

As instructed by Henda, Maria entered the house from behind. She slid down the mound of snow in the rear of the house, landing on the back porch. The rear door was flung open in her face. She stood startled beyond belief: A squad of German solders cheered her. Henda rushed over and spoke first, "My God, Maria, you are safe. It has been years. How did you make it all of this way? You must be crazy to travel in this weather."

Maria brushed the snow from her clothes, then spoke to the group in fluent German. Speaking German broke the ice; the men gathered around her, excited about talking with a girl after spending so much time on the Russian front.

Henda's home was packed with soldiers. The blackout regulations caused the village to be pitch dark, both the streets and the houses. If there had been a moon, Maria would have noticed the German vehicles on her way to Henda's, but she did not.

Henda pulled her away from the troops and suggested, "Come in the kitchen and have some wine."

As they pushed their way through the troops to the kitchen, Maria bumped shoulders with a soldier entering the room. She turned to apologize and looked directly in the face of a young SS officer. Overwhelming shock seized her body. She stood shaking as he stared at her.

He forgot her name, but thought he knew her. He asked, "I have attended school with you, yes? I am Karl Armbrust, Sturmbann Fuhrer Armbrust."

Maria sensed he wasn't sure. She coughed a reply, "You seem so familiar, but I cannot remember from where I know you." He stood rubbing his chin with his hand, holding his head to the side, trying to recall this attractive lady.

Chapter Seven

NAZIS UP CLOSE

Henda rushed in with a glass of wine and tried to distract the SS officer by changing the conversation. "How long will your men be staying, sturmbann fuhrer?"

He responded, "We must leave now, madame. Thank you for all you have done for us."

Karl shouted the order for his men to board the trucks. He told his lieutenant to warm up the engine of his staff car and to keep it running. Henda tried to separate Maria from Karl by handing her some dirty cups and asking her to take them to the kitchen. Karl positioned himself next to Maria, lifted the cups from her hand and set them back on the table. He gently took Maria by the arm and formally requested, "Would you do me the honor of walking me to my car? It is so seldom that I get the opportunity to talk with a beautiful girl."

Maria reluctantly agreed, "I am freezing, sturmbann fuhrer, but I would be delighted to walk with you."

The troops were already in their truck, waiting for their commander. As the two of them walked through the snow to the staff car, it was obvious Karl slowed the pace. Eventually they stopped. He turned, faced Maria and stated, "Maria Zima . . . school teacher . . . spy . . . and soldier. Your country is no longer under what you people call the Jack Boot of Germany. Though I'm afraid that it will soon be under the paw of the Russian Bear. I have lost my dreams through defeat, and you have lost yours through victory. To fight on when victory is close at hand is exhilarating, but to fight on when defeat is inevitable is the personification of a hero: Soldier Zima, I salute you."

Maria, realizing she was exposed, gently touched Karl's arm. She stood dumbfounded in front of him, listening to every word, knowing he was unraveling her life as she stood silent. She spoke softly, "You are correct in everything that you say, except one. I am no spy. It's a long story Karl, maybe someday I will tell you all about it. But believe me, I have never spied on anyone. What will you do now, Karl?"

"Fight them in the streets of Berlin. If you don't mind, Maria, I kept one of your pictures in my briefcase. You are a very popular young lady. Your picture is posted on every street in the country."

Maria looked into his face as he spoke. He was tired and defeated, but he still managed a slight smile. Maria now felt secure, knowing that he wasn't going to arrest her.

She shared her thoughts, "So, I say farewell to Sturmbann Fuhrer Armbrust, my enemy, who is leaving my country for the West while I stand here ready to welcome my enemy from the East. Before you leave, Karl, tell me why?"

"Why what?" he asked.

Maria repeated her question, "Why aren't you going to arrest me?"

Karl inquired, "Have you had any religious training, Maria?"

"Yes, of course," she confirmed.

Karl elaborated, "I will repeat what Jesus said after he was arrested by the Roman Army . . . 'In the time of trouble when you need your friends the most, your enemies will come forward and your friends will stand back and watch.' Do you realize that not one, not one of the apostles stood by him? I have always remembered that. So, the answer to your question is: What good would be served by yet another crucifixion?"

This time a friend came forward.

Sturmbann Fuhrer Karl Armbrust sat in his staff car looking once more at Maria. He saluted, tapped the driver on the shoulder and motioned him to leave. Maria covered her face as the trucks and the staff car hurled snow in all directions as they sped away from the village. She stood for a second longer, realizing, if nothing else, she had lost a friend—a friend who came forward when others would have stood back.

Henda and Maria worked out a plan: The Americans and the British could come during the night. Henda and her neighbors would feed them. They could bathe while their clothes were being washed. Afterward, they could rest near the warm fireplace. They would have to be out of the village in the morning before sunup to avoid detection.

That evening, when Maria returned from Henda's she put the soldiers' names on scraps of paper, then she put them in a pilot's cap and held a drawing. The first six names drawn would go with her that evening. Each night after that, six others would follow in succession. This system made sure each man had his turn in the village.

The men, having something to look forward to, started to relax, and much of their anxiety disappeared. Joe Morton taught Maria English. He used the excuse that Christmas was only a few days away and it was the custom of the American people to all sing together in celebration.

Maria knew the pilots were laughing at her, not with her, but it made no difference, since their morale remained high. The men hummed the tune as Maria tried to sing, *Valking in a vinter vunder lond.*

When she sang, some men would giggle. It was infectious and immediately spread. Eventually, the men would break into resounding laughter. Lt. Green or, sometimes, Major Sehmer would have to quiet the men, fearing the noise would travel through the valley, alerting the Germans of their position.

One night, everyone in the cabin woke up when Sgt. Davis threw someone against the outside wall. Lt. Green and Mac jumped to their feet and flung open the door to see what the commotion was. Davis held a German soldier by the back of his neck. The soldier shouted in German so Davis didn't understand a word and called for Maria. She questioned the German, translating his words for Davis.

Maria reported, "He is a Slovak who was forced into the German Army. His name is Jano Vlasak. He is a deserter."

Maria fired questions at the prisoner. He explained that the Russians did not break through the German positions and were being held in the Carpathian mountains. There was heavy fighting just northeast of their position. He estimated the Germans would hold those positions for another month, unless ordered to withdraw. As he continued and Maria translated, the group listened intently. Most of the German Slovak troops were shipped out of the area and replaced with the *Vermacht* (the old men in the regular German Army).

Lt. Green asked Maria to interrogate him about Allied advances. He replied that as far as he knew the Americans were all pushed back to a place called Bastogne.

He told Maria that he was tired of fighting for causes he didn't understand and just wanted to go home, even if it meant his death. Maria believed him. She conveyed her positive feelings to Davis, who then released the soldier.

He sat and ate with the Dawes Team while Maria translated more military information, updating their news. Maria paused, then asked him, "How did you know that we were here?"

Jano stated, "People know you are here. In fact, they gave me excellent directions."

Maria kept this information to herself, knowing what it meant. She allowed the soldier to finish his meal in peace. Later, outside with Sgt. Davis, she warned, "Davis, I think you should stay and help with this mission, if possible. The Americans are not in good shape, and that soldier told me that everyone knows where we are. We must move again. Some of these men are barely going to make it, including me."

Davis complimented Maria, "You're too tough, they'll never get you."

Maria reluctantly added, "I wish I were, Davis, but I'm beat just like the others."

During the day, Maria, Green, Mac and Lain and some others tried to formulate another plan. They were still rotating the men back and forth to the village. Now, the entire operation would have to be on the move again.

Joe Morton wandered over to Maria. He was always writing in his little black book. He stopped and gazed out over the mountains and then turned to Maria and said, "You know, Lt. Perry and Lt. Gaul are not back from the village. I hope everything is all right."

Finished in the village, Perry told Gaul to stay close to the edge of the woods and wait for him. He was having trouble with the pilots, they wanted to stay longer. It irritated him because they never took anything seriously. He tried to hurry them along, while Gaul hauled food to the timber line. He and the pilots were about to leave when a German patrol pulled into the village and drove directly to Henda's house. Rather than run or give Gaul's position away, the men, unable to continue anyway, stood and placed their hands on the top of their heads. They surrendered.

Joe and Maria watched as Lt. Gaul plowed through the snow with all of the strength that he had. This meant only one thing; they were in trouble. Holding his chest and gasping for air, he exclaimed, "They got Perry and the pilots! The German patrol pulled into the village and went directly to Henda's house. Someone informed on us. How else would they have known where to go?"

Maria convinced Major Sehmer and Lt. Green not to move out that night. She knew the Germans would question Perry. She thought they would lock him up and wait for someone with authority to arrive from Berlin to interrogate him, or they would torture him. Either way, the group would be safe for a day or two, there was nothing they could do to help Perry.

Early in the morning, Maria shook Sgt. Davis. The two of them walked quietly outside the cabin. Maria had to act.

She whispered, not wanting to wake the others, "Davis, I am going to the village to find out what happened."

Davis was upset, "What good will that do? They probably will catch you. Then where will these chaps be?"

Maria insisted, "I'm going. It isn't only for Lt. Perry and the pilots. What about all of the people in that village? They risked their lives, and mostly because of me."

Davis gave in, "If we hurry, we can be back before anyone knows we are missing."

"We?" Maria asked. "I am going alone."

Davis convinced her, "You know you need a handsome paratrooper with you. What gentleman would allow a beautiful girl to go alone into enemy territory?"

"Just how many girls do you know that go into enemy territory?" Maria joked.

Davis gave Maria a little shove with his shoulder, she smiled, shook her head and headed toward the village. They waited on the outskirts of the village until the sun crested over the mountains, lighting the entire valley. They saw some old men from the hamlet crossing the small bridge that lead from the village to the valley.

Maria exposed her position, stepping from behind a snow bank on the edge of the creek. Davis, taken by surprise, was right behind her, brandishing his machine gun. The men stared at him.

Maria walked up to the leading man and said, "Last night, someone in the village informed on the Americans for a few lousy pieces of gold. I want to know who the bastard is. One man who was taken prisoner by the Germans was this paratrooper's best friend. Tell me who it is before he guns down all of you. Make up your minds, and I mean now!"

An old man shouted, "It was the minister and his wife."

Maria demanded, "In which house does the minister live?"

The old men uniformly pointed to a home in the center of the village. Maria pushed her way through the group, walking down the center of the main road. Davis turned the group of old men around and marched them back to the village.

Seeing the parade of men herded through the village, people came out of their houses to find out what was causing the commotion. Davis kept his machine gun pointed directly at them. Women and children gathered around to watch.

Maria slammed her fist on the front door of the minister's house. The minister cracked open the door, barely enough to peek out. Maria turned to the people of the village, and with an outcry heard by most of the inhabitants, addressed them, "This man of God, your own minister, has sold the lives of the men that have come to help our nation. He alone is responsible for their death. He brought disgrace to your village. I will spread the story throughout the mountains that the man of God sold the lives of our liberators for thirty pieces of silver. This village will be known as the scourge of Czechoslovakia. Not more than ten miles from here, the bodies of our Czech soldiers lie blood-soaked in a valley. Meanwhile, this man sits in his warm home. Remember, he plunged the dagger into the heart of our country—for a few pieces of silver."

Maria walked slowly from the house, stopped, looked to heaven and called, "All mighty God, you have a bastard in your ranks. I pray that you send down suffering and illness upon his house and its inhabitants."

She hurried down the steps and walked through the crowd that stood and marveled at the spectacle. Davis slung his machine gun over his shoulder and walked with her. Astonished, he remarked, "Jesus! I thought Churchill and Hitler gave good speeches. . . ."

Venting her frustration made Maria feel better. She pushed through the snow with Davis, as though they were on a weekend ski trip. At that moment, she could care less if enemy fighters swooped down and strafed them. She felt euphoric.

Davis laughed so hard he fell down in the snow. He managed to say, "Wait until I tell Major Sehmer that you put a hex on the village."

When they arrived at the shack, Major Sehmer chewed Sgt. Davis out for leaving without proper authorization. Lt. Green was more subtle with Maria, asking her not to do anything like that again. It would jeopardize the entire mission if she were not there to translate. Maria agreed. She told him it was a once-in-a-lifetime event that would never be repeated. She reminded him of their loss: Lt. Perry was gone from the mission and probably would be put to death, all because of a minister from hell.

To Maria's surprise, a young girl walked out of the shack. Lt. Green introduced Maria, "This is Maria Zima."

The young lady responded, "I'm Marian Rubin, a nurse from New York. I came to visit my grandmother and never made it out. I have been hiding for years. I was with a Partisan group for awhile; we didn't do much, blew up a couple of bridges and blasted a few supply convoys."

Maria listened intently as Marian continued, "I know I am never going to make it out of here. It is just one of those things you can feel. The only thing that really bothers me is that no one will ever know what happened to me. It is such a terrible way to end your life. I must apologize to you, Maria. You are the only woman that I have talked to in months. I really am sorry to bend your ear."

Maria realized Marian was deeply depressed and was venting all of her suppressed feelings. Maria, who was becoming an authority on depression, consoled her, "I know you are Jewish, but come on, tonight is Christmas Eve, we will make things a little better. I have a bottle of vodka stashed in my backpack. We can get that and have one of the guys cut down a tree for us to decorate. Come on, it will be fun."

Marian followed Maria, but the angel of death remained on her shoulder. She no longer knew how to enjoy herself and sat daydreaming most of the time. She hardly paid attention when Lt. Green and Major Sehmer called the men together.

All stood quietly as Lt. Green gave them their orders, "I have decided we will break into two groups. The pilots will go with Lt. McGregor and Lt. Lain. Their group will head west and try to contact the Allies. The rest of us will move east and try to contact the oncoming Red Army. Since tomorrow is Christmas, Major Sehmer and I would like everyone to stay together until then."

Christmas Eve was anything but uplifting. Lt. Gaul delivered a religious service as the men sat with longing faces, each in his own world, thinking of home, family and friends. He was very humble when he addressed the men, "I am not a minister. Now, the only thing that I can think of is what Napoleon said when someone asked him about Christ: 'I know men and I have been with men all of my life and Jesus was no man. I have built great empires, but so, too, did Alexander the Great, Charlemagne and Caesar. But our empires were built on blood and death. And what of the empire of Jesus? His was built on love, and at this very moment there are millions of men who would lay down their lives for him.'"

The men remained quiet and bowed their heads as Lt. Gaul continued with a prayer, "I believe in God, the Father almighty, creator of heaven and earth and Jesus Christ, only son of our Lord, who was conceived by the Holy Ghost, born of the Virgin Mary, suffered under Pontius Pilate, was crucified, died and was buried. On the third day, he arose again from the dead and sits at the right hand of God, the Father all mighty. He shall come to judge the living and the dead. I believe in the Holy Ghost, communion of saints, the forgiveness of sins, the resurrection of the body and life everlasting, amen."

Maria thought how beautiful and how wonderful that Lt. Gaul would remember such a thing. As she slowly glanced over the faces of the British and Americans, she realized with all the sadness and misery this Christmas Eve had, she would remember it as long as she lived.

At sunrise, Mac and Lain had the pilots ready. They kissed Maria goodbye and exchanged addresses back in the United States. Mac approached Maria one last time, trying to get her to come with his group. Even Lain did his best to influence her. She stood hugging the two of them, fearing if she let go she might never see them again. The line of men moved out. As they were almost out of sight, Maria smiled to herself.

Davis looked at her, "In all of this you can find something to smile about?"

She held back tears as she replied, "I knew the last thing I would hear from that group was the pilots bitching. If you listen closely, you can still hear them."

Maria walked back with Davis to the shack where the group formulated a plan. During their discussion, Jano, the German deserter, suggested that the group move to a large, abandoned copper mine he had discovered. It was close; all of them could fit into it; and, above all, it was warm. No one had a better idea, and they were convinced that their stay in the mine wouldn't be for long. The Red Army had to be getting close. If all went well, they wouldn't have to go on another death march. They could sit and wait for the Russians to rescue them.

Jano was sure he could guide the group. Major Sehmer sent a few of the remaining pilots ahead with him. They were the point men. If anything happened, they would give a warning. This arrangement would give the others a chance to take evasive action. The group filed out of the shack, moving in a slow steady line across the mountains to their new shelter.

As they marched through the day and into the night, their feet froze, their lips cracked opened and swelled, miniature icicles formed on their eyebrows. They grew weak and barely could place one foot in front of the other.

Jano wheeled around, tapped Davis on the shoulder and pointed to a roof sticking up through the snow. Davis signaled the rest of the line to move in the direction of the shack. The men helped one another, falling then getting back on their feet. Reaching the shack, they fell on their knees and dug frantically, trying to find the entrance. One man located it, "Here, here is that son of a bitch."

The others gathered around and enlarged the hole. One after another, they moved through the hole into the shack. Lt. Green crawled to a hole dug in the center of the dirt floor. His body trembled with such furor that he looked like he was about to go into a seizure. He tore small pieces of paper from his small note book then, with his military cigarette lighter, lit them. They stayed lit long enough for the men to see the firewood piled next to the door.

They tore the bark off the logs. They knew the bark was easy to light, so they could start a fire with the smaller pieces, graduating to larger ones as the fire started.

Maria sat with Marian, who was almost completely withdrawn. She stared into space and spoke only when necessary. The group's pain and suffering subsided as the fire grew stronger.

Major Sehmer maintained his dignity and military bearing. He suggested, "Men, you know the rules, don't build the fire too high. Jerry might get a fix on our position."

A pilot remarked, "You show me any fuckin' German out in this weather and I'll show you a registered ass."

Jano looked at Maria and said, "Vas?"

Maria replied, "Das ist Amerikanisch." She knew better than to try to explain another American expression.

In the morning, Davis, the most military of the lot, rose and dug his way through the snow that blocked the door. The weather improved slightly, so he organized a scouting party. If the group could find another place to stay while looking for the mine, it would be helpful. Davis wanted to be sure they did not repeat last night's struggle. If they couldn't make it to the mine, they needed to find another cabin.

Lt. Green assigned Major Sehmer, Davis, Maria, Catlos and Dunlevy to the scouting detail. They built up the fire and stood close, trying to stay warm as long as possible before setting out. Maria was worried about Joe Morton. He told her he wanted to go with Maria and her group, but Lt. Green thought that he was too ill and should rest. The lieutenant knew everyone faced another freezing march as soon as the group returned.

Maria was the last out. She felt awful, physically and mentally. It wasn't the usual despair, but a deep, hollow feeling, almost an eerie sensation. She tried to dismiss the feeling and pulled her cap tightly around her ears. When she heard her name called, she turned and there stood Joe with his little black book.

Maria, startled, said, "Joe, what are you doing out here? Go back. You'll catch pneumonia."

He sheepishly said, "I just wanted to wish you a Merry Christmas, that's all."

Maria looked at Joe; tears formed in her eyes. Joe put his arm around her and said, "What's the matter? Come on, don't cry."

Maria rationalized, "I don't know, Joe, sometimes women just cry."

"Why can't I come with you?" he asked.

Maria defended the orders, "Lt. Green is right, Joe. We will be right back. You must save your strength for the coming march."

"Are you sure that I didn't say something to make you cry?" Joe wanted to know.

"No, Joe, you have been one of the nicest people that I have ever met, how could you say anything to make me cry?" Maria affirmed.

Maria, with tears still in her eyes, caught up to Davis. He knew something was bothering her, but didn't want to make her feel worse by asking her about it. He slid his enormous arm around her shoulders and pulled her close. Maria held the back of his jacket as he led the way through the snow.

On patrol for an hour, they were greeted by French Partisans. Maria spoke with them and found they, too, were looking for shelter. Rumors indicated the battle front was breaking up. Units of the Russian Army were moving through the German lines. However, no one had accurate information, it was always hearsay.

The French showed Maria their positions and suggested the Americans join them, at least for the night. It would shorten their march by a day. Maria translated the suggestion to Major Sehmer. He agreed and ordered the group to remain with the French for the rest of the day and night, then he returned to the shack to tell Lt. Green. He asked Maria to thank the French and tell them he would return in the morning with the Americans. The French commander saluted. Sehmer returned his recognition and retraced his steps back to the shack.

At day break, Maria and the men had breakfast with the Partisans. Maria told Davis the French had scouts out and maybe they would return with news before Lt. Green and Sehmer appeared. Soon it was 1000 hours and the Americans had not arrived. Davis told the others he was returning to see what was keeping them.

Maria protested, "If one of us goes, we all go."

The others agreed. They left their gear with the French, then formed a single line behind Davis.

Davis asked Catlos and Dunlevy to walk with Maria, "I'm going to move on ahead and pick up the pace. I want to make sure everything at the shack is O.K."

Maria watched as he pushed through the snow, moving swiftly as though he knew something was wrong. She and the others quickened their pace, fearing Davis was right.

As the group moved up the side of the mountain, they noticed Davis lying flat on the hill across from the shack. He quickly motioned them to his side. They threw themselves prone next to him.

One by one, they peeked high enough to see over the top of the ridge to get a view of the shack. Maria took one look, then dropped her face into the snow.

Joe Morton, sick as he was, tried to hold himself up, but couldn't. He had to be helped by a pilot. Lt. Green stood in line next to Major Sehmer who, as always, stood erect and self-assured. The pilots continued their bitching, this time at the Germans, calling them Nazi assholes, Kraut fuckers and terms Maria did not recognize.

As she regained control of herself, Maria peered over the top of the snow again. She looked over at Davis and shared her observations, "Those troops are Hlinka Guards and Ukrainians, not regular German Army. They are the worst. I'll put a bullet through my head before they take me. There is no use saying that, because they are never going to take me."

Catlos and Dunlevy watched as their friends were forced down the mountain at gunpoint.

Dunlevy raised to his knees, looked over at Sgt. Davis and said, "I guess we should go warn the French."

The little band of four formed a line and headed back to the French base camp. As they walked, Maria asked Catlos if he had seen Marian. He replied he had; she marched next to the pilots, staring at the ground.

The snow returned. Maria walked like she was in a trance. The wet flakes stuck to her face and mixed with her tears, but she did not feel them. Davis looked at her several times, but said nothing. He knew what she was going through. He had seen his friends have their faces blown off. Some were blown to bits without a trace. Others died in his arms. Now, Major Sehmer, his commanding officer, was captured. How terrible, he thought, for this young girl to make new friends, try to get them to safety and then have this happen.

For three days, McGregor, Lain and the pilots moved undetected through the Carpathian Mountains, toward Budapest. The best information they could obtain came from the Partisan units scattered throughout the mountains. They believed that the Allies were closing in on Budapest. Mac and Lain agreed if Budapest were occupied or the Russians were close, they could swing their column west into southern Austria. Mac was sure the Allies would push the Germans from northern Italy into Austria. Once the Allies were in Austria, Mac's group would be safe.

Since Mac's group left Maria and the others, they had moved like a line of robots, planting one foot in font of the other. Each step was deliberate to combat fatigue and the damp winter wind that knifed through their clothing.

Mac halted the line behind a mountain ridge, gathered the men in a circle and addressed them, "We will finish out the day here. At dark, we will head through the valley to find our way out of here. It can't be much longer until we run across a village or people. So hang on. That's all that I ask."

The men huddled together as the wind whistled over their heads. They sat with their heads on their knees. It was no use trying to raise morale. Mac knew they were too far gone. Instead, he maintained strict discipline. At the first sign of discontent, he gave direct orders. The men always obeyed and gave him very little trouble, knowing that it would be useless to do so.

Just before daybreak, Mac had the column on its feet. They moved down the mountain into the open valley below. The men did their best to keep a strong pace. They hoped the entrance to the valley meant they would see a village, or even friendly troops. When they reached the halfway mark, the sky turned brilliant, illuminating the heavens. Pops and bangs echoed through the valley, followed by the familiar sizzling of enemy flares landing in the snow.

Spontaneously, the men stood still. Out of food and weapons, tired, hungry and ill, they raised their hands over their heads as the enemy moved in.

The German officer in charge ordered the men to continue down the valley to the main road. There a convoy of trucks waited. They were herded into the rear of the trucks. Another officer shouted an order and the convoy moved out.

Mac quickly asked the pilots if any of them spoke German. One did. Mac asked him to listen closely to the Germans. He thought they might be close to American or British lines. Any information the German-speaking pilot could gather might be helpful.

The Germans had a temporary camp set up for Partisans, downed pilots, French, Hungarians and political prisoners. The Americans were separated from the others and shoved into one large shack. In the morning, they were ordered to board the trucks again and were driven across the border into Austria. Germany was still in control and no one knew the whereabouts of the Allies.

The trucks pulled into a large camp that the Germans used as a staging area. From it, they shipped prisoners in all directions. Mac, Lain and the pilots were kept together in one large room. One by one, the commandant and his staff sent for them; their interrogation had begun.

The first three pilots questioned were beaten, to intimidate those that followed. Mac was the fourth man called. He stood and walked slowly to the door. A guard pushed him. He stopped, put his finger in the face of the guard, but said nothing. The guard, familiar with discipline, accepted his error and backed off. The interrogator began, "I am Major Oydna."

The Major was a short, fat, shaved-head soldier who wore glasses too small for his face. They were the little, round type and left ridges along the sides of his face.

The two guards slammed Mac into the chair in front of the major's desk. Major Oydna tilted his head to the side as he explained the rules, "I will ask you several questions and you will answer them. What were you doing in the mountains?"

Mac answered, "I was a co-pilot on a B-25 and the Luftwaffe shot my ass down."

The major lifted his head and signaled to a guard. He quickly removed everything from Mac's pockets. Mac was sure he had no identification; he removed it at the Bari headquarters. The major pulled pictures out of Mac's wallet one at a time and asked Mac who each person was. To Mac's disbelief, Major Oydna removed an OSS mess card from Bari headquarters. He turned the card over repeatedly and then asked Mac, "What is this card?"

Mac showed no expression. He asked to see the card. He looked at it with no interest and replied, "That is an Air Corps mess card. You must show that card to eat. I am sure it is the same in your army."

"If it is an Air Corps card, why does it say OSS?"

Mac bluffed, "Those are the initials of the section of the mess hall where I ate, Officers Staff Section."

The major looked at McGregor and dropped the wallet into his briefcase with the other prisoners' articles, commenting, "They will know what all of this stuff is at Wiener Neustadt."

The guards jerked Mac from his chair, but he pushed both of them to the side. Major Oydna raised his hand, as if to say the roughness was unnecessary. Mac said nothing as he walked between the two soldiers back to his prison quarters.

The guards opened the door and shoved Mac into the room. He walked over to Lain who was sitting on the floor. He leaned against the wall and slowly slid down, sitting next to his friend. He looked at Lain and said, "I can't believe it! Son of a bitch! I just can't believe it."

Lain wondered, "Now what? Don't tell me, they want us to join the German Army."

Mac warned, "Don't laugh, I did the most stupid thing possible."

"What did you do, tell them that you are a Naval officer and your ship was sunk somewhere in Austria?" Lain asked.

"You know, you can really be an ass at times," Mac replied.

Lain wondered, "Well, what is it? I mean, Christ, how much more trouble can we be in?"

Mac admitted, "I left my OSS mess card in my wallet."

Lain exclaimed, "You did what! I must be dreaming. You must be twins, one person couldn't be so dumb. How in the hell did that happen?"

Mac explained, "It stuck to the back of my mother's picture. I swear, I went through my wallet at least three times before we left."

"Our worries are over, we're dead. You know the orders from Berlin: OSS personnel are to be shot when captured. What did that Kraut officer do when he found the card?" Lain wanted to know.

Mac responded, "That's it. He didn't do anything. He must have been stationed here the whole war. I don't think he even knows what OSS means. He asked me what it was."

Mac briefed the pilots: All the information gathered on them was stored in a briefcase. He wanted them to retrieve the satchel. Tomorrow, they would be moved and he wanted every man's eyes looking for the briefcase. Their lives would depend on it. Next, he broke the first commandment and told the pilots that he was an OSS officer and that he would be executed at once if the Germans discovered that fact. He told the pilots the Germans would assume they, too, were OSS, which meant they also might face execution. The pilots complained when they heard the news.

In the morning, the guards pushed and shoved the prisoners into the waiting trucks. Mac scanned the compound and noticed two motorcycles, followed by a staff car and two lorries. The pilots looked in every direction, but found no briefcase.

Once in the trucks, the pilots reported: negative, no briefcase.

After traveling for about forty minutes, the trucks pulled into a railroad station. The guards from the first truck filed out and held machine guns on Mac, Lain and the pilots as they climbed out of the truck. The men kept their watch, still no briefcase. One man thought that he saw a sergeant go directly from the staff car to the waiting train carrying something, but he didn't have a clear view. He wasn't sure what the sergeant carried.

The prisoners boarded the last car of the train. The civilians boarding the forward cars watched the weak and bitter Americans being forced on the train. As the train accelerated toward Wiener Neustadt, the pilots whispered to one another. Nobody saw the briefcase. Mac and Lain felt their last hope, the briefcase, was gone forever. They had no defense against such incriminating evidence. Compounding their desperation, they were certain the pilots also would be suspected of being OSS agents and shot.

The train stopped and started repeatedly through the day. Finally, the train crept into its destination. Releasing steam, the engine stopped and the engineer sounded the train's shrill whistle. Guards immediately surrounded the prisoners' car. An officer screamed orders for the men to get off the train and line up on the station platform.

The solemn faces of civilians watched as the men were pushed and prodded with the barrels of the German soldiers' machine guns. Mac and Lain headed the long line. Abruptly, a commotion developed at the end of the line. A German officer grabbed a sergeant by his uniform and shook him, then stepped back, and to the amazement of the other German soldiers, slapped the sergeant across the face.

The commander of the guards shouted for his men to load the prisoners into waiting trucks. Lain and Mac edged toward the pilot standing next to the German officer. He had seen and understood the entire incident. He was the pilot who spoke German, so Mac asked, "What the hell was that all about?"

The pilot explained, "The sergeant got on the train with, get this, a briefcase. I guess a civilian in the first car stole the damn thing. That officer is really pissed."

Lain grabbed Mac's arm, "Remember that prayer that Lt. Gaul gave that mentioned 'I believe in God.' Well, I do now."

Mac joked, "Maybe when all of this is over, you can join the priesthood."

Mac swore, "When all of this is over, I am never going to join anything. I won't even join my mother in prayer, when this is over."

"That might not be too long, you know," Lain cautioned.

"You're an ass, a real ass. I was feeling pretty good and you wrecked it for me. What in the hell kind of thing is that to say to anyone?" Mac demanded.

Lain admitted, "It's true. This may come as a surprise to you, but this is one trip I haven't been looking forward to."

As the trucks bounced down the road, Lain and Mac sat wondering what fate had in store. Their wondering ended when they saw a large menacing castle looming through the mountain peaks. Covered with snow, it looked like an illustration from a book of fairy tales.

The gates of the castle swung open as the trucks approached. The vehicles turned into the courtyard facing the gate, ready to leave after the prisoners climbed out. The prisoners jumped down from the trucks and the small convoy withdrew and waited outside the castle entrance. The officer in charge stood waiting for someone. Mac and the others watched as a tall, handsome, blond SS officer presented himself from one of the huge, wood doors and casually strolled over to the officer standing with the prisoners. They spoke for a few seconds, then the officer in charge saluted and returned to the waiting convoy.

Mac watched as the SS officer walked up and down the line, stopping and starring into each man's face. He halted in front of Mac. They were the same size, both were leaders, both very military and both educated. They were doomed to conflict at their first encounter.

The SS officer took a few steps back and addressed the men, "I am Sturmbann Fuhrer Karl Armbrust. You men will be held here and questioned until I contact Berlin. They will send professionals to question you. If you try to escape, any of you left behind will be executed at once."

He then motioned to the guards to take the men away. Sturmbann Fuhrer Armbrust pointed to McGregor and motioned his sergeant to separate him from the others. The sergeant threw Mac into a room under the sturmbann fuhrer's quarters. There was a small light bulb overhead in the center of the room. The walls were solid stone and the room was ten steps down from the courtyard. A small iron door led outside. Mac walked down the steps to the straw-covered floor, made a pillow from some hay and fell asleep.

When he awoke, he wasn't sure whether it was night or day. He had no idea how long he had slept. His captors had taken his watch, so he couldn't tell what time it was. The huge door at the top of the steps swung open and a soldier left food on the top step, then quickly turned and slammed the door.

It was only black bread and soup, but it tasted like a gourmet French dinner to Mac. After eating, he fell back to sleep. He guessed this process continued for several days. Regaining his strength, he ran up and down the stone steps and did several push-ups. He repeated this exercise all day. It was similar to the exercise he performed as a lacrosse all-American at the University of Delaware.

Sometimes, he did math problems in his head to pass the time. The more difficult ones he worked out on the walls of his cell. During one of his math sessions, he was interrupted when the door swung open and then closed. The sturmbann fuhrer and two of his guards threw Mac to the floor and stripped him. Karl Armbrust opened the small door leading outside while the two guards forced Mac into a miniature courtyard. It was completely enclosed, except the door leading into Mac's cell; there was no roof. The snow and wind circled around him, but he looked up at the black sky and watched the snow fall. Shivering, he kept his muscles in motion by flexing them, then relaxing. Nothing helped, his lips turned blue and his feet were numb.

The sturmbann fuhrer watched him, but said nothing. No questions, no remarks. Then he motioned to the guards and they grabbed Mac by the arms and threw him back on the floor of his cell. The three of them left without a word.

Hours passed and another food tray appeared at the top of the steps. Later, the guard retrieved the remains and slammed the door again. In about an hour, Karl returned. This time, he was alone. He descended the steps and opened the door leading to the small yard. The snow stopped, but the icy winds continued to blow. He walked over to Mac, grabbed him by the neck and led him nude back out into the yard.

Mac stared into his eyes. Karl tugged at his collar to ward off the cold wind. He said nothing and stared back at Mac. Mac was about to collapse from the cold when Karl lead him by the neck back into the cell. He watched Mac lying in the straw, then walked up the steps to the outside.

Mac sat trying to figure out what this sturmbann fuhrer was trying to accomplish. Mac had not been questioned, so the Germans didn't realize he was an OSS officer. Maybe Karl was trying to wear him down before interrogating him. For the moment, Mac's curiosity was satisfied so he fell asleep.

Again, the door screeched open. Mac watched Karl enter. For a moment, Mac was going to challenge him physically, but decided at the last minute not to, realizing he had no escape.

Karl walked over to Mac, but did not repeat the usual routine. He held Mac by his throat and pressed him against the wall. Mac tried to turn his face away, but Karl grabbed his jaw and held his face, looking into his eyes. Mac decided: He was not going to be the first to speak, no matter what.

Karl pulled him away from the wall, then slammed him back into it again several times. Finally, he dragged Mac to the door, opened it and shoved him out. Karl stood inside watching him as he fought the bitter cold. Then Karl closed the door, locking him in the yard.

Mac exercised, doing jumping jacks and windmills, anything to keep his blood circulating. He kept a steady pace until he warmed up. To maintain his temperature, he gradually reduced his calisthenics. It seemed like hours before Karl opened the door. Mac rushed inside and began stomping his feet in the straw. Karl walked over and stood directly in front of him. Mac watched as he put on his black leather gloves. He pulled them tight and made a fist, then drove it into Mac's stomach. Mac doubled over and fell to the floor. Karl stood over him and smiled. He took the toe of his boot and rubbed it along the side of Mac's face. Then he left without a word. Mac was sure Karl was driving him crazy, and he knew no way to counteract this confrontation.

That same evening, the guard that delivered the food added a blanket. Mac refused to speak to the guard, even to ask him where his uniform was. Since he had a blanket, it really didn't matter. Mac was dozing off when he heard the familiar screech of the old castle door: Sturmbann Fuhrer Armbrust was back.

Karl walked directly over to Mac, pulled his blanket off, threw it on the ground and knocked Mac down with one blow. He knelt down beside him and said, "Lt. Lain has told me that you are a spy. Is that correct?"

Mac denied the allegation, "Lt. Lain is a pilot. None of us are spies."

He grabbed Mac by the hair and jerked his head back, "I'll ask you one last time, are you a spy?"

Mac persisted, "No! I am a co-pilot. I was shot down by the Luftwaffe. What else can I tell you? I was captured in Czechoslovakia. What in the hell could be spied on there?"

Karl pinched Mac's face with his leather gloves, squeezing as tight as he could. Then he stood and pulled Mac to his feet. He opened the door to the yard and threw him out into the snow. Mac had enough. This time, he wheeled around and threw a blow to Karl's jaw that staggered him. Karl smiled and walked back into the cell. He pulled off his gloves and removed his dress tunic, folded it neatly and placed it on the last step. Then he calmly walked back out into the yard, shirtless.

Mac looked at him and said, "Think you can stand the cold, fucker?"

Karl smiled and threw a right jab, striking Mac in the chest. Mac bobbed and weaved, throwing several quick jabs to Karl's jaw. Karl fell back, but followed up with a right cross that caused Mac to glance off the stone wall.

Now, Mac realized what it was all about, Karl was a sadistic bastard that enjoyed beating people. He didn't care if anyone was a spy or not. All he cared about was inflicting pain. Mac fought as hard as he could, but the past few months had taken their toll. His energy and stamina were gone. Karl was bleeding only from the side of his mouth. Mac didn't know exactly where he was bleeding from, but blood came from everywhere.

Karl, with the strength of a Teutonic warrior, cocked back his arm and drove his fist into Mac's stomach. Mac buckled and fell to his knees. Covered with blood, he looked up and shouted, "Hey, fuck you! If I had a couple of beers and some good chow for a few days, I would have taken your Kraut ass."

Karl walked back into the cell, put his jacket back on, smiled at Mac and walked up the steps. That evening, the guard placed Mac's tray at the top of the stairs. Mac, with his swollen face and an unidentified pain shooting through his side, crawled up to the tray. When he sat next to it, he tried to laugh, but his face hurt too much. Karl sent him two beers and an outstanding dinner—the good chow he demanded.

Karl didn't bother Mac for the next several days. Using some white lime he found between the large stones in his cell, Mac scratched a checkerboard on his blanket. He also found a large walnut shell in the corner of the dungeon that he broke into tiny fragments. He rubbed one side of the pieces on the stones, making them white. The other side remained black; he now had checkers.

He played for hours. When he lost interest, he switched to math problems. Karl was nowhere. Only the guard came and went, never uttering a word. Sometimes, Mac yelled at him, He ignored Mac, but several times he looked like he might take Karl's place and come down the stairs and beat the hell out of Mac. He always decided, or was ordered, not to contact the prisoner.

One day, the door screeched open and the guard threw Mac's uniform to him. Then he ordered Mac to the main courtyard. Mac saw the prisoners walking in a circle, their morning exercise. The guard motioned Mac to join the others. Lain smiled when he saw Mac and positioned himself next to him.

He asked Mac, "Where the hell have you been?"

Mac complained, "Hey, is that any way to talk? What's wrong with you? Are you O.K.? It's nice to see you, maybe, or go fuck yourself! Not, 'where in the hell have you been?' What an ass you are."

Lain retorted, "Wherever you have been, it put you in a nasty mood. Christ, my guard is nicer than you, and he's a real asshole."

"I'm sure glad I joined this fun group," Mac quipped.

"Well, are you O.K.? I was really worried about you," Lain asked.

"Do you know that big SS officer?" Mac inquired.

Lain guessed, "You mean 'Karl baby?'"

Mac confirmed, "Yeah. That bastard threw me into this tower-of-London cell and then proceeded to beat the hell out of me daily. He never asked me any questions. The only thing that he said was that you squealed on me, telling him that I was an OSS officer."

"The only reason I told him that was, he promised to let me use the car for the weekend," Lain joked.

Mac repeated his usual comment, "You know, you really are a simple ass. Get away from me!"

The two men laughed as they walked, exercising in a circle. The pilots patted Mac on the back as they passed him in the circle. If they only knew how fortunate they were, just to be doing their exercises and not having to duke it out with the camp commander every day, they would be thankful.

The guard called to the men and they filed back into a large passageway. Individually, the guards locked them into their cells. The medieval castle was an ideal temporary detention center. There was no way that any of them could escape, but plans were formulated. If nothing else, it kept the prisoners occupied. Lain gave Mac a quick wave before the cast iron door on his cell slammed shut. They moved Mac to a single cell at the end of the corridor with the others.

Pilots clicked Morse code messages back and forth by tapping on their cell walls. One message reported that General

Patton's armored division was approaching from the south. Someone tapped back a question, wanting to know the source of the information? The reply was, "The shadow knows," alluding to the phantom crime fighter from a radio mystery series. No one wanted to reveal military information to the Germans.

Later, Mac's cell door flew open and three guards entered. One struck him across the face while the other two punched him in the ribs and stomach. Then they dragged him down the passageway through the main door, down another hallway and into an office. Karl sat behind the desk and watched as Mac was slammed down into the chair in front of the desk.

"You are a spy after all. Some of your friends gave us the information. They are in the prison at Mauthausen. Lt. Green and Lt. Gaul, Tibor, Perry, Mican, Paris and Heller. Mauthausen is a death camp and you and your group have been ordered there by Berlin. I just thought you should know so you can prepare your group for the ordeal they face. The *RSHA* (main office of the Gestapo in Berlin) is sending men here to question you and the others."

Karl nodded his head to signal the conversation was over. The guards grabbed Mac by the arms and yanked him to his feet. Karl gave a Mac slight smile as the guards dragged him from the room.

Back in his cell, Mac pondered the situation. Why had Karl warned him of his impending doom? Why hadn't he questioned him or tortured him? Mac knew Green and his team could not hold out forever, and the information that they gave to the Germans would implicate him and Lain.

Why would Karl warn him? He wasn't sure, but put it into the back of his mind as he began to tap out the news on the wall of his cell. In the morning, all of the men were serious, realizing the situation was critical. They discussed plans, ranging from rushing the front gate to taking guards hostage. Mac and Lain tried to assemble information from the pilots. No one knew how to proceed. They were too-closely watched; there were no passages; no openings in the wall or gate and no exits.

All night, tapping continued. The pilots offered one radical plan after another. Mac stayed awake most of the night, realizing their time was running out. The men from RSHA would arrive and then the prisoners would be transported to Mauthausen.

In the morning, the men filed out for their exercise. They moved in a slow circle as Lain grabbed Mac's arm and revealed, "I think I am having a stroke."

"A what?" Mac asked in disbelief.

Next, the walls of the castle caved in. Enormous stones fell in the courtyard. Men ran in all directions. Half the main gate blew open. Prisoners everywhere ran frantically trying to escape. Guards in the tower fired randomly. A tower exploded.

Patton's armored column arrived and blasted their way in. Karl and his staff went out through the back of the castle into the woods before the Americans charged through the front gate.

German guards continued firing until they were driven out the back of the castle through a gigantic hole created by rounds fired from an American tank.

The prisoners rushed to meet the American troops, cheering and hugging them. The Americans handed canned rations to the prisoners, who gulped the food down.

An American officer stood on a tank and yelled to the men in the courtyard, "Get out of here as fast as you can. This is only an armored column, not the division."

The freed prisoners ran through the main gate to the waiting column. Cheers echoed for miles. The tanks roared ahead while the prisoners followed on foot.

Lain and Mac walked together alongside one of the tanks. Lain shouted over the roar of the engine, "Thank God something is going our way, at last!"

The engine of the tank sputtered, the tank heaved and lurched forward. The tank in front of it suffered the same fate. The tank driver used his radio to contact the unit commander, who peeled off his tank and circled back to the two stalled vehicles. Lain looked up at the driver and yelled, "What's wrong?"

The driver shrugged, "No gas. And there is a German armored column ahead, closing in on us."

Mac looked at Lain and said, "You were saying, 'Thank God something is going our way for once?'"

Lain theorized, "I'm telling you, not many people know this, but God has a baseball bat and he keeps hitting certain people with it. We just happen to be those people."

Mac repeated his usual remark, "You're really an ass, I mean you really are."

Then it sounded like a train passed over their heads. An enemy shell landed to their right. The tanks quickly formed a circle, looking like a wagon train forming up against Indians in the Old West. Shells kept falling. One tank took a direct hit.

Patton's armored column, out of gas, could not maneuver. They remained in place and fired at the on-coming Nazi armored column. Tanks went up in flames or exploded while crews and tank captains fired their machine guns into the German infantry units. The battle lasted only twenty minutes. The Americans, finally out of shells and with seventy-five percent of their armor on fire or destroyed, surrendered to the enemy.

Mac, Lain and the pilots marched with the members of Patton's armored column to a prisoner-of-war camp. The men from RSHA would never find out who they were or where they had gone. Lain was right, God was on their side.

Werner Muller was a Gestapo translator, stationed in Berlin. Before the War, he spent vacations in England. He couldn't find employment there, so he always returned to Germany. There, he had no such problem. It was easy to find a job as a tourist guide for the foreigners.

When war came, he was drafted and assigned to the censorship office in Paris. At the end of 1941, he volunteered to join General Rommel's forces in North Africa. He was refused because he failed the physical. In 1943, his physical condition deteriorated so he was discharged. He returned to the censorship office in Paris, this time, working as a civilian.

In the summer of 1944, he was temporarily detached, by order of Abwehr-Leitstelle, to serve as a translator for English, French and Italian prisoners. Then, he was called to Berlin to interpret for the RSHA. Since he was never a member of the Nazi Party, he was always viewed with suspicion.

During his assignment in Berlin, Muller was sent to the Mauthausen concentration camp. He interrogated captured Americans.

Muller was torn with ambivalence, he hated the Nazis, but loved Germany. He enjoyed being with the Americans and the British during his vacations before the War. Caught between mixed feelings, he was bitter over reporting to Mauthausen.

A military staff car drove him from the train station to the gates of the gray, sinister-looking camp. He looked around as the soldier at the main gate shuffled through his papers. A large smoke stack pierced the sky at the rear of the camp. It puked deadly fumes, polluting the air for miles. Muller smelled burning flesh—and death.

He was apprehensive, but decided there was nothing he could do about it—orders were orders. Assigned to the civilian area of the camp, he was given a small room to himself. On his first evening at the camp, a guard knocked on his door and notified him to report to the interrogation rooms in Building 11 at 0700 hours, Sunday, the following day.

Sunday morning, he ate breakfast and hurried across the yard to Building 11. He entered the front door and was shown to an interrogating room. Minutes later, he heard two men approach. They stood at the door, noticed Muller, but neither acknowledged his presence. He felt uneasy as he watched the two officers. One, Sturmbann Fuhrer Schoeneseiffen was tall and gave the impression he might be a university professor. He had a common face—one that could never be recalled.

The other officer was Untersturm Fuhrer Arndt. He was mesomorphic—short and stocky. He would stand out in a crowd. He must have been a laborer; maybe he lifted beer kegs from a truck all day. His haircut emphasized his nose, which had been broken several times but contributed to his well-defined looks.

Major Sehmer was led down the hall to the interrogation room. As he approached, the two arrogant officers stepped inside and introduced themselves to Muller. All three sat behind a large table with Major Sehmer in front. Schoeneseiffen began the questioning. Major Sehmer surprised them by answering in perfect German. He repeated his story: He was an

English officer who bailed out of a plane shot down by German *ack-ack* (anti-aircraft) fire. He hooked up with American downed pilots and was captured by German troops.

Muller did not have to translate so he sat quietly, listening to the major. Muller knew this type of Englishman. They were not going to get any information from him. Sehmer was soon taken to another room and beaten by several guards.

Another American was dragged into the interrogating room. Dr. Arbecker entered and gave Muller a quick look. Then he nodded to the other officers and took a seat behind the table. Before the other officers could say anything, Dr. Arbecker began, telling Muller to translate, "What is your name?"

"Captain L.V. Baranski, United States Army Air Corps."

"What was your mission?"

"I had no mission. I am a pilot and I was shot down."

Arbecker raised his eyebrows to the guard standing on Baranski's right. The guard knocked him from his stool with one blow. They picked him up and put him back in his original position. Dr. Arbecker repeated the question. Baranski stuck to the same answer. Again, the guards slammed him to the floor. This continued until Baranski's face was covered with blood. Finally, Arbecker ordered him taken back to his cell.

Next, Lt. Gaul was marched to the interrogation room and forcibly seated on the stool. He, too, was asked the same question. Gaul answered, "I've had it with you people, go fuck yourself."

Dr. Arbecker leaped from behind the table. The two guards held the prisoner as the doctor beat him. Lt. Gaul reeled back and kicked Arbecker in the stomach. The guards joined the beating. Soon, Lt. Gaul collapsed on the floor. His bleeding body was dragged back to his cell as the guards brought in Lt. Green.

Green looked down at Gaul, shocked beyond expression. Muller noticed no fear in his eyes or face as he began to question him. "What is your name?"

He responded militarily, "Lt. Holt Green, United States Navy."

"What was your mission?" Muller continued.

To the amazement of the officers and Muller, Lt. Green outlined his mission, then added, "I am the only OSS agent here. Joseph Morton is a correspondent for the St. Louis Post-Dispatch. He is a civilian and shouldn't be a prisoner. Marian Rubin is an American nurse and a civilian. The others are downed American pilots; they have nothing to do with me or my mission."

The officers asked Muller repeatedly if he believed Lt. Green. Muller replied that he believed him. The officers decided to review the information Lt. Green gave and terminated the questioning. Muller kept it to himself, but he believed that Lt. Green made up the story to protect the others. Muller knew none of them could hold out long. If they cracked just one man, they could disprove Lt. Green's story.

Muller reported again at 0700 the following morning. This time, the Nazi interrogators hung Lt. Francis Perry in the torture room. They kept demanding, "What was your mission?"

Every time the SS sergeant cracked the whip across Perry's back, Muller flinched. Perry tried to hold back the pain, but finally gave in and began to moan. His body produced its own anesthesia; he seemed to just hang there without emotion, like he was in a trance. The sergeant continued whipping him until an officer signaled to stop. Too much blood was flying around the room; it splashed on their uniforms. When Dr. Arbecker arrived, the others left.

The doctor looked in and saw Perry hanging from the overhead iron bar and smiled. He enjoyed what he saw and remarked to Arndt that he wished he were there during the beating. Muller tried to keep his composure, but felt nauseated. It was a sickening spectacle. He detested the Nazis—especially the SS—now more than ever. Muller told Lt. Green in English that the men torturing him were not members of the regular Germany Army, but were SS troops.

Muller walked back to the interrogation room with the officers as they selected their next victim, Lt. Tibor Keazthelzi, Unites States Army. He sat in front of the table, but before the officers could begin questioning him, he verbally attacked, "What gives you so-called army officers, the right to treat prisoners of war like this? Your asses have already lost the War. What in the hell are you trying to prove by beating these men near death?"

Schoeneseiffen replied, "If you would answer our questions, there will be no need to beat your friends."

Tibor objected, "What questions? I'm a pilot. Ask anyone, pilots don't know a damn thing. We drink and fly planes."

"What about Lt. Green, is he a pilot, too?" Muller translated.

Tibor avoided answering, "I don't know. We all headed to the mountains when Banska Bystrica was overrun. I met him during the retreat with the other pilots."

"What about this man named Jerry Mican?" the interrogators continued.

Tibor responded, "I met him on the retreat, too. Other than that, I have no idea where he came from. I saw him a couple of times at the air base in North Africa."

"Is he a pilot?" they asked.

Tibor assured them, "He better be. I watched him take off in a B-24."

"You can help the others by telling us the truth."

Tibor insisted, "I am telling you the truth."

Muller translated, "Lt. Green is not a pilot. He has already told us that you are a member of his mission."

Tibor denied the allegation, "What mission? All we did was run through the snow for months on end. No one did anything against the Germans."

"Do you know Maria Zima?" they asked.

"I don't know, there were several women in the mountains. I can't remember their names," Tibor responded.

"Here is her picture," Schoeneseiffen pushed a poster with Maria's picture on the front of it toward Tibor.

He looked down at the picture then replied, "She looks familiar, but I'm not sure."

"Do you think Lt. Green knows who she is?" Muller asked.

"I don't know. Ask him," Tibor suggested.

The officer instructed Muller to thank Tibor for his cooperation and then he motioned the guards to return Tibor to his cell.

Schoeneseiffen told Arndt that when the others see he wasn't mistreated, they will believe he gave them vital information, adding, "He will become their enemy. We will then get any information we need from the rest."

Charles Heller was a sergeant in the United States Army. He was nervous and kept swallowing, trying to keep his mouth from drying out. He was dehydrated and so thin that he had a ghostly white look about him. Dr. Arbecker noticed, but continued the questioning. He screamed as loud as he could, "What is your mission? All spies will be hanged. You are a spy, and I am going to hang you!"

The interrogator walked from behind the table and beat Heller in the face and head, slapping him continuously. He threw him to the ground and kicked him in the face and stomach. Heller moaned several times and doubled up on the floor, trying to block the kicks. Dr. Arbecker didn't stop. He jerked Heller to his feet and continued to beat him. The doctor screamed his words at Muller for translation, "Tell him I will have him hanged at once unless he answers my question."

Muller repeated the officer's demands, warning Heller to quickly answer. Heller said nothing. He was scared, but gutsy.

The guards dragged him to the adjoining room and continued to beat him. Muller was horrified at the unmilitary behavior exhibited by the SS officers. However, there was nothing he could do but sit and translate.

The officers and the guards walked out of the interrogation room and down the corridor to select Nelson Paris. He faced them, motionless.

Muller told him, "They have all the information on the Dawes Team. Please tell them what they want to know."

Young Paris knew when Muller mentioned the Dawes Team the Germans had broken some men. He thought it futile to resist and agreed to answer their questions. Already beaten, his young and handsome face was still covered with bruises. His right eye was almost swollen closed and he had a large mark on the right side of his jaw that looked like it came from a ring worn by his attacker.

Muller and the officers returned to the interrogation room. The officers entered first and greeted someone sitting at the table. Muller noticed his pointed face. He was a thin shell of a man. The guest rose and greeted the officers who introduced Muller. For a few minutes, there was idle conversation about

Berlin and the Fuhrer. When they were seated, Muller guessed that the investigation was over. Nelson Paris had given them all of the information he knew. Coupled with the information they had from the others, they knew everything. Consequently, he was surprised when the guards dragged in another prisoner.

Dr. Tost, the new man from RSHA, reached into his briefcase and extracted some papers and a small black notebook. He flipped through the pages of the small book, then handed it to Muller.

Joe Morton knew that it was his reporter's pad. Dr. Tost had the German translation on several pieces of paper. Dr. Tost looked up and instructed Muller, "Ask him where Maria Zima is."

Muller translated all of the questions. Joe answered each time, repeating that he was a war correspondent and had nothing to do with the Dawes Team. When he was asked about Maria working for the *NKVD* (Russian Secret Service), he replied that it wasn't true, that she was ardent anti-communist.

Muller reminded the officers several times that Joe was a war correspondent, not a soldier. His remarks were ignored; several times, Dr. Tost gave him a stern look.

Muller was disgusted with the entire situation. He had been through many interrogations where civilians were caught working with the Underground—blowing up bridges, sniping from the tops of buildings or setting fire to factories. But beating men in uniform was against military protocol. Watching Joe Morton, with his war correspondent identification patch on the shoulder of his uniform, being questioned like a spy was ridiculous. When they slapped Joe across the face, Muller protested. He was told that he was weak and to remove himself from the room. Muller was happy to leave, knowing that the questioning would have to stop since he was the only interpreter.

Joe was unable to answer most of their questions because he never knew what Lt. Green's mission was. He only came along to write their story. All the information he possessed was in the little black book. And the Germans had that.

Dr. Tost walked out of the room into the hall where Muller was waiting. He walked over to Muller and asked, "Are you married?"

"No, I'm not married," Muller answered.

Dr. Tost explained, "Of course not, otherwise you would know how to treat these people who are killing our women and children."

Muller stared at him, knowing that both sides killed women and children. The other three officers left Joe in the room alone and joined Muller and Dr. Tost in the hall. They completely ignored Muller and walked down the hall to the main entrance. Muller followed and heard them say something about calling Berlin.

That evening, Muller returned to see the Dawes Team. Lt. Green was ill. His right side, from his face to his ankle, was swollen badly. His right arm looked broken. Muller summoned the field medical technician and directed him to apply a splint to Lt. Green's arm. The soldier promptly followed orders. Muller told Lt. Green in English that he was sorry for the suffering that the Americans and the British experienced. Muller had only a few minutes to speak with Lt. Green, but he apologized for the terrible treatment and wanted to know if there was anything he could do. Lt. Green asked Muller to please tell the American authorities what happened to his men. Muller promised that he would. This promise seemed to make Lt. Green feel better. Muller was relieved knowing that Green understood his position. Lt. Green thanked him and the German hurried back to his quarters.

The next morning, Muller was called again to the torture room. He hurried down the hall; the officers were already in the room. When he entered, they asked him to question a man. Muller was barely able to watch. The man's wrists were tied behind his back and he was hoisted by a chain halfway to the ceiling. Tears flowed from the prisoner's face.

Muller called to him, saying, "Please tell them what they want to know."

The prisoner agreed. Muller quickly relayed his answers to the officers. They told Muller it didn't matter. The prisoner was to hang there, anyway. That way, they were convinced, he would tell the truth. Muller watched the brutality continue. His stomach knotted up. His feelings of ambivalence now turned to hatred.

How could these men call themselves soldiers? They were a disgrace to themselves and to Germany.

An officer pulled on the man's legs, increasing his pain, but he still concealed his agony. Muller's throat tightened as he watched the young man beg the officers to let him down. He said that he was ready to tell them anything.

Muller excused himself, telling the officer next to him he had to go to the bathroom. The prisoner was cut down and led across the hall to another interrogation room. Muller watched him as he stumbled. His arms were limp and hanging by his sides. He was completely broken; the days of beatings and questioning had taken their toll.

Muller renewed the interrogation. The officers asked only a few questions, most concerning Maria Zima. Then they ordered the guards to return the man to his cell. Muller followed the officers from the room, stopped next to the prisoner and shoved cigarettes into his pocket.

After this incident, Muller began to assert himself. He tried to convince the officers they had extracted all the information the prisoners had. The officers ignored him and brought in Marian Rubin, the American nurse. She was oblivious to her surroundings. She had withdrawn and remained in a catatonic state. Her head flopped on her chest. The guards had beaten her like the others. But her suffering was more mental than physical.

Muller translated, "When did you last see Maria Zima?"

Rubin barely lifted her head to the side so she could see Muller. She mumbled something he couldn't understand. Muller flinched when Dr. Tost screamed at her, though it had no effect on her. Then she muttered a few words, "I am Marian Rubin, not Maria Zima."

Dr. Tost screamed again. This time, Rubin stared at the floor and would not answer. Dr. Tost addressed the other officers at the table, "We already have enough information from this Jew."

He waved his hand at the guard, signaling him to remove her from the room. Muller used the opportunity to ask the SS officer, Arndt, sitting next to him, who Maria Zima was. He said that she was a Russian agent working with the Americans. Several members of Lt. Green's mission were still free and they were trying to find them. Maria Zima was reported to be with them. For awhile, they were sure that Marian Rubin was Maria Zima, but the other prisoners under torture all gave the same story: She was not Maria Zima.

Chapter Eight

THE RUSSIANS

A corporal from the communications building entered the room and handed a communique to Sturmbann Fuhrer Schoeneseiffen. After delivering the paper, he saluted and left the room. The sturmbann fuhrer opened the message and read it. Suddenly, there was a startled look on his face. He passed the message down the table so the other officers could read it. The officer sitting next to Muller handed it to him. He couldn't believe what he read. It was an order for the immediate execution of all prisoners. Muller slowly lowered the paper to the table. He thought aloud, "What is this? They can't be serious."

Arndt looked at him and shook his head, indicating Muller was out of touch with the situation. Muller made one last try and suggested to Dr. Tost the prisoners be put on trial.

Dr. Tost calmly replied, "They have had their trial." The officers stood and left the room. Muller sat for a moment, listening as they made fun of his behavior, referring to him as "Berlin's mama's boy."

Shattered by the execution order, Muller walked alone down the hall, his job finished. Increasing his suffering, he passed Joe Morton who was being led from his cell by a guard. He had a blank stare. Muller knew Joe sensed his fate. Muller didn't have to say a word.

Joe smiled, "Muller, I find myself in the same position as our Lord: I am being put to death, not for something I have done, but because they will not believe who I am."

Muller's heart sank. There was nothing he could do to help this poor man. He just stared into Joe's face. Then the guard escorted Joe down the hall. For the rest of his life, Muller would remember the words spoken to him on that day by Joe Morton.

Across the courtyard was a square cement bunker, formerly used to store ammunition. Wilhelm Ornstein, a Polish prisoner, was assigned to maintain the building. It was Wednesday, January twenty-fourth. A dismal day. The sky was a cold, dark gray. The air was thick and damp and stagnate around the building.

Muller watched as an SS officer dismissed the regular guards from the prison walls and around the building. Eleven members of the American mission, four British soldiers and Marian Rubin were marched across the courtyard to a room where their clothes were taken from them. Naked, each was led alone by an SS guard into the bunker. Lt. Gaul was obviously ill. Green was limping and held his right arm—he was in pain. Joe Morton was calm. At one point, Joe tried to help the Jewish girl, Marian Rubin, but he was restrained by his guard.

Ornstein hardly had any feelings left. He had been dragging bodies out of the building and burning them for over a year. This time, he could not hold back his tears. His heart went out to the poor Jewish girl, standing alone, naked in front of all of the men. She was shivering and tried to cover herself with her hands. Ornstein turned away and faced the wall of his building.

Ornstein went into the cold storage room. In that room, which was connected to the execution chamber, he had drilled a small hole in the wall. He used the hole to identify executed prisoners. He knew that the authorities would be looking for that information when the War ended.

The officer in charge told the group they were going to have their pictures taken before being transferred to a prisoner-of-war camp. The British and the Americans stood silently, as one after the other was taken into the execution chamber.

They were told to face the large camera on the opposite side of the room. Then Arbecker, the cold Nazi executioner, took out his pistol and fired one round through the back of their head as they faced the camera. Ornstein was struck by the fact that the Americans and British stood quietly and died in silence. As usual, Ornstein was ordered to remove the bodies from the execution chamber and move them to the cold storage room. Before removing the bodies, he scratched down the names of those participating in the execution: Franz Ziereis, Bolhorst, Bachmayer, Karl Schultz and Martin Roth. Several of the names he could not remember, and he never saw them again.

Following the executions, Ornstein heard a moan from a victim. It was Lt. Green. Bachmayer noticed and walked over and fired another shot through his head. Ornstein and two of his aids continued dragging the bodies into the cold storage room. Then he noticed several men still had on their dog tags. He quickly jerked the tags from around their necks and shoved them into his pocket. He could not believe the SS had overlooked them.

The bodies were lined up in the cold storage room. As Ornstein scrubbed down the execution room, getting it ready for the next group, he heard whimpering. It was the Jewish girl. Blood was gushing from her head, and she was bleeding through her mouth. She was unconscious and was drowning in her own blood. Ornstein told one of his men to get an officer.

Obersturm Fuhrer Schultz returned. He was perturbed that he had to take time away from his duties to finish off Marian Rubin. He asked Ornstein which prisoner was still alive. Ornstein pointed to Marian. Schulz drew his automatic pistol and fired several rounds through her body. He gave an emotionless instruction to Ornstein, "Next time, just get rid of them, dead or not."

Ornstein then returned to his daily routine: cleaning the blood from the floor and scrubbing the walls. He also had to run the cremation furnaces. As he and his men loaded the bodies on their small cart to transport them to the crematorium, they stopped to watch the officers from RSHA enter their Mercedes and drive through the main gate on their way back to Berlin. Werner Muller rolled down his window and took one last look back at Mauthausen.

On Maria's return to the French Partisan camp, very few words were spoken. Davis walked next to Maria. He said little, knowing she was deep in thought, suffering from the loss of her new friends. She was no longer the innocent young girl from the mountains of Slovakia. She had witnessed the horrors of war and the cruelty of man. He was sure she would never be taken alive. She was becoming a seasoned veteran.

Catlos and Dunlevy, both enlisted men, were now without officers. Davis had lost Major Sehmer, but assumed command of the small unit. They moved close to the French position, but before they rounded the mountain, a French Partisan stopped them. He told them the main body of forces had pulled out. German fighters strafed their unit so their commander ordered him to stay behind to warn Maria and her group. Having delivered his message, he turned to leave. Maria stopped him and asked where Jano, the German deserter, was. He told her Jano was killed during the strafing. He also mentioned the commander ordered the unit toward the Russian lines.

Davis told the group they had to keep moving east. Eventually, they would run into the Russians. Everyone agreed that there was nothing else to do.

They moved on, saddened over the death of Jano; Maria and Davis walked slowly, leading the way. They were soon ahead of Catlos and Dunlevy, so they stopped and waited for them to catch up. Maria looked at Davis and, to his surprise, confessed, "Davis, promise me if we run into the Germans instead of the Russians, you will fight to the death, because I intend to fire your machine gun until they kill me."

Davis disapproved, "You aren't going to kill anyone. Besides, you don't even know how to fire this weapon."

"I was hoping you would teach me," Maria hinted.

Davis refused, "Forget it. There is only one thing worse than a German with a machine gun, and that is a woman with one." He laughed and threw his arm around her. When he did this, Maria always smiled and felt safe.

When Catlos and Dunlevy approached, Maria looked at them and said, "My God, I hope I don't look as bad as you two."

They disappointed her, commenting, "Believe me, Maria, you do."

She touched her face. Her lips had cracked open from the bitter cold; there was an open sore on her right cheek; her hair was matted and she still suffered from the infection in her right leg.

She looked back at Davis, the Bull looked in perfect health. He gave her a broad smile and said, "We think you are beautiful just as you are."

Maria had no answer, she shoved her hands into the pockets of her jacket and walked on, looking like a Chinese peasant moving across a frozen rice field. The others smiled and fell in behind her.

For the rest of the day, they trekked on. About 1400 hours, they came upon a well-traveled road winding through a valley. They approached with caution. Hearing voices, they immediately ran off the road and hid behind the snow-covered stones that lined the path. Maria listened, then reported, "That's Russian they're speaking. They're Russians!"

Davis had his machine gun ready. Catlos and Dunlevy stayed hidden, not convinced they were safe.

Three young Russian soldiers were startled when they saw Maria. She asked them in Russian where their main headquarters was. They weren't quite sure. All three of them had been wounded and were looking for one of their aid stations.

Maria hollered to Davis that it was safe and the rest of the group emerged. She walked with the Russians, trying to get information. All were new recruits. Their heads were still shaved and their uniforms looked relatively new. The one in the middle said they were wounded near the town of Hatvan.

The Germans were pushed back, but the fighting in the area was intense. They had heard there was going to be a German counterattack near Budapest. They had no other information, except there was a schoolhouse on the road ahead. It was an aid station the Rumanians operated. Maria translated the news to Davis, Catlos and Dunlevy.

One of the Russians was in pain. The bandage on his right shoulder seeped blood. Maria asked if she could help. Not wanting to appear unmilitary, he stated he would be fine until they reached the aid station.

Davis, leading the group, called back that there was a building just ahead and to the right, surrounded with military vehicles. It was a schoolhouse.

When they reached the schoolhouse, Maria and the three Russians wanted to know where the Russian headquarters was. The Rumanian officer in charge told her an ambulance driver would transport them to the next town. There, the Russians had taken over the entire village.

Maria and the Americans were led out the front door and directed to the military ambulance. Maria told the driver they were going to headquarters. He looked at her like the crazy truck driver did—the one who had driven her through the mountains months ago to the Partisan camp when she was running messages for Pavlovich. Thinking about it made her smile.

Catlos, Dunlevy and Davis were in high spirits. What Maria learned about the Russians left her still unsure of the situation. She wasn't convinced their worries were over.

Maria stood in the doorway of the headquarters house. The commander, seeing her, walked over and looked her up and down as she stood before him in rags. He leaned forward and kissed her hand, saying, "And how may I help you and your friends?"

Maria answered, "I am Maria Zima. These are sergeants Davis, Catlos and Dunlevy. Davis is British, and the other two are Americans."

The commander repeated, "Maria Zima. You are already a hero to the mountain people of Slovakia. I have heard your name mentioned several times. Where have you and your men been?" he wanted to know.

Maria reported, "Before coming here, Sergeant Davis was in the Carpathian Mountains near the Dukla Pass."

The commander responded, "We had planed to break through there in two weeks, but it took us two months."

Maria told Davis what the commander said. Davis then told Maria to ask him if he knew that the Russians had lost 124,000 men in the Dukla Pass charge. Maria stared at Davis and blinked several times, "Are you serious, Davis?"

"Yes, I was there," he confirmed.

Maria inquired, "But, 124,000 men in one charge. How could that happen?"

Davis assured her, "It happened. I'll bet you he doesn't know a thing about it."

The commander smiled and waited for Maria to translate Davis' statement. When Maria told him, his face elongated. He looked at Davis and changed the subject, "It is not advisable that we discuss such things."

Maria translated and Davis responded, "I have watched your bomber formations come in low and without fighter protection. They were attacked by the Luftwaffe fighters, but not one plane broke formation. They lost fifty percent of their planes, but continued to their target. They are some of the bravest men in the world."

The commander then asked Maria to please ask Davis again if he was sure of the number of men killed. Maria translated and Davis shook his head yes.

Then the commander offered, "Let's not just stand here, come have something to eat and drink."

An enlisted man appeared with bread, cheese and some heavy, dark red wine. They gulped down the food. Between eating and drinking, Maria asked the commander if there were some place they could wash themselves and their clothes.

The Russians had rigged a washing facility in an old wine cellar with huge washtubs made from wine vats. There was plenty of hot water and a place where they could wash and dry their uniforms. The commander gave orders to his sergeant to prepare the tubs and to find someone to wash their guests' clothes while they bathed.

The sergeant left and the commander asked Maria if she knew anything about the Galician Division. She told him that for several weeks they had chased her group through the mountains. He told her, "That division was taking men from the villages, putting them in German uniforms and sending them out in front of their companies. The village men were nothing more than warning signals for the division."

Maria treated the news as though it were to be expected. She kept her grace and charm, but her psychological state caused her to become hard and calloused.

The group headed to the washtubs. Before leaving, Dunlevy and Davis asked if they could use the Russian radio to contact their headquarters. The commander told them he would look into it while they were having their clothes washed.

The commander assigned a young soldier to guard the room where Maria was washing. He stepped in and closed the door.

Maria explained, "I think your commander wants you to guard the door from the outside, not the inside."

He smiled and removed himself from the room. She sank into the hot tub. It felt like being in the arms of God. Nothing in the world could compare to it. She was filthy from head to toe. Her hair was matted and her scalp was covered with lice. She scrubbed and scrubbed. Washing her face and her hair three, four, five times in a row.

The guard kept opening the door, trying to convince her that he should bathe with her. She joked with him, but felt some apprehension. Maria felt at ease when she heard women's voices. The guard stepped back and allowed two Russian women soldiers to enter the tub room.

Maria explained the situation to the women. They laughed and asked her why she didn't let him in. Maria explained that he was only a boy.

Then the older of the two said, "Just use your rank on him, and be stern."

"I can't do that either." Maria told them, "I'm not an officer."

"What are you doing here?" they wanted to know.

Maria replied, "I'm Maria Zima. I was with the CFI until we were overrun at Banska Bystrica."

"Maria Zima, the famous fighting Partisan?" they asked.

Maria corrected them, "I did no fighting, just a lot of running."

"Whatever you did, it made you a legend to the troops and the people of Czechoslovakia," they told her.

Maria was embarrassed. Her face turned red. She was about to tell them there were many heroes and she wasn't one of them, when she heard an English accent from the other side of the wine cellar.

She knew he was English by his complaining. He was trying to tell the guard that he didn't have a towel. Maria called back to him, letting him know that they only had blankets and sheets. He would have to use one or the other.

He called back, "Thank you, ducks."

After soaking for two hours in the warm water, Davis, Catlos and Dunlevy called the guard, asking where their clothes were. Maria heard them and she repeated their question in Russian, so the guard would understand.

The Englishman, hearing the conversation, chimed in, "My name is Sergeant Zenopiean. Are there any Englishmen about?"

Dunlevy called back, "No. There are two Americans and one guy that lives near you, but he is Welsh, not English."

"Yes, dear boy, but he is British," Zenopiean reminded him.

Davis denied it, "Not according to him."

"Really," the sergeant commented.

Maria could hear Davis and his group laugh. The two Russian girls threw Maria a sheet and she wrapped it around her, opened the door and stood, looking like an Arab, as she slung the part of the sheet that was around her head over her shoulder. The young guard smiled. Maria used the advice given to her by the two Russian women and barked an order at him, "Find our uniforms, we have to leave."

Davis, Catlos and Dunlevy came out into the center of the room, also wrapped in sheets. Zenopiean yelled to Maria, giving her orders to find his clothes.

The Russian soldiers finally brought their uniforms and piled them in the center of the room. Davis picked up his jacket, looked at it and slowly turned it around. Their faces dropped. They stood silent for a moment, then howled with laughter. His paratrooper jacket looked like it would fit a teddy bear. The Russians boiled their clothes for the two hours the team soaked in bathtubs.

Zenopiean walked into the room, drying his short, military crew cut with a handkerchief. He complained the accommodations were poor and something should be done about it.

He introduced himself to Maria. He was so thin she asked him if he had escaped from a prisoner-of-war camp. He was insulted and replied, "I have been wandering through these mountains for months. First, with this group, then with that group, hiding in this village, then in that village; running in the middle of the night and sleeping in the snow. Finally, I end up here to find my bath water positively tepid, most unpleasant.

These Russians are short on manners, and I am not sure I trust them."

Davis responded, "I'll do something about our clothes, but you should stick with us."

"Sounds good, old boy," Zenopiean agreed.

Zenopiean held up the sheepskin gloves that used to be his pride and joy. He showed them to Maria, "Look at these. They look like two raisins. I tell you these Russians have no sense of purpose." Maria tried to keep from laughing, but couldn't. She tried to suppress her facial expressions. Davis sputtered, then snickered. Zenopiean looked at him and said, "I fail to see the humor in this situation."

Catlos and Dunlevy turned away and laughed after they saw his dried-up gloves. It had been a long time since any of them were able to enjoy themselves. The laughter was well earned; they enjoyed every minute of it.

Maria asked Davis to go with her down the hall. She stopped the first soldier she saw and asked where the supply officer was. He gave her directions to a large room at the end of the passageway.

A stern-faced officer sat at his desk while Maria explained her situation. He replied there was no army regulation providing for distribution of uniforms to anyone who wanted them. Maria turned to Davis, still standing in his sheet, and told him what the officer said.

He told Maria, "You tell this Russki he better get us some uniforms, or else."

Maria repeated the request to the Russian officer, but it didn't phase him. Maria told Davis, "That won't work. These Russians go by the book and there is no changing their minds."

She turned back to the officer and suggested another approach, "Is there anything in your regulation book that will allow us to exchange our uniforms?"

The Russian searched his manual and admitted, "Yes, you can exchange your uniforms."

Maria took Davis by the arm as they walked back down the hall. The Russian women soldiers gave Davis the eye. Maria noticed and told him. "Davis, I think you are making quite an impression on these women soldiers."

Davis smiled, "It won't do them any good. I'm in love with someone else."

Maria jumped at the chance to poke fun at Davis, "Yes, I saw the way you looked at Sergeant Zenopiean."

Davis was not about to let her get away with the last laugh. As two women officers approached, he opened his sheet. Maria grabbed the sheet and reprimanded him, "What is the matter with you. These Russians will think we're crazy."

"Well, don't you want to know who I am in love with?" Davis asked.

Maria guessed, "I imagine your wife."

"No, I'm not married. I have fallen in love with a beautiful Slovak teacher," Davis told her.

Maria held back, "Davis, please, we are not out of this yet. I know nothing about you, other than I am quite fond of you and you are very handsome. Maybe if things were different . . ."

Zenopiean saw them approaching and started, "What about our uniforms? Are they going to do something about them?"

Maria gathered her things from the floor and answered, "Yes. We can exchange them for new ones at the supply office at the end of the hall. Is that all right, Zenopiean?"

"Do you mean to tell me they have British uniforms here?" he naively inquired.

Dunlevy and Catlos realized they could never use their uniforms and removed the American shoulder patch. Davis told Zenopiean to remove the British emblem from his uniform. This order triggered another of his tirades, "If you think for one minute that I will wear a Russian uniform, you are sadly mistaken."

Dunlevy joked, "You can always sew an emblem on your sheet."

"You people from the colonies have a very strange sense of humor," Zenopiean remarked.

All five, wrapped in their sheets, walked to the supply room and exchanged their uniforms for a set of standard Russian military gear.

The commander joined them to say he had received orders for them to be moved to the hospital. Davis and Dunlevy requested again to use the radio so they could contact their units, but the commander refused. His excuse was he did not have the authority. The commander had been nice to them so Davis and Dunlevy did not want to push him. They thanked him for what he had already done.

A driver pulled a truck around to the front of the building. In minutes, the remaining members of the Dawes Team were on their way to the field hospital. They drove a few miles then pulled into what was once a community hospital. It was bombed out, but the Russians restored it to a functional unit. It was clean, bright and looked well run.

Some nurses wore military fatigues, others wore the standard white nurse's uniform. The doctors had on traditional Russian tunics, white and buttoned from the neck to the right shoulder. The chief of staff wore the long, white traditional doctor's coat. Although men were in charge, there were very few male doctors. Most of the doctors were women.

Maria commented to Davis, "This is not a very good sign."

"What isn't a good sign," he wondered.

"Women doctors," Maria responded.

"Why aren't they a good sign?" Davis wanted to know.

Maria explained her superstition, "Through history, when women took over medicine in a country, the nation declined."

Davis refused to believe her, "We're still in trouble and you are worried about history and the decline of a nation."

Maria explained, "I'm sorry. I was a history major. I always think about things like that."

Davis and Maria were met by an elderly doctor. The commander had called him so he expected them. He addressed, Maria, "You are scheduled for physicals, to make sure you are not seriously ill."

They were directed to an examination room and told to remove their clothes. Zenopiean pulled back the curtain, walked over to Maria and complained, "Do you believe I will be examined by a Russian doctor? A woman Russian doctor!"

"What difference does it make? "Maria asked. "It's only a physical."

Dunlevy and Catlos came to her with the same complaint. They were not used to women doctors and wanted a man to take care of them. The old doctor returned and Maria explained the problem.

Zenopiean rambled, "Just because there is a war going on is no excuse for impropriety."

The doctor asked Maria what his problem was, and wanted to know if he was a member of the British East India Army.

Zenopiean became red in the face as Maria translated the doctor's questions, "What does he mean by that remark?"

Maria looked at the doctor and said, "What do you mean by that remark?"

The doctor elaborated, "When I was in India, many officers in the British East India Army were very close, you know, very close."

Maria smiled and thought, "I'm glad that he didn't ask Davis the same question." She turned to Zenopiean and said, "The doctor was in India and thought he might have seen you there, but he wasn't sure."

Following their physicals, the doctor told the team they should stay at the hospital for a few days of rest. He placed them on a high-calorie diet, hoping to put some weight back on them.

In the next few days, the Russians paid little attention to them. Casualties from the Northern Front poured in, day and night. The group rested and regained their health. In the evenings, they strolled through the hospital for exercise and to watch the Russian medical units in action.

On one of these strolls, Maria stopped and asked a nurse what the horrible screaming was. The nurse told her the hospital had run out of anesthesia over a week ago, and no supplies were arriving. Amputations were performed using vodka—the soldiers drank it before the operation. She met Catlos and Dunlevy walking through the rows of wounded. Dunlevy told Maria about the American Civil War. He imagined that the medical care for the wounded must have been about the same.

He said, "Maria, when you come back to Czechoslovakia after the War, you will have to rename this hospital Gettysburg General. This vodka bit is O.K., but have you noticed all the men are drunk. We helped several back to bed after they fell on the floor. The fall didn't help their wounds."

Maria remarked, "I guess it is better to be drunk than in pain."

The next morning, the doctor sent for the group and told Maria they would be transported back farther from the front to an NKVD camp. All of the people liberated by the Red Army were being sent there for questioning. He assumed that they were trying to get as much information as they could about the Germans. The old doctor had breakfast with them and wished them luck in their travels. He saw them to the awaiting truck and waved as they drove off.

Maria glanced out of the window at the entrance and saw the Lucence Hospital sign. Looking at Dunlevy, she commented, "We should have come out here last night and painted the word Gettysburg over Lucence."

Dunlevy laughed and Davis asked what the joke was.

Maria replied, "I don't know, but two of the nurses told me you look better in a sheet than you do in that stupid Russian uniform and Cossack hat."

Davis gave her a friendly slap on the back and laughed.

All of them were now clean, had new uniforms and their spirits were up as the truck bounced along. Even Zenopiean wasn't complaining. He sat peacefully watching the snow-covered mountains, lost in his thoughts. He was fine until Davis commented, "Were you really in the British East India Army."

Zenopiean snapped, "No! I was never in the British East India Army!"

Dunlevy looked at Catlos, "What in the hell is it with this British East India Army thing?"

"I don't know," Catlos answered.

Davis broke in, "It's the same thing as the Gettysburg Hospital."

Zenopiean moped, "I have never heard such a ridiculous conversation in my life. A minute ago, I was feeling fine and now, thanks to you people, my day has been simply awful."

Davis asked Zenopiean what his assignment was in the British Army. Zenopiean replied that it was probably the same as his. Davis egged him on, "Oh, you're a paratrooper, too?"

Zenopiean denied it, "No, I am not a paratrooper. The thought of jumping out of planes all day is upsetting."

"Well, what did you do?" Davis probed.

Dunlevy and Catlos hung on every word, waiting for Zenopiean's answer. Zenopiean gave a stern look and replied, "Let's just say, Sergeant Davis, that I can't be taken alive."

Maria felt he was sincere. None of them pressed him further.

The truck wheeled into the camp. The compound was surrounded by miles of barbed wire. A young Russian officer met the truck. With him was a private named Nicolia. The officer spoke to Maria, assigning quarters and introducing Nicolia to her. He would be their guide and guard as long as they were under Russian protection.

Nicolia was a happy-go-lucky young man, raised on a farm in central Russia. He took an instant liking to Maria. She used his friendship to gather as much information as she could from him. Contrary to what he was taught, he confided in Maria, telling her that Mother Russia was everything and that the communists were out of their minds. He would have nothing to do with them. He also let her know that he hated the military. He just wanted to return to his family farm and to be left out of politics. "Nevertheless," he admitted, "I intend to carry out my orders to the letter. I may not like it, but I am a soldier."

They were no sooner settled in their room when the officer who met them reappeared. He told Maria they would be moving in the morning to a town near the Rumanian border, Bekescsaba.

Davis complained to the officer, then to Catlos and Dunlevy. He wanted to use the Russian radios to contact the British or Americans. Again, permission was denied.

The refusal, naturally gave Zenopiean another excuse to air his views on the subject. "Ducks. Tell this bald-headed little snip of a man that we intend to use his radios."

Maria translated and then gave Zenopiean his answer. "The officer said he does not have authority to give you permission. It would have to come from, Moscow."

Zenopiean responded, "Tell him, dear girl, to call Moscow."

Maria relayed the message. The officer looked at Zenopiean and left the room.

Zenopiean watched him leave and fumed, "You see, these people have no breeding. It is useless to converse with them."

Nicolia arrived early in the morning and accompanied them to breakfast. He told Maria they had to head southeast. The team gathered their possessions, then walked through the front gate and down the road. After they had walked a mile or so, Maria asked, "Nicolia, where are the trucks?"

He answered, "No one said anything about a truck to me. My orders are to get you to Bekescsaba."

Maria reminded him, "Nicolia, when I talked with the officer, he told me Bekescsaba was two hundred miles south."

"That's right," Nicolia admitted. "But the orders I have said nothing about transportation. So that means we walk."

"Nicolia, do you see that great big strong paratrooper?" Maria asked.

"Yes," he answered.

Maria threatened, "If I tell him what you told me, he will kill you. He has just walked halfway across Europe in freezing weather. So you better think of something quickly, or you're a dead man."

Nicolia looked at Maria and saw that she was serious. Catlos complained that the Russian boots were too tight. Dunlevy remarked that several days ago he would have given his life just to have a pair of Russian boots.

Davis asked Maria what was going on. They had been walking for hours. He wanted to know how much farther to the transportation pool. At dark, Maria pressed Nicolia for a solution. He became nervous and directed them off the road into a bombed-out house for shelter. Maria told him whatever he was going to do, he should do it fast.

Nicolia begged Maria for ideas. She told him there was only one way out: find transportation.

The night was chilling; they huddled together in one room of the destroyed house. In the morning, they ate the food they had with them, then Maria explained the situation to the four men, fearing that harm might come to the innocent Russian boy if she didn't let them know.

Davis was beside himself, "Does this crazy bastard think we are marching two hundred miles?"

The Russians

Maria defended Nicolia, "Davis, those are his orders and he is trying to obey them. It is the same in your army, I'm sure."

Zenopiean joined in, "No one in the British Army would ever give such a stupid order. These Russians are mad."

As the group continued their march, they passed soldiers on their way to the front. Nicolia warned Maria not to get too close to the soldiers. He was only one guard; there were many of them and she was very beautiful. The soldiers seemed more intrigued with Catlos and Dunlevy, who had sewn American emblems on their Russian jackets. All the trucks that passed were headed to the front with supplies or troops, nothing was going toward the team's destination. So, they walked all day and into the evening.

They decided the next morning, they would commandeer the first truck or car headed in their direction, despite the consequences. Maria relayed their decision to Nicolia, who just shook his head.

When morning came, they assembled on the road. The thick fog was eery. They had to strain their eyes to see the road in front of them. Soon, they heard an unfamiliar sound echoing through the fog. They knew the sound of tanks, trucks, troops and panicked civilians, but this noise was different.

The sound became more pronounced as it approached. Suddenly, it was directly in front of them. The sun broke through the fog so they could see. They couldn't believe their eyes. In front of them were thousands and thousands of Mongol troops on miniature horses, all trotting in a line, as far as they could see.

Dunlevy mumbled, "Talk about Gettysburg, if I didn't know better, I would swear we were watching Genghis Kahn passing in review."

Zenopiean remarked, "My God, every one of them looks exactly alike." He was right. Every man wore the same hat and carried the same Russian machine gun. Each carried a rolled-up blanket across his chest, secured by a leather strap. Maria asked Nicolia who they were.

He responded, "I think they are part of the 3rd Army, under General Yeremenko, but I'm not sure."

The team pushed on and that afternoon they reached a railroad supply depot. Thousands of trucks were being unloaded and lined up, ready to be moved to the front. Dunlevy examined a truck and told Maria they were American trucks. He showed her the name *Ford* on several parts. Then he pointed out the Russian red star had been painted over the American white star on each door.

Maria told Nicolia the trucks were American, given to the Russians by the American government. He told her that wasn't true and called a guard, who wasted no time in telling them that the trucks were made in Russia. Adding that the Americans had given them nothing toward the war effort.

Maria and the group demanded to see the commanding officer. The guard thought nothing of it and told them to follow him. They were guided to a small, wood office building near the tracks. The guard knocked and motioned them in. Maria took charge. She shared their story one more time with the commanding officer. The young major's tailored uniform made him stand out from the others.

He stated there was no way they could have a truck without an order. He didn't have the authority. She insisted the trucks were American, and that they had a right to one. He told her she was mistaken; the trucks were made in Russia. Maria did not repeat the conversation to Davis or the others. She thought that Davis was reaching the end of his patience and might try something physical.

She asked the major, "If they were made in Russia, why does it say *Ford* and *USA* on the parts? The red star is painted over the American white star."

He told Maria that he did not have to answer any questions put to him by a woman, let alone a Slovak woman. Then he started asking her questions, wondering why she was with military troops. She told him that she didn't have to answer any of his questions, after all, he was only a Russian. The battle continued as the two British and the two Americans watched, not understanding a word.

Realizing Russians back down in the face of authority, Maria bluffed, "When I was General Yeremenko's interpreter with the 3rd Army, he ordered me to accompany these men."

The major quickly changed his attitude. Her trick worked. He ordered a guard to bring a truck to the shack. Now, he couldn't get rid of them fast enough. He stood next to the truck as the group boarded. As Davis helped Maria into the cab, the major looked up and defended his country's honor, "If these are American trucks, they were paid for by Russian gold."

The group drove all day, passing numerous Russian units. When they saw a village, Maria bought food, offering the gold pieces Lt. Green had given her. But the Slovak people always refused the gold and gave the group any food they could spare.

On the first night, they stayed with a Czech family in a Russian-occupied village. The house was warm and free from the cold night winds. Maria was uneasy and stayed awake most of the night. Several times, she noticed Davis looking out the window. He was afraid someone would steal the truck.

At sunrise, Nicolia summoned Maria. Davis asked her what he wanted. She told him he said to get ready to move out.

Davis complained, "Get ready to move out! What in the hell does he mean, 'get ready?' We are wearing everything we own." He pulled his Russian fur cap forward and said, "There, tell him we are ready."

After a few hours of watching Davis grind the gears in the truck, Maria griped, "After driving all this way, you think you would know where the gears were."

"Do you want to drive?" Davis offered.

Maria admitted, "No. I don't know how."

They noticed a large camp to their right and pulled in. The guard motioned them through. Davis, still grinding gears, pulled up in front of the central office. The people in the village had been moved. There were only Russian soldiers and civilians held for questioning.

Maria told her story again to the officer in charge. She requested permission to use their radio. The captain said he had no such authority. He called several Russian soldiers and had them take the group to an empty house.

Maria told Davis and Dunlevy she could not get permission to use the radio, causing them more frustration than they could handle. Maria had to calm them down, telling them she would try again later. Zenopiean increased the tension by remarking that no one knew where their unit was, and that they were getting farther and farther away from the Allies.

The Russians sent food to the house. Following the meal, a sergeant arrived and asked Dunlevy to accompany him to the information center. Dunlevy looked at Catlos, as if to say, they will get very little information from me. Seconds later, another sergeant appeared for Catlos to follow. Then one for Maria.

Maria was shown to a room with a bright overhead light, a desk with a single chair in front of it and a colonel behind it. The colonel welcomed her and asked if she would mind answering a few questions. Maria assured him that if she could help to liberate her country from the Germans, she was willing to do so.

"Where were you born?" the colonel began.

Maria responded, "In Slovakia."

"Is your family still there?" he wanted to know.

"No," Maria told him.

He asked, "Where are they?"

Maria explained, "I'm not sure. They moved several times during the War. We used to live in Banska Bystrica. I am not sure where they are now." To Maria, none of these questions were relevant. She answered in vague terms, not sure what the Russian probed for. She certainly wasn't going to volunteer information about herself or her family. She became suspicious when he asked what the American mission was. She suggested that he get that answer from the Americans. At the end of the seesaw questioning, Maria told the colonel that the Americans requested the use of a radio. His reply was that he would look into it.

That evening, the group discussed the situation. Before they had gone too far, Maria covered her ears and pointed around the room. She was sure that the Russians were listening electronically to their conversation. They immediately changed the topic. Zenopiean began to flatter the Russians, saying how nice he had been treated, and what wonderful food they were served.

The questioning continued for five days. Davis and the Americans complained constantly, repeating their demand to use the radio. Zenopiean quoted the Geneva Convention, as though they were prisoners of war. On the fifth day, Maria was not returned to the group, but was kept isolated and guarded. Several times, she saw Nicolia march back and forth, accompanied by two Russian soldiers. Apparently, he was questioned, too.

The Russians started waking Maria at 0200 hours and again at 0400 hours. They would wait for several hours then get her up and question her again, always with the same questions.

"Why are you helping the British and Americans?" an interrogator asked.

"Those were my orders from General Viest," Maria responded.

"Why didn't you go with the Russian Partisans?" they wanted to know.

"My orders were to stay with the British and Americans, not to join the Russian Partisans. I couldn't be in two places at once," Maria explained.

"Why didn't you leave them on their own?" they asked.

Maria defended herself, "They speak English and nothing else, that's why I was ordered to stay with them."

The questioning lasted fourteen days. The only new question was, "What are you going to do after the War?"

Maria answered honestly, "Go home to my liberated nation and return to school."

The colonel politely said, "Maria, with your knowledge of languages and your ability to do this kind of work, you would find a great opportunity in Russia."

Maria's heart leaped into her throat, thinking of what might happen.

He smiled and continued, "I have been asked if you would care to join the NKVD. It will offer you a great opportunity. I don't want to disillusion you about the liberation of Czechoslovakia: I am sure it will remain under Russian control for quite sometime. With your family and friends there, perhaps you should think this proposition over."

Maria, trying to stall, told the colonel she would think about it. She realized the NKVD (Russian Secret Service) was pushing the man when he slid a paper in front of her. "Here," he said, "Maria, read this and sign it. Then we can take care of your group."

The paper read, "I volunteer my services to the NKVD and the Red Army. I promise to obey all orders without question; never to reveal any confidential information that is given to me; to take all assignments without question or refusal. Failing to adhere to the above, I will be subject to all laws governing the NKVD and those of the Soviet Union."

Maria realized you face death if you deal with these people. She pushed the paper back and told the colonel politely she would like to think it over that evening and give him an answer in the morning.

Back in her room, she walked the floor. Davis was God knows where. She hadn't seen him in two and a half weeks. There was no one that she could talk to, and she knew there was only one answer the Russians would accept. She had to tell them yes.

Maria was allowed to sleep the entire night. In the morning, she was called to the colonel's office again. He had the paper sitting in front of him and next to it was a pen. Now, three colonels were present. They introduced themselves; the one standing to the right of the desk said, "It is very important to us that you sign the paper. Naturally, it is equally important to you."

Maria knew exactly what he meant. She smiled, making it look like she agreed with them. She signed and then they told her she could be excused. She left the room, walked down the road leading to the quarters of the men. This time, there were no guards and she was apparently free to roam about. She thought the Russians might have made a mistake. She all but ran to the house, walking by the sentry, acting as though he wasn't on duty.

She hurriedly told her story to the others, explaining she was forced to sign. She said she wasn't sure what would have happened to them if she didn't. Davis was concerned. He told her he thought she made a mistake, but that it was too late to worry about it. His main concern was for the group. He asked Maria if she had any idea what would become of them. She didn't know and told him so.

Davis gathered everyone and announced, "Listen, here is what we are going to say: Maria and I were married in the mountains. Lt. Gaul was the minister who performed the ceremony. There are no papers, but he recorded the ceremony and the date in his book. It was all legal, so she is a British citizen."

Everyone agreed. At least their story would throw a wrench into the Russian machine. Maria also mentioned she thought the Russians forgot to put a guard back on her, but she should return to her quarters. She was out the door and back to her quarters in a flash.

Shortly after Maria returned, the colonel came to her room. He was formal in his report, "You and your group have been ordered to the repatriation camp. From there, the rest of the group will be turned over to the British and American authorities. You will receive your orders from the NKVD when you arrive."

In typical Russian fashion, he wasted no time. He informed her transportation was already waiting. The group would be picked up on the way. Maria thought the truck would drive by the group, which meant she would never see them again. She relaxed when the driver stopped in front of their quarters and they entered the truck.

A whistle blew and someone called out in Russian to hold the truck. Seconds later, Nicolia, with his machine gun hanging around his neck, climbed into the truck. He confided in Maria that he was absolutely convinced the communists were out of their minds; they treated him like the enemy.

Maria assured him they received the same treatment. But, he reminded her, he was a Russian soldier not a foreigner. She replied, "You are in Czechoslovakia, that makes you a foreigner."

Nicolia objected, "I didn't mean that."

"I know what you meant. I am only joking with you, Nicolia," Maria laughed.

Maria told Davis she was worried. They were moving closer to the Russian border. Davis temporarily convinced her that all would be straightened out when they reached the repatriation center. Maria had her doubts.

The driver turned off the road into the center. It was an enormous camp. There were Poles, Jews, Hungarians and Rumanians. The truck did not pull directly into the camp, but to one side. The passengers were told to exit the truck and enter the building to their left. It was a barracks and the group filed in.

Settled in their new home, they waited for the Russians' next move. On the second day, Maria was ordered to the central office. She was about to file a protest on behalf of Davis—he was still trying to borrow a radio—when the commanding officer of the camp informed her she was working for the NKVD. She was to start questioning Polish families. He wanted to know why they refused to return to Poland.

Maria complied, not wanting to upset the Russians. Questioning the Poles, she was always told the same thing, "We left when the Russians came."

She took a break from her work and returned to the group. Davis told her to extract some information from the Poles and to give the correct information to the officers. The Poles could be a plant. They could be testing Maria to see if she gave the right translation. He suggested she continue her duty until they could find their way around in the new situation.

Maria gave only selected information. She did not want to jeopardize the Polish families. Knowing she could not do this long, she was anxious, but continued. One evening, she told the group she could not stall much longer. To make matters worse, Zenopiean convinced the group that they were going to be sent to Siberia and never heard from again. Maria felt he might be right. She knew one thing, she was not going to Russia.

The next evening, Dunlevy and Davis requested to see the commander. When he refused to let them use the radio, they left his office and formulated a plan. They were going to escape from the Russians.

The next morning, Maria, walking across the camp grounds to the interrogating room, bumped into a man. She turned to excuse herself and recognized John Schwartz. She knew that he had been captured and she also knew that he was not part of the Dawes Team. He was with the mission called Houseboat. He looked at her, but she said nothing, fearing she would expose him if he were still on a mission. Maria walked on and never looked back.

That evening, Maria told Davis and Catlos what happened; they couldn't believe he was there. They heard he had been captured by the Germans. But Maria was positive that it was him.

Davis, Dunlevy, Catlos and Zenopiean soon agitated the Russians. First, they demanded to see the commander, then they wanted to talk to someone from the NKVD and the American Red Cross. Zenopiean told the colonel to ring up the British Ambassador in Italy. He was sure that the ambassador would take immediate action. The Russians became furious and told the group to remain in their quarters until they received orders.

Two days later, the Russians told the group they would be shipped to Odessa. When Maria visited with the group on one of her breaks, they asked her where Odessa was.

Maria responded with fear, "My God, Odessa! That's on the Black Sea. If we go there, Zenopiean is right, we're finished. We will be in Russia. That will be the last anyone will ever hear of us."

On her way back to the interrogating room, Maria stopped to see the commander. She asked him what time she would be leaving.

He informed her, "They will be leaving, Maria, not you. You are needed here."

She left his office. Instead of proceeding on to the interrogating room, she crossed the compound and entered the NKVD office and demanded to know why she was being separated from her husband, Sergeant Davis. Maria's question caused a mild panic in the office. The officers looked at each other. This news baffled them and they were not sure how to handle it. The officer in charge asked, "Why haven't you told us this before?"

Maria explained, "No one ever asked me. I thought you knew that I was a British citizen."

They looked at her records, flipping through the pages. Finally, one officer told the others that she was right. Nothing showed up in her record, and no one ever asked her.

Maria took advantage of the confusion by adding, "It is out of the question for my husband to be sent off to God knows where while I remain here." Davis was summoned at once. Maria was sitting in the office when he arrived.

He went to her and asked, "What's the matter, darling?"

Maria gave her best wifely performance, "These men are trying to separate us."

Davis walked across the room and put his chest as close as he could to the NKVD officer. His rugged strength from years in the paratroopers showed. His face was anything but calm; he intimidated both officers. They assured him that they would contact Moscow and see what should be done. Davis threatened, "I know you don't have authority! Well your asses better get authority, because I am not leaving here without my wife. I don't know what in the hell you are running here, but we don't want any part of it."

He walked across the room, grabbed Maria by the arm and pulled her to her feet, demanding, ". . . and another thing, you are not returning to that interrogating room. Let these bastards ask their own questions."

Maria's act continued, "Yes, darling, I was only trying to help."

As they walked through the camp, Maria thought aloud, "Davis, we have to do something. We can't go to Odessa. And after what you did, we can't stay here."

"What do you mean, 'after what I did?' I just saved your ass, that's what I did," he reminded her.

Several hours later, Maria sat with the group. Davis wouldn't let her return to the office. A colonel from the Red Army came to their quarters and told Maria she would join the group and go to Odessa. He wasn't quite sure what it was about, but told her the NKVD officers no longer wanted to talk to Sergeant Davis.

Catlos and Dunlevy were totally confused. They assumed Russia was on the side of the United States. Maria told them Stalin must be from another planet. He assumed everywhere the Russian Army stopped was new Russian territory. No exceptions. He doesn't trust anyone, not even his own people, she explained.

Maria went on, "You must remember the Russians have been invaded throughout history. That is why they are isolationists. It doesn't work, but you can't tell them that. The NKVD is worse. They suspect their own mothers and there is no changing them. Our main problem is getting the hell out of here. Forget that they are Allies. We have to look at them like we looked at the Germans: as enemies. The sooner we get rid of these people, the better off we will be."

Trucks lined up in the morning from the main gate to the center of the camp. Roll call started as the civilians boarded the trucks. The Russians assigned the Dawes Team to the first truck. Davis slid down the bench in the back of the truck to be close to Maria. She was scared that she would be yanked off at the last minute. When the convoy moved out, she held Davis' arm, knowing she was safe for the time being.

The team was driven to a town close to a railroad station. The trucks were emptied. Other civilians joined Maria's group in a hotel. As they gathered in the lobby, the officer in charge announced once they were in Odessa, they would be sent home by train or ship, depending upon their destination.

The hotel was overcrowded with Russian soldiers. There was no electricity or heat. The furniture had been burned long ago by Russian troops. They slept on the floor, in hallways and in the lobby. Civilians were assigned to different sections of the hotel. Maria waited with her group in a large vacant dining room. As soon as they sat, five Russian officers entered.

The Russians wanted to appear hospitable since this was the first time they had seen American and British soldiers. One Russian officer was a drunk Asian major. Maria knew he was a Tartar because he was so tall.

The Russians brought drinks to the table. Since Maria was the only one who spoke Russian, she had to carry the conversation. She thanked them for the drinks on behalf of the British and Americans. The major sat close to Maria and put his arm around her, giving her a squeeze. He told her she was beautiful, and that he always wanted a blond.

Davis kept asking what he was saying. Maria lied, "He is snockered, and isn't making much sense."

"Tell him to get his arm off of you," Davis ordered.

Maria lifted the major's arm from her shoulder, but he persisted, dropping it to her knee.

Davis stood and said, "You tell this Mongolian simpleton to back off."

She told the officer she was tired and had been sick. She just wanted to sleep. The officer in charge saved her by announcing that the group could go to their rooms. The major's personality changed in seconds. He shouted at her in Russian. She had never heard some of the words and thought they must be part of the Russian's crude military language. Without notice, he grabbed her and pulled her from the room.

Davis leaped to his feet, took the major by his collar and threw him on the floor, yelling, "You bloody bastard."

Catlos and Dunlevy stood and faced the other officers, warning them to stay back.

Zenopiean, sipping his vodka, raised his glass to those who had gathered, trying to see what the commotion was. He condemned them, "Appalling, absolutely appalling. These Chinese types always seem to lose their composure when they meet a lady of breeding."

Davis lifted the major by his shirt and threw him into the corridor. Several Russian officers intervened and broke it up.

Another major appeared and told Maria to move her group to their rooms. The newly-arrived major asked Maria who escorted them. She pointed to Nicolia. He walked over to Nicolia and ordered him to follow the group to their rooms.

Catlos, Dunlevy, Zenopiean and Davis were put in one room. Maria was shown to the adjoining room. The major ordered Nicolia to stand guard outside her door. He told Nicolia that he would be held responsible if anything happened to any of them. The last thing that the major wanted was an international incident. As he closed the door, he added that Maria was NKVD, and he didn't need any trouble with those people.

The major then knocked on Maria's door. When she opened it, he amended his instructions, "On second thought, I am going to have the guard stand his post inside your room. I am sorry, but I feel it is necessary."

Maria, not wanting to cause any trouble for herself or Nicolia, offered no objection. Nicolia apologized, saying there was nothing that he could do.

A few minutes later there was another knock at the door. Nicolia opened it to see the major apologize again and inform Maria that he must assign another person to the room. He introduced the English woman who would share the room. The English woman told Maria she felt ill, so ill she might faint. Maria helped her into bed and covered her. She refused Maria's offers to get her food, explaining she could not keep anything down. She said she just wanted to sleep.

When everything was settled, Maria decided to remain in her Russian uniform. Nicolia sat in a chair and tried to stay awake, but his head kept nodding. Maria was almost asleep when the peace of the night was shattered by a thunderous pounding on the door.

Nicolia flew out of his chair and hollered, "What is it! This is a restricted area."

It was the Tartar major. Maria asked Nicolia why the MPs hadn't detained him. He told her he was an officer, so the MPs could not detain him.

"Well, why didn't they just lock him up?" Maria asked.

"It would be unheard of to lock up an officer," Nicolia informed her.

Maria commented, "Oh, I see. Forget law and order. Some system you guys have."

Finally, Nicolia shouted, "Do not try to enter. My orders are to shoot, and I'll do just that."

The drunk major complained, "You lousy son of a bitch. They have converted you to a capitalist." Then he left.

It was quiet again, except for Zenopiean, who shouted almost as loud as the major, "The man has no sense of propriety."

Several times during the night, the major returned, banging on the door. Each time, Nicolia shouted that he would open fire if the major entered. Finally, the major gave up.

At 0600 hours, two MPs knocked on the door and told Maria they were assigned to escort the group to the train. The Russians gave the group breakfast in their rooms. After eating, they departed through the rear door of the hotel to an awaiting truck. The MPs jumped in behind them. At the station, they told Maria to board the train and then to remain hidden until the train left.

Maria asked, "Why? Who am I hiding from?"

The MPs told her, "That Tartar major is on leave. He made threats against you and the big paratrooper. Our officer doesn't want anything to happen to your group. We have had quite a bit of trouble with the Tartar troops. This major is typical. The problem is all of his troops are very loyal to him. So he could make trouble, if he wanted to. His men would follow his orders over those given by regular Russian Army officers."

Maria understood. When they arrived at the station, she joined some Dutch women sitting on the floor, waiting for the train. Davis told Maria to tell the MPs that if the major showed up, he was going to kick his Tartar ass.

Catlos and Dunlevy remarked that it all seemed like a nightmare. How could everything go wrong all of the time?

Zenopiean tried to explain to the Dutch women why he was in a Russian uniform. After a few minutes, they were sorry they had asked.

The MPs left the group to see if they could find their driver. As soon as they left, Maria looked up and saw the dreaded major. He was walking with six other Tartar officers. They stopped while the major's interpreter questioned the people waiting to board the train. Each group of passengers shook their heads.

Maria knew the Dutch passengers had seen her, but they deliberately refused to identify her. None of them would even look in her direction, fearing they may expose her to this questionable lot. She was relieved when the major and fellow Tartar officers continued down the platform.

Nicolia told Maria that he could hear the train's whistle. Following his instructions, he told the group to stay put until the train came to a complete stop. Then they were to board the car directly in front of them. Nicolia felt their chances of detection by the Tartars would be minimal if they followed his plan.

Hundreds of people moved onto the platform, offering perfect cover for the group. Davis still mumbled about beating the

Tartar. He wanted to stand and fight. Catlos and Dunlevy added fuel to the fire by agreeing to join him.

The major spotted Maria as she boarded and pushed through the crowd. Nicolia saw what was happening and told Maria to tell Davis and the others he would shoot if the major tried anything. However, Davis wasn't boarding, he was trying to push his way through the crowd to meet the major. Maria called to him. She reminded him he was outnumbered and should get on the train.

The crowd was so thick that even if Davis could reach the major, he wouldn't be able to raise his fist, let along start a fight. Nicolia pulled Davis back to the train. They floated with the human tide and ended up where they had begun.

Once on the train, the group saw a compartment door open. An NKVD officer from the interrogating camp recognized Maria and motioned her and the group into his compartment. Maria was surprised to find that he only knew that she was an NKVD agent, nothing more. He had been ordered to another base.

Several Russian officers pushed their way through the hordes of people along the passageway. They noticed the American emblems on the group's uniforms and wanted to meet the British and Americans. They shoved their way into the team's compartment and offered a toast, "Vodka, vodka do na (to the bottom)." They passed the bottle around the compartment.

Zenopiean was the first to take a drink. His complaint followed, "Good Lord."

The Russians asked Maria what he said. Her translation was, "Good, very good."

Next, they handed Maria the bottle. She knew, according to Russian custom, she must drink or she would insult them. She thought the group already had enough trouble for one day, so she downed a healthy gulp and smiled. Her stomach went into spasms as she handed the bottle to Davis, suggesting, "Please, Davis, just take a drink. Don't make a scene."

"What are you smiling about?" he asked.

Maria confessed, "The nurses were right, you are cute in that Russian fur hat."

"What nurses? Who told you that?" Davis demanded.

Maria added, "Well, you are cute."

Davis downed half the bottle and then dried his lips with the sleeve of his uniform. He passed the bottle to Catlos, who raised the bottle and toasted, "To General Yeremenko, hero of Stalingrad."

Maria translated the toast and the Russian officers stood and repeated his words. Then they raised their glasses and said, "To Roosevelt and Churchill."

They all drank another round until it turned into a never-ending series of toasts. Dunlevy and Catlos apparently knew every general in the Russian army; they offered toasts to Generals Govorov, Purkaev, Zhukov, Gokikov and Vatutin.

Maria stopped them when she noticed the NKVD officer scrutinizing their uniforms. The group made their first real mistake: They stood out.

Maria was convinced if she had another drink of vodka, she would be blind. An officer asked her if she had read any American novels. She told him that she had not and stood to leave.

"Where are you going?" he asked.

Maria slurred her words, "I am going to find some oil to drink, so I won't absorb any more vodka; either that, or I am going to sleep, I haven't decided."

Maria needed fresh air and pushed her way through the crowded train to the open platform at the rear. Once on the platform, she drew in a deep breath. She saw a stunning Dutch woman standing with a young, beautiful girl, oblivious to her surroundings.

The lady invited conversation, "Hello, I'm Mrs. Phillips. I'm Dutch, are you?"

Maria answered, "No, I am a Slovak, but I speak Dutch. Is your daughter well?"

Mrs. Phillip's face filled with a sorrowful expression and replied, "We were in Budapest when the Germans came. They allowed us to remain since I was from a wealthy family. Then, when it was overrun by the Russians, they went house to house, raping everyone. They raped my daughter several times before leaving. She hasn't spoken since the incident."

Maria gasped, "How awful. Why are you being sent from Budapest to Odessa?"

"I wish I knew," she said. "We were all rounded up like cattle. They keep saying we will be sent back to Holland, but we keep moving toward Russia. I was hoping to meet British or American soldiers and get her some medical help."

Mrs. Phillip's eyes dripped tears. She was not concerned for herself, only for her daughter. She told Maria that everyone between twelve and seventy-five was raped. The Russians also looted the houses. They took everything that wasn't nailed down. They tried to get gold and silver so they could buy vodka.

She said most of the troops occupying Budapest were from the convict battalions. They were Asians who were wild and uneducated. Only their officers were able to keep them in line, and they had a difficult time.

Maria touched Mrs. Phillips gently on the shoulder and consoled her, "I hope I see you on the next train. Maybe we could talk more."

Mrs. Phillips said she would look forward to it. Maria left her to join the others. When Maria saw Davis, he was drunk and teaching everyone the words to the song, "There will always be an England." Catlos had already passed out and Dunlevy was right behind him. Just before Dunlevy fell into a drunken stupor, he notified the group that he was Irish and that any Irishman could drink them all under the table.

Zenopiean looked down and criticized him, "You know, the Irish are the same the world over."

Davis, on the other hand, showed no ill effects from his drinking. Nicolia drank with the others, but refused to drink too much, recognizing his commitment to his duty. The group would have to change trains in less than an hour, and he wanted to make sure they didn't interrupt their schedule.

Nicolia woke Maria to tell her they were coming to the town of Giurgiu, on the Russian-Rumanian border. He reminded her that they had to change trains there. Maria moaned and told him to wake her when they reached the town, not before.

Nicolia remained alert, but the rest of the group, including the Russians, fell asleep. He shook Maria, telling her to get the group together; they had arrived in Giurgiu. Nicolia helped Maria to the platform.

The Russians wanted her to translate, since they had a wonderful time talking with everyone. Maria passed the message on to the group, who were in no mood for anything other than silence.

Nicolia confided in Maria that since he had been with the group, the Russians would not let him alone. He had heard that any Russian soldier serving outside of Russia during the War had to be reeducated. Those who came into contact with the Allies were suspect. He was nervous as he continued, "I like your group; they are good people. You need to act. Once you are inside Russia, that will be the last of you."

Maria had reached that conclusion already. Nicolia impressed upon her that this would be their last chance. Once on the next train, it would be too late.

In minutes, the train they had been on for hours stopped and the mass of passengers left the train.

On the train platform, a Rumanian man saw the arm patches on the group and spoke to Maria. He told her that once they boarded the train for Odessa, nothing could be done. Word filtered back that no one was repatriated. Everyone disappeared. Many Russian soldiers sneaked into Rumania, rather than return home.

Nicolia found out their train would arrive in an hour. During that hour, they had to form their plan. They entered a large terminal building where Maria saw Mrs. Phillips waving to her through the crowd.

Maria motioned the Rumanian man closer. She asked him if he knew of any Allied units in the area. He told her that there were rumors that they were in Bucharest, just north of the train station. She asked him to please try to find them and tell them that Americans and British were being detained against their will. The Rumanian man assured her he would find the Allies, but wanted to know what she was going to do in the meantime.

Maria answered, "One thing we are not going to do is to get on the train."

He told her, "If you miss it, there is only one place they will take you, the Russian overnight military quarters, over there." He pointed to several military-looking buildings.

Maria begged, "Listen, bring anyone you can. I don't care if it's a Partisan outfit, but bring someone."

The man seemed to work for the railroad, but Maria was not sure in what capacity. Quickly, he vanished into the crowd. All their hopes rested on one little Rumanian man that she had just met.

Maria gathered the group and explained the situation. Finishing, she asked, "Are there any suggestions?"

Catlos and Dunlevy wanted to jump the Russians. Davis wanted to slip away from the station and try to move west with the Russian troops headed for Germany.

Maria told them that they could discuss those plans later. The immediate problem was to miss the train. She emphasized they had to miss that train to Odessa.

Nicolia figured out that there was only one other guard watching them, besides him. He told Maria that she had to distract that guard the moment the train arrived.

Maria pushed her way over to Mrs. Phillips and relayed their situation. Maria asked her to help create a distraction by taking her daughter into the bathroom and pretending to throw up. Maria would accompany them and tell the guard she was too sick to board the train. Maria would then act as a nurse and inform the guard that what she had might be contagious. That should excuse them from boarding the train.

Mrs. Phillips was more than happy to help. She just wanted to get her daughter to American doctors.

Chapter Nine

LIEUTENANT MARIA

Maria explained their escape plan to Sgt. Davis: "Mrs. Phillips will cause a commotion on the right side of the station. You guys have to disrupt the left side. Nicolia will tell the other guard they assigned to us that Mrs. Phillips is too ill to get on the train. What can you do to distract the remaining station guards?"

They thought for a few minutes, then Zenopiean broke the silence, "We could start separate fights. One between Davis and Dunlevy and one between Catlos and me. The Russians will think it's Americans against the British, which isn't uncommon, you know."

They agreed. Maria returned to tell Mrs. Phillips. She was to wait until the train was loaded and then begin her act. Her daughter would stay close by her side. Maria also told her that Nicolia was with them and not to be concerned about any of his actions. If Nicolia was watching her, she was safe.

Maria knew Nicolia didn't want to return to Russia, so she trusted him. The other guard was only recently assigned; Maria wasn't sure how he would react.

The crowd moved onto the platform when they heard the whistle from the approaching train. Davis and the group moved to the left side of the station and Mrs. Phillips and her daughter entered the bathrooms on the right, as planned.

The train was packed. Civilian and military passengers stood shoulder to shoulder. Mrs. Phillips was nervous, but controlled her emotions. She began her act in the greatest performance she would participate in. She gave it her best, splashing water in her face and acting faint. A young Dutch Jewish girl hiding in the washroom came out, thinking Mrs. Phillips was critically ill. She placed her arm around Mrs. Phillips and asked her if there was anything that she could do to help. When Mrs. Phillips told her what they were doing, the Jewish girl began to throw up. She wet her hair and began a deep bronchial hack.

She was a natural actress and even convinced Mrs. Phillips, who called the new guard, "We are ill. It must be food poisoning. The poor girl in there is deathly ill."

The guard looked in the waiting room where the Americans were fighting. On the other side of the station, the train's whistle sounded its departure warning. Nicolia did not wait for the other guard to react. He went out to the platform and signaled the train to leave. It chugged off, while passengers watched in amazement as Zenopiean rolled over benches, pretending to choke Catlos. Dunlevy had more sense; he kept running away from Davis' apparent attack, adding to the confusion.

There would not be another train for a day, and, just as the little Rumanian man predicted, they were placed under guard and moved by truck to a military camp south of the train station. All the way to the camp, the Jewish girl continued her convincing act. She was so good the cough she invented kept the guards at bay.

The Russian officer in charge billeted the group, ordering his men not to come into contact with any of them. The group of five, the Jewish girl, Mrs. Phillips and her daughter met to plan their next move.

Maria did not want to rely solely on the old Rumanian, there were too many uncertainties. Perhaps, there were no American troops in Bucharest; he could have been detained by the Russians; or maybe the task was too much for him, at his advanced age.

Most of the day, they huddled together trying to decide what to do. Nicolia was more nervous than the others. Maria surveyed the compound. Dunlevy wasn't worried about breaking out. He wondered, what they would do once they were out. With only the Russian Army in the area, Davis thought, if they could get out they could mix in with the portion of the Russian Army heading west—they still wore their Russian uniforms.

Maria offered to use her newly-acquired NKVD status. It was good for, hopefully, something besides her death. Davis suggested they use her plan only if they couldn't come up with anything else. Maria reminded Davis he had to consider the Jewish girl, Mrs. Phillips and her daughter, too. They were no longer a group of five. It was their duty to assist those who had helped them.

The group spent the rest of the night trying to decide what to do in the morning. Mrs. Phillips and the Jewish girl voted for moving west with the Russian Army, hoping to make it to Rumania. If they made it, they could send forces to Odessa to rescue the others.

The Jewish girl, realizing her acting ability was appreciated, suggested, "I can convince them my father is the Ambassador to Tunisia. That should throw them off; it will take them plenty of time to check that story."

Maria proposed they start an uprising with the other people in the compound detained against their will. She tried to convince Davis that the Russians wouldn't dare fire on them, fearing an international incident.

Zenopiean was positive that his plan was the best: They should march to the front gate, demand the guard open it and simply walk out.

The snow reflected the sun's morning rays through the window. They were all still awake. Davis called for a vote, "Well, what is it to be?"

Before anyone could answer, jeeps and trucks crashed through the main gate. The group ran to the windows to see what the commotion was. It was the Americans. They had taken the Russians by surprise. Catlos threw the door open and waved the convoy in his direction. The Russian guards standing watch lifted their machine guns, then looked at each other, not knowing what to do.

Maria yelled in Russian, knowing the guards would hear, "Our troops are here. Finally, the Allies have arrived."

The Jewish girl kissed the Russian guards on the cheek, "Thank you. Thank you for being so kind." Maria translated for her, confusing the guards even more.

An American colonel walked over and shouted, "My name is Ross. I am an American. Are any of you Americans?"

Catlos and Dunlevy acted military for the first time and saluted. The colonel yelled, "Get your asses in the trucks."

Maria looked at the convoy. There was the little old Rumanian man sitting with members of the Rumanian Underground. Apparently, the Americans were already having trouble with the Russians and had gathered information on them.

The last truck in the small convoy had a British major in it. When he learned there were British soldiers present, he marched into the barracks. Davis and Zenopiean identified themselves. He ordered them to board the trucks before the Russians could figure out what happened.

Maria walked up to the trucks with the Jewish girl and Mrs. Phillips. Davis was looking for her in the barracks when the British major ordered him out.

Davis asked, "Have you seen a beautiful blond in a Russian uniform?"

The major didn't take him seriously, "No! Listen, old boy, this is no time to be thinking about that."

"Christ, major, I'm not thinking about that. This girl saved our lives," Davis responded.

Davis looked in the back of the American truck and asked Catlos and Dunlevy where Maria was. Catlos answered, "Don't worry, she will be all right with these people."

Davis pulled him out of the truck and threw him into the snow and shouted, "You dirty bastard. After all that girl has done for us, do you think I'm going to leave her here with the Russians?"

He struck Catlos across the face. The British officer hurried over and broke it up. He warned Davis that if he continued he would be court martialed. Davis stopped fighting and continued looking for Maria. He spotted her on the other side of the trucks.

Maria welcomed him, "Davis, they were going to leave me. I can't believe it. They were actually going to leave me. I know I'm not an American, but I can't believe it. I'm not leaving Mrs. Phillips or the Jewish girl, and they are Dutch."

Davis grabbed her, "You are coming with me."

Maria hesitated, "I'm not British, either."

Davis persisted, "So what. Get into the last truck. You will be British as soon as I marry you."

Maria helped the Jewish girl, Mrs. Phillips and her daughter into the last truck, then boarded herself.

Zenopiean was already in the front seat holding a machine gun. He hollered to Maria, "I could have told you. Never trust anyone from the colonies. They have no breeding."

Many civilians ran past Zenopiean to get in the truck. As each passed, he said, "Don't worry, you are under British protection."

The driver reminded him there were only eight Americans and three British subjects in the convoy.

As the trucks rolled out of the main gate, Maria told Davis that since she was not a British citizen there might be trouble.

Davis doubted her, "More trouble? How can there possibly be more trouble?"

As the convoy rolled through the countryside, Maria patted Mrs. Phillips on the back, as if to say at last we are away from the Russians. Zenopiean informed them they were on their way to Bucharest.

Mrs. Phillips asked Maria how she was going to get out of Bucharest if the Americans hadn't taken it over. The British officer told Mrs. Phillips that the Americans and the British had several missions operating in Bucharest. Those missions could move them out, using their own people. Mrs. Phillips returned her demeanor to the poised lady from the prominent wealthy family that she was. She was also told doctors were available. This news seemed to cheer her up more than anything else.

Davis became bitter toward the Americans. He mumbled that they had no honor, no sense of decency, no responsibility to others and were self-centered. Maria learned long ago that when he became upset, there was nothing to do but let him babble to defuse himself.

As she rode to Bucharest, Maria's fatigue and emotional strain caught up with her. She felt weak. Her mind drifted back to her escapades in the mountains, especially that terrible night when they descended the mountain. What happened to the thirty-seven men that she had started with? Were they still alive and moving through the mountains? Were Mac and Lain dead, or did they make it? Was her nation free or another puppet state of the communists? Did the eighty-three Czech soldiers that froze that horrible night realize they may have died in vain?

And what of her life? She could not return home, the Russians would find her. There was no way they were going to allow her to escape. Maria knew too much about the Russian Army and its commanders from her interpreting work in Banska Bystrica. She also had signed papers stating she was an NKVD agent.

Since Maria was forced to leave her little schoolhouse in the mountains, she was hunted by the Germans, turned on by the Americans, and now she was chased by the Russians. That left only the English, and Maria wasn't sure about them.

When they arrived in Bucharest, Colonel Ross drove them to the mission headquarters. Here, Russians, British, Americans and other soldiers worked together.

Mrs. Phillips and her daughter were sent immediately to an area south of the city where the Dutch gathered, waiting for the War to end so they could return home. Maria was disappointed to find they had already departed; she missed the opportunity to say good-bye. The convoy's second stop was Sophia, Bulgaria, where the British had a large field hospital. The Jewish girl was sent to a private home in the city. In all of the turmoil, Maria never found out her name.

Bucharest was the next stop.

Colonel Ross returned with papers from the mission administration office and handed them to Davis, Zenopiean and Maria. They were to report to the home of Anton Escu, President of The Consul of Ministers. Maria looked down at her papers and read the address: 33 Street Batispe, Bucharest. They were assigned a jeep and driver.

Davis and Maria waited in the jeep for Zenopiean, who was being detained in the administration office. An English captain appeared at the entrance and addressed them in their jeep, "Sergeant Zenopiean will be flying to England on a priority flight. He wanted me to convey his best regards to you both. He said that if you are ever in Prestwick to ring him up."

Davis jumped out of the jeep and began to walk toward the entrance. The officer ordered him to stop, "Sergeant! Remain in the jeep and follow your orders. Sergeant Zenopiean has already gone."

Maria wanted to see Zenopiean, if only for a minute. With all of his complaining and bitching, he was still a wonderful man. He had hung in there when others would have failed. He complained, but endured; he was English.

Davis was disappointed, but Maria tried to cheer him up, "Look, Davis, the sun is out, the snow is melting and the sky is as blue as your nose."

Davis produced a slight smile, nothing more. They rode in the jeep to the outskirts of the city. Here, there were rolling hills and thick rows of trees. To their surprise, the driver turned the jeep into the driveway of a mansion. It was beautiful.

Maria asked Davis, "What is this 33 Street Batispe?"

"Maybe they don't want anyone to know where we are," Davis suspected.

Colonel Carter, the former Governor General of Palestine met them. Mary Carter, his wife, was President of the Senate of Rumania before the War and a descendant of King Michael. She showed them through the mansion.

Maria had never seen such splendor: pillars of Italian marble, a rosewood piano, mirrors from floor to ceiling. The dining room table looked like it continued for hundreds of feet. All the chairs were hand carved. Down the center of the table were sterling silver candelabras, interwoven with Baccrac crystal.

Mary Carter walked with them, moving as a vision of womanhood. Her steel gray hair was perfect, not a strand out of place. Her skin looked like it had never seen a ray of sunlight. She looked years younger than her age, and was charming and hospitable. She pointed out the oil paintings that she was very proud of. Not because of their monetary value, but because of the history behind each painting.

Mrs. Carter ended the tour by showing Maria and Davis their rooms. As they climbed the stairs, she said, "We have the commanding General of the Russian Army for Rumania with us and his staff."

Davis asked, "Mrs. Carter, we have been on the move for months and have had very little news. What is the situation?"

She reported, "The Americans are at the Elbe and Mulde Rivers. Soviet forces have circled Berlin and the Germans are fighting in the streets. I'm sure it will all be over within a month."

Maria changed from English to Rumanian, asking Mrs. Carter why the Russian Army hasn't moved on. Mrs. Carter replied that she wasn't sure. It was obvious to Maria that she wanted to stay away from the subject, probably because she didn't know who Maria was or why she was there.

The bedrooms were enormous. The beds must have been carved over a hundred years before. There was a large dressing table, silk sheets, lounging chairs, and even a side reception room for breakfast or tea.

After the tour, Mrs. Carter accompanied them to the huge reception hall. Civilians and military personnel were engaged in conversations, reading or trying to gather or send information. It seemed like everyone in Europe was trying to find relatives.

Colonel Carter asked Maria and Davis to report to the administration office. As they walked together, Davis said, "I knew it was too good to last. They probably will ship us off to some camp. I feel uneasy here. I think I am the only enlisted man in the place, and that colonel keeps treating me as his equal. This just isn't done in the British Army."

When they reached the administration office, they were surprised to be handed an envelope containing a large amount of money. They returned to the reception hall, where Colonel Carter told them to take the jeep and go into the city and purchase anything they needed. He gave them an address to go to.

In the city, Maria asked directions from men on the street. Eventually, she and Davis turned down an alley, found the address and knocked on the door. A large man with a hat pulled down, covering half his face, opened the door. Maria greeted him in Rumanian and he let them enter.

She looked around and said to Davis, "So this is the black market."

They saw everything imaginable in the underground warehouse: bolts of cloth, food, guns, ammunition, gasoline, canned food and shoes. Davis remarked that the best store in England didn't have this much stuff before the War, let alone during it. He looked at leather military gloves, starring at them for a moment. Then he looked at Maria and said, "I sure wish I could have seen Zenopiean before he left."

Maria wandered off, looking at beautiful dresses and women's blouses. She tried on attractive high-heel shoes. Davis picked out some new military shirts—American ones, not as coarse as those the British Army issued. He couldn't believe his eyes when he saw bars of soap. He instinctively picked up two, fearing someone might come and snatch them.

After an hour of shopping, the two paid the exorbitant asking prices and returned to their jeep with their treasures. Davis wanted to know what Maria bought. She delicately unfolded the paper from around her riches.

Davis laughed, "You spent all of your money on that?"

"No. I also have a dress and shoes in the other package," she added.

"What is all of that junk?" Davis wanted to know.

Maria exclaimed, "Junk! Are you crazy? There isn't a woman in all of Europe that wouldn't cut your throat to get their hands on this."

"On what?" Davis asked.

Maria explained, "This one is face cream; this one is a moisturizer and this one is lipstick. You can't find these things anywhere. And look at this, rouge! My God, it's priceless."

"You know, you women are really crazy," Davis concluded. "For months, we have been without food, damn near killed everyday, and every son of a bitch in Europe is chasing us, and the only thing that you can think about is face cream and eye stuff."

"To a woman, it is very important, even more important than food, sometimes," Maria told him.

Davis shook his head, "You don't even need that stuff. You are beautiful as you are. Just ask that Tartar major, he'll tell you."

"Come on. I am just starting to feel better and you start in with that stuff."

"I'm sorry," Davis admitted. "Let's go."

Out of the city, on the way back to the mansion, Davis pulled the jeep to the side of the road.

Maria asked, "What's the matter, now?"

"Nothing. I just want to ask you something," he said.

"What?" Maria asked.

Davis surprised Maria, "I want to marry you, that's what!"

"Why wouldn't I want to marry you?" Maria responded. "You're handsome, thoughtful, you care about others and, above all else, I love you. But remember, my father is a priest. He will have to marry us. I have to notify my family, if any of them are still alive. You have to get permission from the military. I will have to get permission to enter England."

Davis agreed, "All these things have to be completed before we can think about getting married. However, I am willing to do whatever is necessary. And I do love you very much."

It was cold again. Spring was around the corner, but Mother Winter was still reigning supreme as Davis pulled Maria close and kissed her tenderly on the lips.

The next afternoon, Maria disappeared for an hour. She soaked in a warm tub, fixed her hair and applied her makeup. Looking in the mirror, she realized the past two years showed. She tried to massage away the lines forming under her eyes, with some success. She tried each shade of lipstick, to see which one matched her complexion.

After restoring her original beauty, she donned her new dress—a cocktail dress, slightly off the shoulders, formfitting at the waist. It came just below the knees and was slightly iridescent. Depending on the way the light touched it, it would flicker, dancing between emerald green and a rich crimson.

Maria glanced at the old French clock on top of the fireplace mantel, it was dinnertime. She closed the door to her room and walked to the dining hall. Davis was about to enter when he saw her. He looked astonished and complimented her, "Oh my God, Maria, you are more beautiful than I realized."

Maria joked, "That's what those Russian nurses said when you flung open your sheet."

"If you don't stop talking about that . . . you know that isn't what happened. I don't want to change the subject, but I am not going to share this dinner with a bunch of officers. I still believe that I am the only enlisted man here. When you look at most of these officers, I seem to be the only man here."

They walked into the dining hall and all the officers stood when Maria entered the room. She acknowledged their courtesy and took her place at the table. She was engaged in conversation in a matter of seconds. The general on her right spoke to her in Russian. The officer across from her spoke Rumanian. She kept both conversations flowing until the officer to Davis' right leaned across Davis, trying to get Maria's attention. This did not sit well with Davis. He did not appreciate the French officer leaning in front of him every few seconds.

During the conversations, Maria kept an eye on Davis. He handled himself very well, he had perfect manners, tasted wines like an expert—most unusual for a Welshman. She was proud of him. He started a conversation with a Rumanian officer sitting across from him. Maria tried to hear what they said. As far as she could gather, Davis did not think much of President Roosevelt.

He told the officer that Roosevelt must have known that the Japanese were on their way to Pearl Harbor. There was no way he could be president and not know. The speculation continued, English families in Hawaii had Japanese servants. Several weeks before the attack, their families in Japan sent them telegrams, telling them to return home immediately. If these events weren't a warning, what were they?

After dinner, the conversations centered on the War. When would it end? Where was this unit and that unit? Why was the

American military leader, General Patton, held back from entering Berlin, allowing the Russians to take it?

Admirers surrounded Maria most of the night. Davis tried not to show his concern and engaged himself in military conversations with the officers. Mary Carter managed to separate him from the brandy-sniffing officers. She was fascinated with him and he was fascinated with the brandy. But, as a good soldier, he was always in control of himself.

The evening entertainment dissolved; the guests retired to their rooms. Maria said good night to Davis, who was having the time of his life, and retired to her room. She tried for over an hour to go to sleep in the huge feather bed with silk sheets, but it was impossible. For the rest of the night, she covered herself with blankets on the floor and fell sound asleep.

At 0530 hours, a Russian sergeant, an aide to the general, was out polishing the general's Rolls Royce. The general confiscated it as one of his war trophies. When the sergeant finished polishing the car, he notified the general who plopped himself in the front seat and started blowing the horn repeatedly. He stopped, occasionally, and switched to rolling the windows up and down. His finale consisted of opening and closing the glove compartment. Then he grabbed the steering wheel and jumped up and down in the front seat. Maria watched in amazement and laughed.

She hurried down the luxurious corridor to breakfast. She wanted to find news of the War. A young English officer greeted her in the hallway, "Did you hear that stupid barbarian and uncultured twit of a Russian general this morning?"

Maria answered, "Yes, lieutenant, I did. What is the matter with him?"

The lieutenant went on, "He causes much apprehension. You know, Mrs. Carter suffers from migraine headaches. The man has no consideration for anyone. Colonel Carter calls him a dumb commie with a blood clot for a brain. By the by, are you English?"

"No, but I am going to marry a Welshman," Maria explained. "That's almost English."

He disagreed, "Not quite. But where would we be without all of their coal?"

At breakfast, Maria noticed that Colonel and Mrs. Carter spoke only French, never Rumanian, which they believed would identify them as low class. The music they played was always French; the decor of the mansion was French; one would have thought they were French.

When Mrs. Carter spoke, she always talked of the good old days. She believed that everything was going to be just as it was before the War. Maria tried to warn her that things may be much different in Europe after the War. Though Mrs. Carter listened attentively, she never permitted such thoughts to enter her mind. She would simply change the subject, relieving herself of worrisome thoughts. Maria understood. She never discussed it again.

Davis entered the dining hall late, hung over. Even the noise of coffee cups chattering on their saucers bothered him. Maria smiled; he just shook his head. They took their coffee and walked to the administration office.

Colonel Carter summoned them. He faced them, cocked his right eye and reported, "The Russians sent a formal complaint to Washington and London about the raid on the detention camp where you two were. They said, mind you, such action would not be tolerated. Can you believe it?"

Maria, who did not trust Americans and was suspicious of the British, tried to guess what would happen to her. She asked Colonel Carter, "I am not American or British. I cannot return home. I am considered a Russian NKVD agent. I must do something soon, colonel. Sergeant Davis has asked me to marry him and requested the necessary forms. I know you are a busy man, but maybe you could help us?"

The colonel suggested, "Since you are going to marry a British citizen in the military, you will have to follow some specific procedures. You should contact the headquarters of Davis' command."

Davis told Maria he would handle the processing. He was a soldier and knew the procedures. He did not approve of her discussing their problems with the colonel.

At the administration building, Maria asked if the office had received a response to their request. The communications officer assured them that everything had been sent, but no response was received. He agreed to contact them the minute he heard anything. He handed Davis mail forwarded from his last duty station in England.

Maria wondered when she would hear from anyone. No one knew where she was; she was not in contact with family or friends; her life was in limbo.

Her thoughts were interrupted when Davis dropped several of his letters. He was busy reading one, so Maria stooped and picked up the ones that fell. She noticed the return address on the top one. She read: Mrs. B. Davis.

Maria handed the letters to Davis. He looked at them; all but one was from B. Davis. He looked at Maria, then turned away and mumbled something about going into the city. His face was flushed and he could not look into her eyes. Davis was married.

Maria's heart sank. She felt nauseated, nervous and depressed. Worst of all, she felt betrayed—again. Davis attempted the lame excuse that B. Davis was his mother.

Maria knew better and confronted him, "Davis, you're married, aren't you?"

He admitted, "Yes, but let me explain. I was only married for thirty days before I was sent overseas. I hardly know the girl. I was going to tell you. I'll file for divorce as soon as I return. Then I'll send for you."

Maria refused, "No, Davis. Remember, I told you my father is a priest? I have a strong belief in God. You stood before the Lord and took an oath to stay married until death do you part. It means just that. The bible tells us that once we divorce and remarry, from that day on we live an adulterous life. I love you dearly, Davis. You are a wonderful man, but when I take the oath of marriage, it will be once and only once. Stay with your wife. God knows I have enough troubles."

Maria looked for Colonel Carter, now in the communication section. He was processing dispatches when she interrupted him. Explaining her situation, she concluded there was no hope of getting to England. Her last hope was with Davis, and he had just crushed it.

The colonel understood her problem and was very sympathetic. He felt sorry for her and called over a civilian worker. He asked him to drive Maria into Bucharest. He assured her

Lieutenant Maria

she needed new a environment. It would make her problem fade away. Maria agreed. At least, she would be away from Davis. She couldn't handle him now, fearing that she may give in to his proposal.

The colonel withdrew money from the military budget and handed it to her. He offered help, "Look, Maria, I know that you are trying to figure things out. Let me help. Go to the city while I send a few messages. By the time you return, I should have something."

Maria thanked him, "You don't know how much better I feel, having someone on my side, colonel."

As Maria started to her room to get her coat, she called back, "Thank you, colonel. Tell the driver I will meet him at the front door in a few minutes."

Maria tried not to think of Davis, but it was impossible. She was so hurt she could not push him out of her mind. She just wanted to get away. The driver was waiting as she hurried down the steps.

He asked, "Where would you like to go, miss?"

"Do you know where to find a beauty shop?" Maria asked.

The driver replied, "Yes, ma'am, I do. There is one on this side of the city. I see the Russian women soldiers going there all of the time."

The driver was right. The shop was full of Russian women soldiers. It was almost as though things were back to normal. The women giggled and tried to talk above the noise and laughter. When each finished, they looked into the wall mirror and smiled. Each was positive that she was the most gorgeous creature walking the earth.

The girl washing Maria's hair looked like a competitive weight lifter. She had enormous arms and strong hands. Maria got the full treatment. The big woman washed Maria's hair, then applied hot towels to her face and massaged her neck. Maria's mind wandered. She relaxed and fell asleep.

"Miss, Miss . . ." The Rumanian girl shook Maria to wake her. "I hate to wake you, but we need the space. There are many others waiting."

The girl finished the treatment by combing and brushing Maria's hair. Maria looked in the mirror and applied lipstick.

The hairstylist stood with her mouth open, looking at the cosmetics Maria had in her purse. Maria noticed and handed her a tube of lipstick. She carefully slipped it into her pocket, so the others wouldn't notice. To her, it was worth more than gold. She refused to charge Maria, and even asked her to come again, any time.

Maria walked out into the noon sun feeling reborn. Back in the car, she asked the driver what the date was. He replied, "It's the eighth of May, why?"

"Because I want to remember this day as long as I live," Maria told him.

They drove a few miles farther into the city. The young chauffeur was delighted to have the day off and did not care when he returned to the mansion. He told Maria that his orders from the colonel were to make her happy and give her anything she wanted. Suddenly, he got a thought in his head and smiled from ear to ear.

Maria recognized the look and responded, "I'm sure the colonel meant in your capacity as a driver. Look, over there, a sidewalk cafe. Pull over, I would like some wine."

Maria's strong personality intimidated the driver. He enjoyed being with her anyway. She asked him to order a heavy red wine, remarking she loved wine more than life itself. Maria used the opportunity to question him about Colonel Carter. The driver had nothing but praise for the colonel. This news delighted Maria. Maybe she found someone she could trust. But, she had been wrong before and could be wrong again, she could only wait and see.

Without explanation, the waiter screamed and came running from the kitchen. The chefs and the kitchen help followed. People called from windows in the apartments that lined the avenue. Others ran into the streets. The young driver asked Maria what happened. Maria asked two Russian officers sitting near them.

The Russians shouted, "The War is over! Russian troops entered Berlin and Germany surrendered."

Music flowed from every building on the street. A little old man who looked like he might have been a waiter at the last supper played an accordion. Russian soldiers danced the old two step.

Maria grabbed the young driver and kissed him on the cheek, ordering, "Quick! Get us back to the mansion. I'm not going to miss this party."

The streets filled with people blowing car horns, dancing, kissing and screaming. The crowds tried to pull the driver and Maria from the jeep, but Maria forced the driver on. As soon as they left the city, the noise faded. They sped through the countryside back to the mansion.

When the two of them approached the mansion, they saw the guests file out the front door, getting into jeeps and military trucks. They yelled for Maria and the young driver to follow. The group headed back to the city to a large hotel that Colonel Carter and his wife frequented. The convoy flew down the road. In no time, they drove through the crowded streets to the resort.

The international mob disembarked from the trucks. Russians, French, Rumanians, British, Americans and people Maria had not met dissolved into the crowd already occupying the hotel. There was music, dancing, food and shouting everywhere.

A young American lieutenant dragged Maria onto the dance floor. Then his buddy handed him a pitcher of beer. While he stood and drank it, his friend took over, dancing with Maria. The lieutenant staggered around the center of the dance floor, gulping his beer.

As she left the dance floor, a waiter approached Maria, trying to shout above the crowd, he asked, "Would Madame like some caviar? I saved it for this day."

"Caviar! You have to be kidding?" Maria turned to ask him where he had obtained it, but he had already disappeared into the hysterical crowd.

Russian officers poured into the hotel. Toasts continued until 0500 hours. The Russians, drunk, had no inhibitions. They danced and kissed men and women; it made no difference. They fell over the tables, breaking glasses and bottles.

At 0530 hours, Colonel Carter, the backbone of the British empire, with his stiff upper lip, void of any sense of humor, shouted at the top of his lungs for everyone to fall in. Then he led a march out the front door of the hotel and through the city.

Breakfast came much later. Most of the people at the mansion suffered from the effects of the previous night. Maria was one of the first to arrive in the dining hall.

Mrs. Carter, having coffee, said, "Maria, I am glad that I have this chance to talk with you in private. You won't believe what I am about to tell you."

Maria's heart raced as she listened.

Mrs. Carter continued, "General Eisenhower, I can't believe the man is in his right mind. General Eisenhower has put out an order that any person helping the Allies during the War is to be returned to their country of origin. What is the man thinking of? Doesn't he realize that those people will be put to death? The man can't be that stupid! There are already rumors that Polish officers are committing suicide. What could Eisenhower be thinking of?"

Maria realized what Mrs. Carter told her. If she were forced to return home, the Russians would execute her.

Mrs. Carter was worried. She told Maria that she had requested the colonel to act at once. In a few minutes, the colonel came in and elaborated, "Maria, as you know, the Russians will occupy every territory that they can get their hands on, including Czechoslovakia, Hungary, Rumania and Poland. God knows what else Roosevelt gave them. All those countries are already under the Russians' control. I tried to get you an exit visa, but the Russians refused. Did Mrs. Carter tell you about Eisenhower?"

Maria forced a response, "Can you imagine what history will say about that decision?" She added, "What excuse did the Russians give when you asked for the visa?"

The colonel repeated the Russians' answer, "They said you are a Slovak citizen and they have no jurisdiction over you."

"That's great," Maria frowned, "The government in Slovakia is Russian. We have no government of our own. It is impossible to obtain a visa from a government that does not exist."

Colonel Carter filled their coffee cups and they strolled out on the balcony. The colonel, now serious, suggested they could fly her out of the Russian zone or she could try to drive out, or maybe they could put her in a mail bag and drive her out. Anyhow, he wanted her to be ready to move at a moment's notice.

Maria asked, "Are you telling me, colonel, that I am on the run?"

The colonel confirmed her suspicions, "I'm afraid so, Maria. Stand by, we will come up with something soon."

That afternoon the colonel was excited. He received a message stating the Czechoslovakian government had a representative in Bucharest. When he contacted Maria, he already had a jeep and driver waiting. He ordered her to go at once to obtain a visa from the Czech representative.

Maria was off. The colonel must have told the driver that time was important because he maneuvered the jeep at high speed.

They found the headquarters for the Czechoslovakian representative. Maria was sure that it was a communist-backed office used by the NKVD to gather information on Czech citizens. Nevertheless, she was going to try hard to obtain a visa.

The secretary welcomed Maria and showed her into the office of the representative. He was an old man in his seventies. His red face provided contrast for his snow-white hair. He had a pleasant smile as he greeted Maria.

She remembered and followed the advice given to her long ago by Lt. Green: only offer enough information to answer the questions. She was surprised when he informed her that he had no connections with the Nazis nor the Communist Party, and was free of any pressure from Rumania.

As their conversation progressed, Maria found him to be anti-communist. He assured her he would assemble all the information the Russians had on her. And he would make sure she received her visa. He asked her to report the next morning at 1000 hours. Maria thanked him for his consideration and assured him that she would return the following morning.

That evening, Davis was not at dinner. By this time, everyone in the mansion knew what had happened between the two of them. Maria carried on as though nothing out of the ordinary had happened. During the meal, Maria asked Mrs.

Carter if she knew where Sergeant Davis was. Mrs. Carter said she had seen him earlier, but that was hours ago.

Maria turned heads when she said, "It looks as though Roosevelt has given Germany to the Russians, along with all of Eastern Europe."

The table fell silent. Then the English-speaking Russians translated for the Russian general. He gave her a stabbing look. Maria ignored him, and continued to drink her wine. She excused herself from the table as Colonel Carter rolled his eyes toward the ceiling and shook his head.

Maria felt alone again as she fixed her bed on the floor. Before she fell asleep, she made herself a promise. If the crazy general jumped up and down and blew the horn in the morning, she would throw a grenade out the window. In seconds, she was sound asleep.

Before she realized it, the sun drew lines across Maria's face as its rays slipped through openings in the velvet curtains. She got up, dressed and hurried downstairs to breakfast. She requested the jeep from Colonel Carter and told William, the driver, to drive her into the city. She was excited, but nervous. She thought the Russians might grab her before she could get out of the country. If the old man couldn't get her a visa, she had to go on the run without papers.

At the government office, Maria was invited in. As he promised, the old man had the information about Maria on his desk. As she sat, he looked over the top of his glasses and asked, "My dear child, what have you done to the Russians?"

Maria denied the accusation, "I've done nothing to the Russians. Why do you ask?"

He explained, "They stamped 'no' all over your request for a visa."

Maria's hopes sank again.

The old man noticed her revealing facial expression and said, "Cheer up, young lady, I told you I don't like these communists, and I don't." He stood up from behind his desk and walked over to the window. With his hands holding the lapels of his coat, he looked out over the city and confessed, "My world is gone. There is nothing left for me in life. The old ways are being replaced with these criminal communist types. Our nation over the years, Maria, has fought seven-hundred wars for freedom, and we just lost another one."

He stood for another moment in silence, then returned to his desk. He pushed all of the Russian papers aside and extracted new papers from the drawer on his right. He stamped one paper after another with a large rubber stamp.

He warned, "You must never return to Slovakia or Rumania as long as you live. As for me, the Russians probably will solve my worries. It's been an honor meeting you and helping you. It has been my pleasure. Like I told you, Maria, the Russians will be right behind you. I was supposed to call them the moment you walked into my office. I told them you weren't due back for another week, and I didn't know where you were."

He handed Maria her visa and wished her luck. Maria stood motionless for a moment and wondered where does a man get so much courage. This gentle, little old man had the heart of a lion. She walked around the desk and put her arms around him, holding him tightly, and said, "You make me feel proud to be a Slovak. I will remember you in my prayers for the rest of my life."

He wished her luck and told her to trust no one. She thanked him again, then left the office.

The driver returned Maria to the mansion. She told Colonel Carter that she had her visa and was going to run for it. The colonel was concerned. He told her the Russian general was already asking about her. He had probably received some inquiries about her. Maria asked for suggestions where to go. He told her about a new OSS Headquarters in Wiesbaden, Germany.

He scribbled on a card he took from his wallet and handed it to Maria, explaining, "Here, this is the location of an American friend of mine named Ruby. He was a professor at the University of Chicago before the War. I met him several times during the North African campaign. He seems like a nice chap. If you head in that direction at least you can look for him."

Maria placed the card under the seam of her wallet, where it would be hidden from those who might search her at checkpoints. Mrs. Carter wrapped some food for Maria to take with her. Maria could not thank her enough for all that she had done.

Mrs. Carter took Maria by the hand and said, "What I have done is nothing compared to what you have been through. It was the least I could do for you."

Maria gathered the few things she had in her room and hurried downstairs. William, the driver, was sitting in the jeep waiting for her. He told Maria that a train was leaving in about forty minutes. Then added, "I don't know where you are going Miss Zima, but I wish you all the luck in the world."

Maria pontificated, "William, luck is a foreign word to me. I've never had any, I've never seen any and I don't believe there is any."

On the way to the train, William tried to cheer her up, reminding her that the War was finally over. Things would be better soon. He watched her train leave, waving good-bye until she was out of sight. The train headed northwest, toward the Hungarian border.

While she rode, Maria pieced a plan together. It would be quicker to cut directly across the country. If she could determine that her mother and father were safe, or even inquire about her sisters, it would set her mind at ease. She decided to take the risk, knowing she was risking her life.

In Budapest, she waited for another train headed north. Changing trains was nothing new to her. During her courier experience, she would change direction, back track, and then proceed to her objective.

Changing trains in Bratislava, she remained calm and fit in with the peasants traveling home. Two women who traveled this train frequently boarded in Imava and sat behind Maria. Everyone in the car looked at them suspiciously. Conversation stopped. The passengers just gazed out the windows or stared straight head, as though they were in a trance.

The two women spoke to each other softly, "I can't believe they are picking up the Czech soldiers. Our men have done nothing but fight for the nation."

Maria turned and questioned the two ladies, "Excuse me. Who is picking up our soldiers?"

The two women glanced at each other, wondering if it was safe to talk to Maria. Finally, the taller of the two said, "The Russians. They have a black book of names. My brother was only three blocks from our home when I saw him. I warned him that his name was on the list. At first, he didn't believe me. Then his traveling companion, a fellow officer in his regiment, came to us in a coffee house. He, too, was warned. They were waiting to pick him up so he warned my brother."

Maria asked them when this practice started. They told her, as far as they knew, the moment the Russians occupied the cities.

Maria, fearing an inspection, left the train at the next stop. Her hopes of returning home were gone after hearing the two women. She took the bus north to Prague. Here, with her forged papers, she boarded a train that crossed into Germany. Now, she was out of Rumania, so the visa given to her by the old man was useless.

Germany, the nation that had wrought misery on thousands and thousands of people, lay in complete destruction. Its people were devastated. Maria traveled for miles seeing nothing but the remains of once-beautiful cities. The art and culture were gone. The futuristic designs of Albert Spears were wasted. Not a single edifice he constructed remained. People searched garbage cans for food, and the sick and dying walked the streets.

When Maria was in the administration office at the mansion, the colonel showed her startling figures. Counting the military dead from all nations, twenty-five million people perished. The real shock was the estimated civilian deaths—twenty-four million. War was a disgrace to man and God, but Maria knew the bible predicted war would exist until the end of time.

She reached Weisbaden, questioned only twice during her trip. Her papers permitted her passage at each check point. When the bus to Weisbaden stopped, the driver told the passengers they had to get off and walk. Roads from that point on were under construction.

The Germans were left with few radios. They managed to connect the ones they had to loudspeakers, strategically placed on top of huge piles of rubble, easily found on many streets. As the German people were busy rebuilding their cities, music played over the speakers. Every so often, the radio stations broadcast a news bulletin, then the music returned.

Maria walked through the pieces of stones and bricks that was once the city of Weisbaden. She asked people where the American offices were. They directed her north a few miles, where part of the city remained intact.

As she started north, a news bulletin flashed over the makeshift public address system, "Anyone knowing the whereabouts of Maria Zima, Slovakian citizen, please report to the Russian authorities."

Maria paid little attention to the announcement. She convinced herself that she was no longer Maria Zima. She looked again at the address that the colonel gave her. The building was in front of her. Maybe this time the luck that William, the jeep driver, wished her might come her way.

There were many Americans in the building. Maria worked her way from office to office, looking for Mr. Ruby. She found him seated in an office with a corporal in front, serving as receptionist. She explained to the corporal that she had business with Mr. Ruby, adding that she had been sent by Colonel Carter.

Ruby, seeing Maria in his outer office, walked out and asked if he could be of any help. The corporal quickly explained who she was and who sent her.

Just as the colonel had described him, Mr. Ruby looked and acted like a university professor. He had a slight potbelly and blinked his eyes rapidly. He moved about like he had hidden energy. One second, he would jerk his head around and the next moment he would rearrange the papers on his desk, stacking them in neat piles. These obsessive actions reminded Maria of Joe Morton. Thinking of him made her face sad. What happened to poor Joe?

Mr. Ruby said something to Maria that drove a spike through her heart. She became light-headed as her blood rushed into her legs. Ruby reported, "I was really sorry to hear about your group. All those men being executed while they were still in uniform."

Maria moved her lips, but felt the muscles in her throat tighten. Was it Mac and Lain's group, or was it Lt. Green and Joe Morton? She nearly fainted when he handed her the communique. Her hand shook as she grasped it.

With terror in her heart, she read, "Berlin . . . Eighteen members of one Anglo-American group of agents, headed by an American named Green and an Englishman named Sehmer, who posed as a major, were caught on Slovakian soil in the hinterland of the German fighting sector, competent German sources announced. Investigations revealed their objectives were sabotage and economic and political espionage in Slovakia. Agents, who wore civilian clothes when arrested, were sentenced to death by court martial. They were executed by shooting."

Maria's eyes watered. Her hand shook as she returned the communique back to the desk. Ruby suddenly realized that Maria never knew what happened. Watching Maria's face, his eyes filled with tears. He quickly brushed them aside, fearing Maria would notice.

Ruby called the corporal and asked him to bring wine for his guest. Clapping his hands, he pointed to Maria, "Don't you realize this young lady is a hero?"

"Sir, I don't know where the wine is," the corporal informed him.

Ruby left, directing the corporal, "Come on, I'll show you."

Maria realized Ruby was just being kind. He thought if she were alone for a few moments, she would feel better. He returned shortly with wine. Maria welcomed it.

After her first sip, she said, "I don't know how many more horrible things await me, or whether I can handle them, but I'll tell you one thing, Mr. Ruby, the Russians are never going to get me."

Ruby consoled her, "When the colonel told me you were coming, I spoke with some of our high-ranking people and have an idea what you should do. First, read and sign these papers."

Maria read the documents and smiled. She shook her head and remarked, "Do you realize, Mr. Ruby, that I signed similar papers for the Russians, making me an NKVD agent? When I sign these papers, I will be an American OSS agent. I am neither American nor Russian."

Ruby explained, "By signing these, it will be simple. We can always say you were working for the Americans."

"What about that stupid order put out by General Eisenhower?" Maria asked.

"Oh, you heard about that?" Ruby answered, embarrassed.

Maria was uneasy, "Yes. If they know I am a Czech and working for the Americans, they will return me to Slovakia, the Russians and my death."

Ruby continued, "That brings me to the second part of our operation."

Ruby gave her more papers and asked her to fill them out. Maria read them and noticed, "These papers are for a student visa?"

"That's right," Ruby revealed. "You are going to school at Vassar, in the United States."

Maria requested, "Mr. Ruby, I am most grateful for your help and I hate to ask you for a favor, after all that you have done. But do you think there is a chance I could return home before I go? I haven't seen my family in so long; I'm not even sure they are alive, but I would feel much better if I could find them."

Ruby promised, "I'll work on that the rest of the day. The corporal will billet you for the night, and I will see you here at 1000 hours tomorrow."

That evening, Maria tried to rest, but it was impossible. She thought: first she had run from the Germans; then she ran from the Russians and she was forced to become a Russian agent; then she was made an American agent. The Germans turned on her, the Russians followed suit, the Americans tried to leave her with the Russians. Now, the British dumped her on the Americans again. She had no idea where she belonged. She knew governments had ruined her life, intentional or not. They were still destroying her life, and there was nothing she could do about it. She reminisced about the old bunch and started to cry.

At breakfast, Maria pulled bits and pieces from her muffin and slowly sampled the tasty, imported American coffee. She was not depressed, on the contrary, she smiled to herself thinking, "I wonder what they will have me doing today? Probably signing papers for the French Foreign Legion."

Mr. Ruby appeared and came over to her. He sat and briefed her, "O.K., here it is. I am really worried about you trying to see your family. It is your business. If you have it in your head, there is nothing I can do. That part of the plan is up to you. I had papers forged last night and everything is ready to go. Your name is now Maria Davis, Lieutenant Maria Davis. The corporal in my office has your uniform. You are now an American Army lieutenant. Can you drive a jeep?"

Maria exaggerated, "Yes, of course." She had driven a jeep only once and was all over the road, but she wanted nothing to stop her from trying to see her family. She appreciated the fact that Mr. Ruby had worked all night assembling the necessary papers and transportation for her exit. After she sat at the table for over an hour, Ruby had her student visa to the United States. Finally, she had her military papers and jeep.

Ruby told her that once she visited her family, she was to head straight for the coast of France to the American debarkation center in Bordeaux. He suggested that she act like she was returning from duty with the US Army. She had all of the appropriate papers, so no one should question her.

They finished their coffee and Maria followed Ruby down the hall to his office. The corporal handed Maria her uniform and showed her to the ladies room. He waited for her in the hall.

When she reappeared, he smiled and said, "Ma'am, your biggest problem is going to be keeping the American soldiers away from you, not the Russians."

"Is that a warning or a compliment?" Maria inquired.

"Believe me, it's a compliment!" he assured her.

Ruby escorted Maria to a large mirror in the hall. He instructed her in the proper placement of the military cap and what each emblem on the uniform represented. Then they returned to the office. Ruby walked with Maria to the main entrance. He warned, "Everything you have is forged or stolen. No one knows who you are and there are no records of you anywhere. If you find yourself in trouble, show the Americans the card I put with your papers. But that is only in an emergency. If the Russians stop you, take my advice, let loose with everything you have. Just keep telling everyone that you are an officer in the US Army, and, indeed, you are, we just can't prove it!"

He walked with her to the entrance and down the steps. Maria stopped and said, "Mr. Ruby, if you don't mind I would really enjoy another cup of that American coffee. I just haven't had anything that delicious for years."

Ruby escorted her back to the mess area where Maria poured another cup and they sat for a few minutes. Ruby expressed his sorrow over the loss of the Dawes Team. Maria tried not to think about them. She finished her coffee and thanked him, "Mr. Ruby, thank you again for all of the help. I can never repay you for your kindness. I really appreciate everything you have done. It isn't necessary for you to walk me to the door. I'll say good-bye here."

They walked out into the hall together, then Maria headed outside. Thank God, she thought, Ruby went to his office without seeing her to the jeep. She had no idea how to even start a jeep. Maria stopped a soldier on the street. He saluted. Not knowing what to do, she returned his salute with the palm of her hand facing forward, like the British.

The soldier looked shocked and hesitantly inquired, "Yes, ma'am?"

"See that jeep?" Maria asked, pointing to the vehicle.

"Yes Ma'am," he responded.

"Start it, please," Maria ordered.

The soldier gave her an inquisitive look as he slid behind the steering wheel and turned the engine over. He assisted Maria into the driver's seat and saluted her again. She returned the British salute and started grinding the gears. The soldier watched, then laughed. Maria was embarrassed. Her face was flushed, but, finally, she found a gear that moved the jeep forward. For the rest of her trip through Germany, she floored the jeep in second gear, wondering why her top speed was only thirty miles an hour.

Maria made the trip through Czechoslovakia, questioned frequently by Russian checkpoint guards, always managing to confuse them. She was abrupt and stated she was under orders. When they asked why she spoke Russian so well if she was an American, she responded, "In the United States, only the highly educated and those in authority speak Russian."

Realizing that the Russians respected those in authority, Maria used this technique repeatedly; it worked every time. She reached Prague undetected. The US Army opened a small communication station in the Czechoslovakia capital. Maria went there and told the officer in charge of the operation that she was under special orders. He questioned her no further and asked if he could assist.

The office was directly across the street from the Presidential Palace. Edward Banes, the president, was still pro-western and he was trying to hang on to what was left of the republic. Maria met John Masaryk, the Minister of Foreign Affairs, who was educated in the United States. He explained to Maria that it was his hope that Czechoslovakia could remain free and that somehow they could keep the Russians from taking over their nation.

Maria painted a dismal picture of the Russians for him. Explaining that while she was the interpreter for Major Studenko, Commissar Nickolai Popov mentioned to her several times, ". . . wherever the Army of the Socialistic Republic stops, behind that line is Russia."

Masaryk listened as she continued, "When the uprising took place, I asked Major Studenko why the Russian forces were not attacking as they had promised. His reply was, 'If the CFI could rise against the Germans, they could rise against Russia. Better that they die now.'"

Masaryk had a long face. He commented, sadly, "I guess I was only dreaming of a free Czechoslovakia. The Russians already occupy most of the nation. Since we have only a small army, there is nothing much that we can do. I am really disappointed in the United States, the people are so uninformed. The CARE organization is sending truckloads of food, but, and if you can believe this, you have to show your Communist Party membership card before they will give you a package. Not only that, the Americans have set up radio stations throughout Europe. They call it Radio Free Europe, but the stations are manned by communists. At the end of their broadcast each day, when they sign off, they play the Russian National Anthem. I think Eisenhower is out of his mind. If he isn't, he is the most ignorant man alive. No, I take that back, the American taxpayer is."

The Presidential Palace was untouched by the War. All of the hand-carved furniture, mirrors trimmed in gold, crystal and marble, and even the maids were intact. Maria was surprised when she was introduced by John Masaryk to an OSS officer living in the palace. He had a wife and two children, but was with his mistress, a well-known whore. She was also the mistress of a former Nazi officer that preceded him in the palace.

Maria, when introduced to her, said, "When this American major leaves, you will have to learn Russian."

Maria was cold to her and the two never spoke again. The woman knew what Maria thought and always avoided her.

Every morning for the past four days, Maria checked in at the OSS headquarters building to see if there were any new dispatches. On this morning when Maria checked communications, the officer in charge gave her a message, "Maria, there is an American, born in Slovakia, looking for you."

Maria was puzzled, "I can't imagine who."

"I have a file on him. Let me see . . . 'John Schwartz, fought against the initial invasion by the Germans, escaped to France, fought against the Nazis at the Maginot Line. Captured by the Germans and escaped after three weeks. Made his way to the US where his parents lived. Entered the US Army and volunteered for duty with the OSS. Became leader of a mission called Houseboat. Permanent address, 1774 Eastburn Avenue. Bronx, New York. Married, no children. Occupation, teacher.' " The officer's voice dropped as he continued, "At present, he is under suspicion for collaborating with the enemy."

He stopped reading and looked at Maria. He took the folder and replaced it in the file cabinet, locking it and testing the drawer several times to make sure it would not open.

Schwartz was never part of the Dawes Team, when his operation failed, he joined Lt. Green and his group.

As Maria was leaving the office and heading for the Palace she heard, "Maria!" It was John. Under suspicion or not, Maria ran to meet him.

He held her as she remarked, "I thought you were dead."

He told her, "No, they took me prisoner, along with some pilots and Czech soldiers. I sat out the rest of the War in a POW camp."

"I guess you know about Lt. Green and the others," Maria sadly mentioned.

Schwartz went on, "For awhile, I thought that you were the woman they executed. I read some reports, but then I stopped, I just couldn't go on. If they got the information from them, why did they have to kill them? Why hang them with wire and beat them? Well, enough of that. What are you doing here, and in an American Army officer's uniform?"

As they walked along together, Maria told him the story from beginning to end. When she finished, she inquired why he was in the area. She thought, perhaps, he was on another mission. In which case, he would not discuss anything. But he told her that he was doing the same thing she was trying to do—make sure his relatives were safe. When he found that Maria had a jeep and was told to drive it all the way to France, he suggested that they travel together. They had papers, but Schwartz warned Maria that the Russians were very suspicious of Americans. She already knew that, but felt they both could handle any situation.

That evening, Maria thanked John Masaryk for all of his help, wished him well in his fight for liberation, knowing it was useless. The Russians already occupied the nation.

The following day, John Schwartz and Maria drove through Czechoslovakia, trying to avoid the Russians, who seemed to be everywhere. They reached the home of John's grandparents in Nitra at 1600 hours.

Everyone at their house talked at once, so no one could hear what was said. The family brought out food they had hoarded for such an occasion. John carried in his duffle bag from the jeep. It was full of soap, sugar, bread and every kind of canned food imaginable. Maria did the same. She had traded cigarettes for a variety of food, which she now shared.

Nitra was a small, beautiful town. It was hit hard by the War, but the Slovak people were tough and recovered from the hardship. Schwartz knew that he could not stay long. He promised when he returned to the United States that he would mail them whatever they needed. Maria and John were treated like royalty by John's grandparents for three days. John felt it may be dangerous for his grandparents if he and Maria stayed any longer, so he told them good-bye. He held them close as they cried. They knew they would never see him again.

Maria sat in the jeep, grinding the gears, trying to find first. She saw the look on their faces as they walked with John to the vehicle. Despair, fear and sadness were reflected in their eyes. At this point, Maria wondered if it was worth going home. She felt so sad that she wanted to jump out of the jeep and console the elderly couple. John didn't take it well either, so she decided the best medicine would be to depart as quickly as possible. The two old grandparents stood waving as Maria floored the jeep, speeding away at twenty miles an hour.

That evening, they covered seventy-five miles and arrived in Maria's hometown of Jakubiany. She pulled in front of her parent's house, turned off the engine and sat for a few minutes. Schwartz turned to her and asked, "What are you waiting for?"

Maria hesitated explaining, "I haven't written in so long. I had no way of mailing letters. If I had written, the Germans would have intercepted the letters."

John brought her back to reality, "Are we finished rationalizing now?"

John and Maria walked to the door and knocked. Maria's mother opened the door with caution, peeking out to see who was there. She screamed and clutched her chest as if she were having a heart attack. Maria's father rushed to the door to see what the commotion was.

Seeing Maria, he blessed himself, making the sign of the cross twice, then said, "Dear God, we thought you were dead. Oh, dear God, you're alive."

They rushed to greet John Schwartz, thinking that he, in some way, may have saved Maria's life. They held him, squeezing him, saying repeatedly, "Thank you, thank you."

John looked over at Maria, opened his eyes widely and arched his eyebrows as if to say, "What's happening here?" He broke their death grip and returned to the jeep. He carried in Maria's duffel bag, walked through the living room and left it on the kitchen floor. Seeing the food that Schwartz unpacked, Maria's mother and father stopped crying at once. Their full attention was given to the food. They hadn't seen so much food since before the War. It was too good to be true.

Maria's mother poured wine and searched the kitchen for something to serve the two guests. Maria handed her two large cans of soup. Schwartz handed her the opener attached to his penknife. She wasn't quite sure how to use it, so John opened both cans. He told her he would leave the opener with her, and if she wanted to use any of the cans of food, she would have to learn to use it. Maria's mother and father sipped the soup like it came from heaven. Her father noticed the two of them were exhausted. Mrs. Zima excused herself and hurriedly straightened up rooms for John and Maria.

Her father sampled his wine like he had just finished a banquet. Then he said, "You are both tired. There will be plenty of time tomorrow for you to bring us up to date on everything."

It was late, so neither of them argued about retiring.

The American jeep sitting next to the house caused quite a stir. Not being able to stand it any longer, friends and neighbors knocked on the front door. The word was out. Maria's friends all showed up wanting to wish her well. To Maria, it was like going back to her school years. Old stories were rehashed to the laughter of her old school chums.

In the midst of the laughing, one girl remarked, "It was too bad that they hanged that poor girl, thinking it was you."

The entire room fell into a deadly silence. The blood drained from Maria's face. Her mother held the bottom of her apron and began twisting it with both hands. She was hoping to keep the news from Maria: The Germans hanged her girlfriend, thinking it was her.

On the third day of their visit, Catrina Liska, one of Maria's old schools friends, came to the house. She told Maria that a member of the Communist Party in the village was asking questions about her. Why was she there, and in an American uniform? Who was the man with her? What had she been doing during the War? Maria's parents knew she had to leave. They assured her they would be safe and for her not to worry.

Schwartz and Maria had no alternative. They had to leave. Safety for all was their primary concern. Catrina Liska asked if she could go with them as far as her home. She lived some distance from the village. They assured her that it was no problem; it was on their way.

While he waited for Maria to say good-bye, Schwartz selected the least-traveled roads through Germany and France for their escape. They would follow his planned route to the coast.

With their belongings in the jeep, they helped Catrina Liska into the back seat. Schwartz said good-bye to Maria's mother and father and checked the water and oil levels in the jeep. Maria remained with her mother and father for a few moments. Her father pondered, "I will never understand all of this. I still don't know why you are in an American officer's uniform? Who were all the Americans and British, and what were they doing here in Czechoslovakia?"

Maria put her arms around her mother and told her, "I love you so very much. Try to understand that I have to go because of the Russians. Someday, when we have time, I'll tell you all about it."

She held them both. Who knows what was ahead, or if she would ever see them again. Before she broke into tears, she ran to the jeep.

Schwartz drove for a half hour, then Catrina said, "There, pull in there, please."

Schwartz swung the jeep onto a small side road, then pulled in front of a two story mountain home and stopped. He helped Catrina from the back seat.

Catrina looked at Maria, "Maria I have a surprise for you, wait here."

She disappeared into the house and returned with Olga. Maria was overwhelmed. She hadn't seen Olga since the days of Anna at the old school house. They hugged and kissed and cackled like two chickens in a barnyard. Chattering without

Lieutenant Maria

stopping, each tried to get their questions in first. Finally, Maria stopped and introduced her sister Olga to Schwartz.

Olga invited them in, "Come in, I want you to meet someone."

Schwartz gave Maria a look, indicating they should not stay too long. Maria acknowledged his expression by tilting her head back slightly. They entered the house and Catrina showed them into the main room, while she went to get wine.

A big man appeared from upstairs. Olga rushed over to him and held on to his arm. She introduced him, "This is Rudy Casarian. We expect to be married. Right now, we are moving up into the mountains to fight the Russians."

Maria couldn't believe what she heard, "What do you mean, fight the Russians. The War is over and we have lost, again. What are you going to fight the Russians with? There is nothing left of the Czech Army. The country is all but starving. Fight with what?"

Schwartz cut in, "Rudy, you should know better. Try to survive under the Russian occupation. Eventually, you can get the people organized for elections. That is the only way you can win, now."

Rudy appeared arrogant, telling Schwartz and Maria that they didn't know what they were talking about. Schwartz interrupted and replied that the Czech people had been through too much. The last thing they needed was another war.

Maria tried in vain to convince Olga not to go with Rudy. It was apparent that Olga was infatuated with him and nothing would change her mind. Maria felt if Rudy wanted to wage war against God, Olga would have joined him. However, Maria tried one last time to dissuade Rudy.

He spoke down to her, "Being a man, I know what has to be done. Perhaps it would be better if you and your American friend would leave."

Maria looked over at Olga who was silent. Her master spoke. She firmly embraced her sister and warned, "If this is what you really want to do, be careful. There isn't anything that you can do, except get yourself killed."

Catrina and Olga walked with Maria to the jeep. Maria turned to Catrina and asked, "You're not in this mess are you?"

She affirmed she was, "Yes, Maria. We are moving into the mountains tonight. We were told that General Viest was still alive and that he and the remainder of our army are now fighting the Russians north of here."

Schwartz gave one last pitch, "Catrina, you are making a big mistake. You would be much better off leaving the country and moving west. You could work in France or Italy. Why stay here and die for a lost cause? It just doesn't make any sense."

Catrina explained, "It is better to die on the soil of one's homeland, than to flee to another country with your tail between your legs."

Schwartz and Maria knew further attempts to persuade her would be useless. They all kissed and hugged. Schwartz helped Maria into the jeep and they drove off. Maria looked back one last time at Olga and waved.

Chapter Ten

CITIZEN MARIA

Instead of feeling elated over visiting their families and friends, Schwartz and Maria felt lonely. They remained silent, each in their own world. Schwartz had his parents in New York, but Maria had no where she could be safe. Before the War, she never left Czechoslovakia. Now, her whole life faded in the distance. The jeep moved steadily down the road, but brought her closer only to the unknown. Behind her was a life destroyed, ahead an unknown future.

God was on Maria's side. The Russian radio continued broadcasting inquiries about her whereabouts and news of a warrant for her arrest. They hadn't discovered she was in an American officer's uniform and that her new name was Maria Davis. If they had, the news would have been broadcast. Schwartz assured Maria that things were fine and that the Russians would never suspect them. Maria, not as confident as Schwartz, told him that Lt. Green's group probably felt the same way before their capture. John quickly changed the subject.

Inside the Austrian border, they felt much safer. They had driven for hours and were hungry. Looking for a place to have lunch, they realized Austria was better off than Germany, but not much better. The Austrians rebuilt their nation, bit by bit. They cleaned the streets and restored their buildings. Many hotels were already open, securing business from the foreign military forces occupying the nation.

Schwartz stopped at a hotel on the Austrian border. He was heading for Stuttgart, but thought the Austrian hotels might be better than those in Germany. They ordered lunch and beer. A thin waiter limped his way to their table. He spoke very little English so Maria spoke German.

He had stored questions about the War for over a year. Instead of taking her order, he asked her if President Roosevelt was insane. Why had he divided Europe, giving half to the Russians? The Yalta Conference was the biggest disaster in history! Stalin walked away with everything and Roosevelt and Churchill went home with nothing. He stood and waited for Maria's answer.

She could only say, "I agree."

The waiter was dumbfounded. He turned to the patrons and publicly called out that the American lady officer was the only person in the Allied forces who knew anything.

The people in the restaurant who spoke German smiled, but were afraid to laugh. In German, the waiter added, "These Americans and British think that we are all Nazis. Only six percent of the total population of Austria were registered Nazis."

Maria smiled and responded, "You should be happy the American and British forces are here and not the Russians."

The waiter explained, "We are happy madame officer, but Austrians like to complain and discuss. It keeps one's mind active. Don't you agree?"

"Yes, I agree. Now could we have some of your Austrian beer while we are discussing world affairs?"

Schwartz leaned over to Maria and said, "Do you think that I should ruin his whole day and tell him that I'm a Jew?"

Maria shook her head, "That's all we need, another gang chasing us across Europe."

Maria liked John and decided to break her rules and ask him some personal questions, "John, I don't mean to pry and I know that you are still under orders, but what happened to you after the Germans captured you in the mountains? If you don't want to talk about it, I'll understand."

Schwartz answered, "No, I don't mind. I have already filed my report as, I am sure, you have. It is on record, so I don't see any harm in telling you."

Maria told him, "The only reason I ask is, before I met you coming out of the OSS office, an officer told me that someone was looking for me. When I asked him who, he picked up your file and read a little of it. At the bottom of the page he let it slip that you were under investigation or observation for being a collaborator. I was really shocked. Did something happen when you were captured?"

Schwartz elaborated, "When I joined you, I was part of the Houseboat Team. I had nothing to do with the Dawes Team. Our team never went into operation, so I stayed with Lt. Green and you. When I was captured, my commanding officer was Lt. Taylor. He was captured before I was, but we all ended up in the same prison. Taylor and his group were tortured and beaten daily.

"Reports filtered back to our headquarters in Bari, Italy, that I was being treated like a double agent. And, indeed, the Germans did not torture me like the others. I tried to convince them that I would work with them. You know, no matter what you do or how you try to hold out, they are going to get the information from you. I just tried to convince them that I could be a double agent, hoping the War would end soon and someone would rescue us. The officers questioning me said that both radios from the Dawes Team were destroyed. That happened on the day I was captured. As you know, several pilots were captured with me on that day, but no one suspected them. I told the Germans that I was only a courier for the plan, nothing more. I believed they were going to ask me to be a double agent. So I kept stringing them along. We were freezing, fighting and running for months on end. Then what? We are suspects. The hell with them."

Getting into the jeep, Schwartz suggested, "Listen Maria, we're not far from Weisbaden. Maybe they have some new orders or information for us. Why don't we stop there? It's almost on our way. Now that they are settled in, we could pick up some more travel money. After all, we need money to travel and eat. If they won't advance us any, we can always pick up a few cartons of cigarettes. They are more valuable than money, anyway."

Maria agreed and he swung the jeep around and drove north.

Maria smiled, "I wonder what Ruby will think? Probably that we are on vacation."

"Screw 'em," Schwartz decided aloud.

Maria wondered, "Why do you say that? He has helped me more than anyone. The man made decisions on his own, decisions he could suffer for later. He issued my papers, not the United States Government."

Schwartz explained, "The United States Government is slower than the second coming of Christ. If you waited for the government to issue you your papers, you would still be sitting there."

Maria was concerned, "What if he wants his jeep back? We could be in trouble."

Schwartz dismissed her concern, "I'm sure this jeep is not on anyone's books. We'll just hide it. If he doesn't inquire, we won't mention it."

When they entered the OSS Headquarters in Weisbaden, Maria was embarrassed. Her orders were to continue to the French coast, not to return to headquarters. Contrary to her guilt, Mr. Ruby was delighted to see them both. They quickly explained the ordeals and pleasures of their trip and their reason for returning. Ruby greeted Maria, saying, "I am so happy you returned. During your absence Allan Dulles from Roosevelt's staff arrived. Also here is Frank Weisner, a United States Navy commander and high-ranking official with the OSS."

Ruby was excited as he told her that Dulles approved her forged papers. Now everything was legal. Ruby knew that Maria had no where to go. Her name was now carried on the Russian NKVD black list. They intensified their search, so he ordered her to remain in uniform and leave Germany the following day. Four members from OSS Headquarters Weisbaden were leaving in the morning and Maria was ordered on the same truck. Ruby was afraid if the NKVD caught up with Maria an international incident would result. He was also worried about his own position. He realized that Maria never volunteered her services. From the beginning, she was forced into the War. With practically no military training, she carried out her orders. She risked her life for the Americans, and he reasoned it was his responsibility to aid her.

Ruby then addressed Schwartz, "John, I am afraid that your news is not so good. They would like you to report to operations."

John and Maria knew what that meant. He was about to receive new orders. His face saddened. He thought he was returning home; it had been so long. Maria walked to the operations office with John. He was already depressed.

Maria tried to comfort him, "It really must be important, otherwise they wouldn't keep you from returning home."

He picked up his orders and smiled at Maria, "They just want me to have a physical, clear up my debriefing and then I fly home."

"How long is all of that going to take?" Maria asked.

Schwartz rambled, "If they start taking X-rays, blood and sending me for a psychiatric evaluation, who knows?"

Maria was positive, "That's not so bad. I heard that many men developed TB. Maybe taking a physical is a good thing. I have to take a boat to the United States, you get to fly. You will be there before I am out to sea."

In the morning, Maria sat in the front seat of the army truck. The three men in the rear of the truck had no idea whom she was, only that she was an Army officer. As they drove through Germany, Maria stared through the large windshield, mumbling.

The driver asked her to repeat what she said, "What's that, ma'am?"

Maria still mumbled, "The destruction."

"What's that?" the driver asked again.

Maria remarked, "The destruction; it is unbelievable. There are no buildings, only rubble."

The driver agreed, "I know. Aren't you glad you are a woman and never had to see any combat?"

If he only knew, thought Maria.

Traveling through Frankfort, Maria felt sorry for the German people. The Nazis killed the citizens, destroyed their freedom, ruined their art and imposed their Reich on everyone. Seeing Frankfort helped her forget her misery.

People walked the streets endlessly. Only one road was open, one that went through the center of the city. Maria saw it all. Displaced soldiers returned home while the wounded and the sick wandered from street to street looking for medical care that did not exist.

The soldier driving commented, "If I didn't know where I was, I would swear I was on the moon."

They crossed into France and headed for the debarkation center. Schwartz was gone, the last of the original group. All that Maria could think about was that she was driven into exile, to a country that she knew nothing about.

The debarkation center on the coast of France was overcrowded with American personnel returning home. Maria was assigned to the women's barracks. She was billeted with an American USO troupe, mostly singers and dancers, who never stopped talking. She spent most of her time in the mess hall, drinking coffee and waiting for her orders. Sometimes, she walked alone along the harbor. She did not enjoy the cackling, giggling and snickering of the women in the barracks.

Each morning, she would report to the harbor office and ask when she would depart. Each morning, she was told her name was not on the list.

One morning, a young Navy officer inquired about his orders. He, apparently, was having the same difficulties as Maria.

When she walked outside, he was right behind her, "Excuse me, lieutenant, are you having any luck?"

Maria responded, "No, lieutenant, I'm not. I can't understand what is causing the delay."

"The military is always buried under reams of paper," he said to excuse the government delay.

He asked Maria if she would like to go off the base and have lunch. Maria missed having good wine and since she thought the French had the best food in the world, she immediately accepted his invitation. They walked to his jeep and drove to the city.

Maria asked, "How do you pronounce your first name?"

"It's pronounced Bent, but you spell it B-e-n-d-t. It's a Norwegian name," he explained.

He asked her questions about what she had done during the War and what she thought of the Russians. She knew at once he was either OSS or Naval Intelligence. But she was out for the afternoon and decided to enjoy the day, regardless. Anything was better than sitting on the base, listening to the women in the barracks. He paused, ceased his questioning and mentioned he had a new Buick waiting for him at home. Maria asked him what a Buick was. He laughed. Not a joyful laugh, but a condescending one.

Maria ordered the meal in French, then asked Bendt if he spoke French. He said he didn't, so Maria returned his condescending laugh. Agitated, he was silent during most of the meal, but managed to throw a couple of questions at her. He asked her why she was going to the United States and what she was going to do when she got there.

It was difficult, but Maria kept her voice low, "Look, I am going to American because I have no place else to go. My life has been destroyed. I have no country to return to. All of this was caused by others, not me. And no, I don't enjoy the Andrew Sisters. I don't even know who the Andrew Sisters are. And I could care less about your Buick."

Bendt sat with his mouth open as Maria stood and pulled the strap of her military purse over her shoulder. She walked a few steps away from the table and called back, "You can tell Naval Intelligence that you wouldn't last five minutes with the Germans or two minutes with the Russians. Tell your superiors that a fifth grader could have extracted more information than you. If they are all like you, God help the Office of Naval Intelligence!"

She left the lieutenant sitting in the restaurant. As she passed through the main entrance, she was stopped by a short man with a smiling face, thinning black hair and a slight pot belly, "Lieutenant, you might have trouble catching a cab. Fuel is difficult to obtain, so there aren't many cabs around. Let me introduce myself, I am George Bookbinder."

Maria, still upset with the Navy lieutenant, was short with her remarks, "I suppose you, too, are from the Office Of Naval Intelligence! I can tell that you are an American, but I have never heard such an accent."

He told Maria, "I'm from New York. And, yes, you are right. I am intelligence, but OSS, same as you."

"Maybe you can tell me what is going on?" Maria asked.

Bookbinder reported, "It seems the Navy is spying on the Army, and the Army is spying on the Marines."

"How did you people ever win the War?" Maria wondered.

"We just made the Czechoslovakians do all of the work," he joked.

Maria laughed. She felt at ease with Bookbinder and accepted his offer for a ride back to the base. He didn't ask any more questions. He mentioned he knew Ruby and that Ruby wanted to make sure she was on a ship headed home. He assured her that he would do everything possible to help. Maria paid no attention to him. This promise had been made repeatedly, always with the same enthusiasm and never with any substance.

While Bookbinder drove Maria back to Le Havre, she asked him to use whatever influence he had to get her on board one of the troop ships. She only had a month to report to Vassar College and was becoming worried that her student visa wouldn't be any good if she didn't arrive in time. She would miss an entire year if she had to wait for the next class to begin.

Ships continued to leave. Maria checked the passenger lists, but her name never appeared. She tried every way possible to find transportation, including speaking with the harbor master, the commander of the base and even Army intelligence. She stayed away from the Navy.

Three more days passed. Maria watched as the SS George Washington was loaded. Soldiers marched up the gangway, headed to the United States. She watched for a minute, then something inside her clicked.

Maria hurried back to the barracks, packed her duffel bag, put on her dress uniform and reported to the dock. She was going on this ship, or else.

Maria joined an all-male line waiting to board the ship. The men helped her with the heavy bag and laughed at her accent and joked with her. When she reached the officer checking the men on board, she knew that her name wasn't on the list, but that didn't bother her. She stepped up to him with confidence.

He asked in a monotone, "Name?"

"Davis, Maria, lieutenant," she said matter-of-factly.

The officer flipped through several pages, looking for her name. He glanced at her repeatedly, then said, "I don't see your name here, lieutenant."

Maria was stern, "What do you want me to do about it."

The officers behind her started complaining, yelling that he should let the girl on.

The officer persisted, "Lieutenant, none of the Davis' first names are Maria."

Maria bluffed, "Maybe they used my initial."

"There is an initial, but it is J not M," he told her.

Maria insisted, "Can't you see that they made a mistake; it should have been M, not J."

"Who knows? Go ahead," he shrugged.

The line of officers cheered as Maria boarded the ship.

On board, she searched for the women's officer quarters. She located them on the port side of the ship, two decks down. She remained in her quarters all day. Several women officers tried to get her to go to the chow hall, but she refused to leave until she heard the whistle of the ship signal three times, indicating they were underway.

The women officers soon realized Maria was not an officer. She did not understand military terminology or expressions. They resented her, thinking she was a prostitute smuggled into the United States by some high-ranking officer.

Maria knew she would be exposed. Rather than have them think she was a prostitute, she sat with the three other officers in her cabin and told them her entire story. They listened in disbelief. When reality sank in, they helped Maria, bringing her food. They kept her secret.

The seas were rough during the crossing. Waves broke over the bow. Sometimes, the stern rose completely out of the water, exposing the churning props. Maria and the three women officers confined themselves to their quarters. One at a time, they crawled to the bathroom, throwing up and praying God would take their life. The ship clanged, banged, rattled and echoed unfamiliar sounds.

Maria believed it was an old wives' tale that people turned green when they became seasick. She changed her mind when she looked into the mirror. If the Tartar officer could see her now, he would run through the crowd in the opposite direction. After seeing herself, she drank some water. Her face was so dehydrated she could have used it as a sponge. For the remaining few days at sea, she prayed. God had not finished making her suffer.

The storm ended, leaving the seas serene. The sun shone brightly as the ship approached New York harbor. The captain ordered, "All ahead one-third."

The four women walked out on deck. There was the Statue of Liberty. Maria, still recovering, lifted her head and addressed the monument to freedom, "Instead of that crown on your head, you should be wearing an ice pack."

Tugboats came alongside, guiding the ship to her berth. Fireboats sprayed water into the air, whistles blew and passing ships dipped their flags in respect for the troops. Sirens filled the air, military planes zoomed overhead and people along the shore cheered. Military bands played as thousands sang out.

The ship moored her lines to the dock and the troops filed down the gangway. The three officers with Maria got dressed and gathered their belongings. They shook Maria, trying to wake her, but it was useless. They decided to leave her, telling her she could wait and be the last one off. That way she could have a few more hours of rest. Maria did her best to say good-bye. The others understood and wished her luck at Vassar College.

The music died down, the crowds dispersed and quiet returned to the dock. Maria, finally, showered and put on her uniform. It was impossible for her to carry her duffelbag. She dragged it behind her like a heavy log. A sailor, seeing her predicament, assisted.

As he helped Maria down the gangway, she said, "I will never go to sea again as long as I live."

The sailor set her bag down and replied, "I know just what you mean, lieutenant. That damn ship going up and down, back and forth, up and down..."

Maria ran to the side of the dock and threw up in the ocean.

She looked around the docks. In which direction should she go? Where should she go? And whom should she see? It was a terrible feeling: being in a strange land, unfamiliar with the language and with little money.

Several sailors leaving the troop ship walked with her to the bus and accompanied her to the train station. They wrote down the information she needed to get to Vassar.

The train leaving in the direction of Vassar was ready to depart, so she thanked them for their assistance. They saluted—this always made Maria feel uneasy—and she returned their salute.

The train crawled through the city, stopping frequently to board passengers, then picked up speed as it left the big buildings behind.

Northern New York was beautiful. Maria watched the dairy farms vanish in a blur as the train sped through the countryside. How different it was.

She was still tired and felt ill from the trip. Her eyes blurred as telephone poles flew by the window in a rhythm matching the clanking wheels. The undulating side-to-side movement had a hypnotic effect on her, soon she was asleep.

"Lieutenant, lieutenant, wake up, this is your station," the conductor called, "this is Poughkeepsie."

"Pou... what?" Maria stammered.

The conductor repeated, "Poughkeepsie, you are going to Vassar, right?"

"Yes, I am," Maria admitted.

"Then you have to get off here," the conductor instructed.

The conductor pulled her duffelbag down from the overhead compartment and helped her from the train. He looked up and down the station then announced, "All aboard, all aboard."

Maria inquired, "Sir, which way to Vassar."

"Check into the main station," he suggested. "They will give you directions. Good luck, lieutenant."

Maria enrolled in Vassar College on the twentieth of January 1946. At last, she was preparing for her life dream of becoming a history professor. For the next four months she studied day and night, mastering English and the freshman curriculum. Her roommate, Cynthia Banks, was a track and field athlete. They became close friends during Maria's first semester.

Before the summer vacation, Maria received a letter inviting her and her family or friends to West Point. Cynthia was excited. Maria invited her to go along, since she was the only person she knew in the United States.

On the twenty-fourth of May 1946, the two girls packed their suitcases and were ready to leave. Cynthia asked why they were going to West Point. Maria said she didn't care, she was glad to get away from school for a few days.

Maria caught Cynthia packing her discus and said, "Where do you think you are going to throw that?"

Cynthia responded, "Maybe in some field. You know West Point has a football field."

Maria condemned the decision, "My God, you can throw that thing all year, we are going to have fun, not trounce cadets on the football field."

Cynthia agreed, "It doesn't matter. Since we will be away from here we will have fun. Exactly what did your telegram say?"

"It said they were holding a semi-formal ceremony," Maria told her. "I think it might be like a reunion."

Cynthia didn't understand, "A reunion of what? You don't even know anyone."

"Who cares, you and I will have a reunion. What difference does it make?" Maria asked.

They left for the train station. Cynthia was still confused about the telegram.

Maria asked Cynthia if a blue suit was considered semi-formal. She replied that it better be because she packed a gray one almost identical to Maria's.

As they departed the train, Cynthia carried the luggage. She told Maria that it kept her in shape.

Maria looked at her and said, "In shape for what? Throwing cannon balls?"

They called West Point and were told they were guests of the Point. They were both happy and welcomed the news. It meant that they could spend what little money they had on having a good time, instead of a hotel room.

They took a cab to the Point and were dropped at guest housing. Their room was a large one overlooking the grounds. After unpacking their things, they wandered down to the main lobby and asked the cadet on duty if he had information on the following day's events. He reached under the counter and produced a schedule. He looked up and said, "Could I please have your name, miss?"

"Maria, Maria Zima."

He looked down at the paper and then at Maria.

Finally, Maria said, "Is something wrong, cadet?"

"No. No, it's just an overwhelming honor to meet you," he stammered.

"What does he mean, Maria?" Cynthia asked.

"I don't know. Maybe there is another Maria Zima," Maria responded.

"At Vassar . . . I'm sure! What is going on?" Cynthia demanded.

"It probably has something to do with the War," Maria guessed.

"The War? Let me see that paper," Cynthia reached for the program.

Cynthia read the schedule aloud while the cadet stood still, watching. Her mouth dropped open. She slowly lowered the paper and said, "What is all of this? I thought we were coming to a dance. Now I find out that you are another General Patton. I wish I had my discus, I would drop it on your foot."

Cynthia sat through dinner, looking at Maria and shaking her head. She asked for an explanation, "I don't suppose you are going to tell me anything about this?"

Maria explained, "There really isn't much to tell. Anyway, I don't like recalling it."

"I understand, Maria. You should have told me what we were getting in to. My God, the entire cadet corps passing in review. You must have done something," Cynthia surmised.

Maria bit her bottom lip and swallowed several times. Cynthia knew Maria always did this when she was trying to suppress deep feelings, so she dropped the subject.

Cynthia looked at the schedule one more time before placing it into her purse: "25 May 1946. Maria Zima will be the first woman in the history of the United States to be honored by the Cadet Corps of West Point, passing in review at 1300 hours this date. The Bronze Metal, with full military honors, will be presented to Miss Zima by General William Donovan."

Cynthia was up most of the night trying to make sure everything would be ready for the next morning. She was still confused, but enjoyed the excitement.

Reveille sounded, the drums and bugles echoed through the labyrinth of the academy. The cadets assembled in formation. Mess call sounded, the day had officially begun. Cynthia watched from her window. Maria headed to the shower making her usual statement about dying if she did not get a cup of coffee.

They decided to dress casually and wandered about the academy after a leisurely breakfast. Cynthia delighted in viewing the cadets, her only concern then. Maria was fine until Cynthia asked her if she were nervous.

Maria searched the academy for a familiar face. If she were going to receive a medal, where were Mac and Lain, Catlos and Dunlevy? Surely they must be here, somewhere. She looked at visitors and passers-by, no familiar faces. On their return, they stopped in the lobby to ask the duty cadet if he had any information on others that might be receiving medals. He handed them all the information he had. Maria looked over the papers, but did not recognize anyone's name. She wanted to question someone, but who? She knew no one there. Even the dignitaries were strangers. She never liked calling attention to herself and always tried to keep her life private. She was sure that she was going to see the men she struggled to survive with. She had her heart set on a reunion.

Cynthia reminded Maria they were late and should get ready. Maria was calm, but disappointed and somewhat perturbed. How could they have singled her out for a medal and not the others?

Cynthia put her makeup on two or three times, changed her hair style twice and tried to darken her eyebrows. Maria stood at the window and watched detachment after detachment pass on their way to the parade ground. She looked at herself in the mirror and fluffed the lace on the collar of her blouse. She was ready.

Cynthia looked into the mirror, disappointed. She concluded, "No matter what I do, I still look like a linebacker. But you never know, maybe one of these cadets might have the hots for a linebacker."

Maria didn't understand, "A linebacker, what is a linebacker?"

"It's an expression meaning a beautiful, strongly-built woman," Cynthia explained.

The day was beautiful, with a tepid breeze. As the two of them started for the parade ground, the warm air felt good blowing on their faces. Maria closed her eyes and pointed her face to the sun. It reminded her of the day that Olga and Julius came to the little schoolhouse. That seemed a thousand years ago.

Cynthia bumped Maria's arm to get her attention and asked, "What are you thinking about?"

Maria responded, "Nothing, really, just wishing that all of this was over so we could go back to school."

Cynthia disagreed, "Not me, I wish this would never end. I have never seen so many handsome men in all of my life."

Maria reminisced, "Yes, Cynthia, I know what you mean. I once knew many wonderful, handsome men, too. One was named Joe, just like in the movies. He was a dear and wonderful man, one that I will not forget."

Cynthia wondered, "Why is it that you never told me about any of this?"

"I keep those things to myself," Maria told her.

They moved along with the crowds forming around the reviewing officers, who were standing behind the microphones.

Maria asked an officer directing traffic to the reviewing area where she and Cynthia should go. He checked Maria's name off his list and seated them on the right side of the reviewing officers.

The crowds quieted down and the Commanding Officer of West Point stepped up to the microphone, "Ladies and Gentlemen, cadets of West Point it is my privilege to present to you this afternoon: General William Donovan, Commander of the Office of Strategic Services."

Cynthia watched General Donovan walk up to the microphone. Then she leaned over to Maria and whispered, "My God, that man has more decorations and ribbons on his uniform than General Patton."

The OSS Commander continued speaking, "There are few events in the life of a military man that give him great pleasure. Today is one of those rare opportunities. Please have the color guard escort Maria Zima to the presentation area in front of me."

The cadet color guard marched over to Maria and Cynthia. The soldiers mistook Cynthia, the big and strong one, for Maria. Maria, sitting in the sun, looked like a frail, young school girl on vacation with her mother. Cynthia loved it; she was, finally, close to the cadets.

Maria stood as the color guard surrounded her and walked toward General Donovan. The wind changed and blew the edge of the American flag across her shoulder. Hearing it snap in the breeze, she turned and looked. It was more like a prayer than a thought that flashed through her head, "It is for you, the men of Dawes Team and those crazy pilots, so dear to my heart, that I am accepting this medal."

She faced General Donovan and looked into his eyes as he read,

> From: Harry S. Truman, President of the United States. To: Maria Zima, Czechoslovakian Citizen. Subject: Award of the Bronze Star. General Order number 26, 14 May 1946, by direction of the President, the Bronze Star Medal, for distinguished heroic or meritorious achievement or service in connection with military operations against an enemy of the United States, is awarded to Maria Zima,

Citizen Maria

Czechoslovakian Partisan, guide and interpreter, Dawes Team, Czechoslovakia, Company B, 2677th Regiment, Office of Strategic Services, Provisional, for meritorious achievement in connection with military operations in Czechoslovakia from 30 October 1944, to 8 May 1945. Maria Zima, who was serving with the Czech Brigade in the heart of enemy territory was recruited on 30 October, 1944, to assist an American intelligence mission in that territory in the capacity of guide and interpreter. She served with the mission until the capture and subsequent execution of most of its members.

Following the capture of most of the party, on 26 December, Maria took the lead in planning and executing the further movements of the survivors; her unswerving courage, plus her knowledge of the land was, in a large part, responsible for keeping the little party of two British and two Americans together and alive. In particular, on 6 January, it was she who decided, against the best local advice obtainable, that they could and should pass through the remaining German-held territory and cross the Russian lines. At this time, her leg was so badly swollen that, on at least one occasion, she had to be carried. After a few days of convalescence, it was Maria who explored the German lines for an escape route and an interim hiding place.

On at least six occasions between 6 January and 20 January, she explored and foraged for food, bringing her into direct contact with German patrols and with local fascist sympathizers who were ready to betray her. On each of these occasions, she escaped thanks to her courage, quick wit, and resourcefulness, and returned to her comrades. In the company of two Americans and two British paratroopers, she made her way through enemy lines to the Russian forces. The mission, although enduring the greatest suffering from exposure to the elements and extreme hazards from enemy action, contributed intelligence of distinct value to the war effort and effected the rescue of a considerable number of Allied flyers downed in enemy territory. Maria Zima, through her complete disregard for danger and faithful and effective performance of her duties, was instrumental in making these contributions. By command of Major General Taylor."

General Donovan stepped forward and pinned the Bronze Medal on Maria's lapel. He shook her hand and said, "A grateful nation thanks you for what you have done."

Maria shook his hand and then did an about face. General Donovan stood to her right while the other officers formed a semi-circle around her.

The military band played and the commanding cadets shouted orders to their companies. The long gray lines of cadets gradually moved forward. Soon, a gigantic wave of cadets marched across the West Point drill field. As they approached Maria, she heard the "eyes right" command. The cadets drew their sabers and their heads snapped to the right. Maria Zima, Czechoslovakian Citizen accepted, for the first time in US history, the highest honor ever bestowed on a woman by the cadets of West Point.

Cynthia stood and applauded with the crowd as the photographers' flash bulbs popped in Maria's face. Tears flowed down Cynthia's face. All these months, her roommate was a hero to the world and she never said a word. Cynthia stayed back as Maria was congratulated by well wishers. It looked like every important person in Washington was there. When they departed, Cynthia stood drying her eyes.

She walked up to Maria and put her arms around her, "Oh my, what a terrible part of history, and you were right in the middle of it. I don't know if you noticed, but that cadet carrying the flag was gorgeous."

When they returned to Vassar, the dean sent for Maria. An invitation for Maria from Eleanor Roosevelt was sitting on the dean's desk. She told Maria that it arrived during her absence. Maria read the invitation and asked the dean if she had to accept. The dean explained it was a great honor to receive an invitation from the White House, especially from Eleanor Roosevelt. Maria confessed that she never saw eye to eye with the Roosevelts, but would attend the tea party out of respect.

More invitations arrived from newspapers, radio shows and speaking opportunities. One came from Hollywood. Cynthia read the letters and tried to convince Maria to take advantage of the opportunities, but Maria wasn't interested. Friday, before leaving for Mrs. Roosevelt's tea party, Maria told Cynthia that she did not want to accept the offers because it had taken her time to push her terrible ordeal from her mind. She did not want to relive it all.

Cynthia understood, "Since you accepted Eleanor Roosevelt's invitation, see how that one goes. You have to do something for money, you just can't go on like this—with nothing."

Maria agreed and decided that if she survived the tea party, she would consider other offers.

While at Vassar, Maria designed and made several dresses. Her training with Madame Zolkoff came in handy. She had something to wear to the garden party. It was a navy blue dress patterned after a Chinese design, with a high Mandarin collar, trimmed in white. It was form fitting, with a slit showing her left leg. She added oriental designs on both sides of the collar and trimmed the dress with white tape. On the right side, she hand stitched a small peacock, using every color thread she could find. The dress was magnificent. Cynthia sat in awe, watching as Maria tried it on. She was beautiful. . . .

Cynthia remarked, "Those people are expecting to see someone like me. Wait until they get a load of you. If there are any wives there, you'll never get to meet their husbands."

Maria elaborated, "Cynthia, this is a garden party for women. Men don't attend tea parties. However, I'd feel much better if men were there, at least I could have a beer and a few laughs. I never got along well with women."

Cynthia was envious, "Well, I can see why. If you show up in that dress and there are any men around, there is going to be big trouble."

Sunday morning, Cynthia drove Maria to the train. The trip was turning into more of a chore than a pleasure. Maria had a bad feeling about it, but decided to make the best of it. She knew that she did not belong with the women of society. Many of them were probably wonderful people, but she did not want to take the time to find out which ones. She accepted the invitation mostly for the dean and Vassar. The dean told her that the publicity would benefit the school. Maria felt she should help her school.

With her invitation in her handbag, Maria checked into a hotel on Pennsylvania Avenue. On time, she walked through the lobby and had the doorman signal a cab. He opened the door to assist her and said, "I don't know where you are going, miss, but wherever it is, you're going to be the center of attention."

Maria smiled and said, "I wish you hadn't said that, but thank you for the compliment."

Maria presented her invitation and was shown to the rose garden of the White House. Women were everywhere, standing in small groups, holding cocktail glasses and cackling like hens at feeding time. Mrs. Roosevelt welcomed her and introduced her to senators' and congressmen's wives, none of whom Maria had ever heard of.

It was warm as they walked past the outdoor bar. Mrs. Roosevelt suggested they pause and have something to drink. Eleanor Roosevelt leisurely moved her fan back and forth trying to generate a breeze. She ordered tonic water over ice. Maria ordered a shot of vodka, causing Eleanor to drop her head slightly and squint her eyes. Several women noticed and watched as Maria tilted her head back and allowed the Vodka to disappear. She politely placed the glass back on the table and the two of them continued their promenade through the garden, stopping several times to admire the flowers. Mrs. Roosevelt continually referred to the Russians as those poor helpless people.

Maria responded, "Helpless people! They have more courage than a wounded lion. Their pilots, with a minimum of training, took the Luftwaffe on and did a damn good job. When they charged, it was to the last man. When they held a position, that, too, was to the last man. They are far from helpless, Mrs. Roosevelt."

Several women gathered around them. Maria caused quite a stir and most of the women were inquisitive. They asked, "Tell us about your experiences."

Maria admitted, "There isn't much to tell. I was placed in a situation that required me to do what I did."

"What about all of those wonderful men you were with?" they wanted to know.

"Yes, they were wonderful men," Maria confirmed.

"I'd shiver to think what I would do in that situation," one woman commented.

Maria said facetiously, "That's exactly what I did most of the time, shiver."

They pressed Maria, "I don't think you understand what we are asking, my dear. You know, you're the only girl and all of those handsome young men, alone at night..."

"Oh, I understand," Maria answered. "You want to hear about me and the boys."

"Yes, tell us all the dirt," they insisted.

Maria began, "When the city of Banska Bystrica fell, I moved to the mountains with the Americans, handsome pilots and other members of the Army and Navy... you know."

Now Maria had their attention. They listened intently as she continued, "We were attacked by German aircraft. They machine gunned people on the road. There were dead and dying everywhere. For months, we traveled in a blizzard, our feet were frozen and turned black. I urinated in my pants and it dried on my legs. At night I tried to heal the scabs on my lips and face. When I had a few minutes to myself, I removed the lice from my hair. My right foot and leg was frozen, but a wonderful man named Joe Morton, a war correspondent, carried me out into the snow so I didn't have to defecate in front of the handsome men.

"One night, during a freezing gale, I tried to pull some Czech soldiers to their feet, I actually stood and watched them freeze to death. Eighty-five of them died that night. You were probably wondering if I slept with any of the young handsome men? Well, ladies, the answer is, yes. I slept with the handsome Americans. I slept with them almost every night. We would hold one another trying to keep from freezing. One or two of the pilots threw up on me. It really didn't matter because they were all put to death anyway. Is that what you wanted to know?"

They watched as Maria walked over to the bar, ordered another shot of vodka, faced the women and raised her glass in a salute then downed the drink. She put the glass back on the bar and left the tea party. She was upset. What was the dean going to think? Maybe Mrs. Roosevelt wouldn't mention the incident, and maybe the Hindenburg never blew up over New Jersey!

Heading home on the train to Vassar, Maria stared out the window. The trees flashed by with such speed that they were barely recognizable. She thought to herself, "Cynthia was right." Maria was out of money, had no one to turn to, and wasn't a citizen of the United States, so she couldn't work. She must do something. Maybe one of the offers from New York would help. At least she would get paid for her interviews, even if she were not a citizen.

Cynthia was waiting for her at the train depot. She questioned Maria about the tea party. Maria lowered her head and shook it negatively. Cynthia knew not to continue; the tea party had been a disaster.

On the drive back to the college, Maria told Cynthia that she was thinking of taking the New York interview offer. Cynthia acted like she was jolted with an electrical shock. She started babbling about the Radio City Hall. None of it made much sense to Maria. Cynthia convinced her that since it was June and she was on summer vacation, why not go to New York.

The following day, Maria called New York and told the radio station manager that she would accept his company's offer. Wednesday of the following week, she was on a train. She found her way to the radio station and sat for a short interview. They wanted a short version of her life that would be played by actors working for the broadcasting company. The producer was abrupt and uncouth. He wanted her to give names of people who were in the Czech Underground. He told her that it would make the story more interesting and realistic if they used actual names. Maria explained to him that the Russians had taken over her country and if she mentioned the names of those people it would be disastrous. They, including her sister, were now fighting against the Russians instead of the Germans.

She told him that her story was very interesting—one the Americans and British would love to hear. After all, it was about their men. She wanted to tell their story so the people of the United States would realize what they did for her country.

He insisted that people wanted to hear about the Russians, not the Germans. The conversation stagnated when Maria refused to put any of the people in the Czech Underground in jeopardy. She then refused to give him any story. He made a phone call and asked Maria to wait.

Moments later, a driver arrived and asked Maria to go with him. She still had her suitcase and hadn't had time to check into a hotel. The driver took her to an airfield on the outskirts of the city then drove for several hundred yards, stopping next to an old, two-seat biplane. He threw Maria's suitcase into the back seat, returned and opened her door. He directed her, "This way, miss."

Maria walked over to the plane with him. He helped her into the back seat. Somewhere between her feelings of disbelief and amazement Maria asked, "Is this for some kind of publicity?"

The driver responded, "No, honey, it isn't. You should have listened to the man and sold your story. You know, a buck is a buck."

A pilot appeared and started the airplane. He revved the engine then slowly taxied the plane onto the runway, threw the throttle forward and they took off.

Maria looked down at the airport, then at the back of the pilot's head. The intense wind pulled the skin of her face back. Her blond hair trailed the open cockpit. She stared for a moment, almost in shock, and laughed. Higher and higher they climbed into the massive cumulus clouds that were forming above the city. She glanced down at her feet, resting on mail bags. Her laughter increased and she shouted, "I'm going to kill that Cynthia."

Maria felt the flight took forever. The pilot landed at several airports, picking up and dropping off packages. The weather was beautiful, and for the first time, Maria realized what a magnificent country America was. The mountains, rivers, wheat fields and canyons, and the orchards with trees standing in rows like soldiers. Flowers covered the land and trees stood shoulder to shoulder for miles. It was beautiful.

The plane bounced along the runway when it landed for the last time. Maria had enough flight time to last her for the rest of her life. As the pilot helped her from the plane, she asked, "Does everyone in New York get fired this way, or just me? When you think about it, this is crazy, I mean, really crazy.

That man telling me that a buck is a buck, what does that mean anyway?"

The pilot fumbled for an answer, "Miss I don't really know. They called the office and paid to have you flown home. I just thought that you were a friend of someone and needed a lift."

Maria spoke loudly, "A lift? Is that what you call flying in the back of this freezing, World War I fighter plane? I thought they stopped making these things after the Kaiser gave up."

The pilot apologized, "Sorry, ma'am, but we are still using them."

Maria took a cab from the airfield to the train depot. She still could not keep from chuckling. If she wasn't on a train going nowhere, she was on a plane going nowhere, then back on a train again, and for what?

She decided to leave Vassar. The struggle was becoming too much for her. The only clothes she had were the ones that she made. Maria felt, too, that she couldn't keep up with the other girls. She always made excuses why she couldn't attend parties or go on outings. What little money she had went to purchase books or lab equipment. She wrote letter after letter to her family. There was never a response.

The Dean of Vassar tried to convince Maria to stick with her studies. She had outstanding grades in all of her classes. Maria was well read and had an outstanding background in several fields. On her first summer at Vassar, the dean sent her to represent the college at an international meeting in the Catskill Mountains. Educators from around the world attended. Since Maria had command of so many languages she was the ideal choice to attend. Regardless, Maria dropped out of school.

Having left Vassar, Maria took a train to New York and looked for work. During the day, she searched the want ads of the newspapers. Mr. Ruby gave her several names of business men in New York that had connections to the OSS. When she sought them out, each either refused to meet with her or acted as though they had never heard the name Ruby or the OSS.

She, finally, found a job with a conservative magazine. They had an opening for a sales representative, however, she had to move to Cleveland. Since she didn't know where else to go, she accepted the position and left for Ohio. During her first week, she met a young Navy officer, Eugene Peck. He was tall, handsome, intelligent and possessed the key to Maria's heart, a sense of humor.

For the next few weeks, Maria lived a peaceful life. She settled in and channeled her energy to her new life. Eugene called for her in the evenings and they walked arm in arm discussing music, politics, the military and the movies. She was, for the first time, at peace with herself and in love.

During this time, Maria felt she was being followed, she wasn't positive, but she had a feeling—women's intuition. On one of their evening strolls, Maria asked Eugene if he had been assigned by the Navy to watch her. It caught him completely off guard. He was surprised, "Is something wrong? Why are you asking me a question like that?"

Maria was uneasy, "I don't know. For awhile there, I thought that I was being followed. I guess I am becoming paranoid."

"Well, don't become paranoid over me. I'm just a Navy lawyer," he said sternly.

The following morning Maria walked around the corner to her favorite coffee shop and stopped at the newspaper stand to pick up a copy of the New York Times. She sat, sipping her coffee. As she slowly turned a page of the paper, she peered over the top of it. She noticed two men sitting in a car directly across the street from her and identified them as a surveillance team.

All sorts of things came to mind. Maybe they were NKVD agents sent to get her. The Office of Naval Intelligence must be looking for her. But she had done nothing wrong. If anything, she should have been looking for them, not the other way around. When was she going to be finished with all of this? She was sure that the United States Department of Immigration was stalling on her application for citizenship. They gave her one excuse after another, and now this.

Her newspaper was full of articles about the McCarthy hearings. Pages of stories about people being dragged before the hearings from all over the United States. Everyone was suspected of being a member of the Communist Party. The first week of McCarthy's investigation into the United Nations in

San Francisco, some two hundred workers resigned. Maria assumed if the communists were running Radio Free Europe, they sure as hell were in everything else. She paid no attention and turned the page.

That evening there was a knock at her door. She opened the door with caution. There stood two very tall men, both were wearing sport coats and though they were indoors they failed to remove their sunglasses. The darker of the two men asked, "Maria Zima?"

"Yes, I'm Maria Zima," she answered.

They handed her folded papers and quietly left. Maria locked the door, then sat in her favorite chair. She unfolded the papers and began to read, "The people of the United States vs. Maria Zima."

Maria was on the phone immediately to Eugene Peck. He was preparing some legal papers for the Navy, but told Maria that he would leave that until later. Her subpoena was more important.

It was the twentieth of September 1952, at the Federal Building, Cleveland, Ohio. A Federal agent grasped Maria's arm and escorted her down the long, marbled hallway. Spectators lined the entrance to the building. They gathered in large numbers directly outside the hearing room. Maria was mortified. She was a pale and frightened woman, clutching her black patent leather purse that complemented her dark gray dress. She tugged several times at the petite feminine bow on her blouse, an outlet for her tension.

Her face was tense. The worried look in her eyes was evident to the crowd. She glanced from side to side, into a sea of unfamiliar faces. She hoped someone would step forward and say, "Maria, let me help you."

There was no such person. Maria stood alone, facing her accusers. Trying to gain her composure, but slightly shaken, she sat on a cold marble bench. She looked around the room and thought to herself, "Who are these people? What have I done?"

Norman Thompson of the Department of Justice pointed to the chair at the end of the table where four members of the Justice Department sat and directed her, "Maria Zima, would you please be seated in front of the Justice Department members, right there. Yes, in front."

Maria stood with her legs quivering. The nauseating feeling in her stomach was becoming more acute. She gently sat.

Eugene Peck entered the court room and took a seat against the back wall. He was conspicuous in his Navy commander's uniform. He gave Maria a quick glance, trying to signal he was there for her. Mr. Thompson began questioning, "Are you a communist, Miss Zima?"

Maria denied the accusation, "No, I am not a communist."

"Have you ever been a communist?" Thompson asked.

"No, I have never been a communist," Maria answered.

"Do you ever read communist newspapers?" Thompson wanted to know.

Maria rotated the small gold ring on her finger—one given to her by her grandmother. Her voice cracked, whispering, she answered, "Yes, I do."

Mr. Thompson raised his voice, "Do you mind speaking louder we can barely hear you."

"Yes, I do read communist newspapers," Maria repeated.

He continued, "Why do you read communist papers?"

Maria was candid, "I like to know what is going on in the world."

Thompson demanded, "Can't you find that out by reading the American newspapers?"

"Not always. How do you know what is going on?" she asked.

"Well, Miss Zima," he explained, "I read our American newspapers."

"You mean the ones that told you that President Roosevelt knew nothing about the Japanese attack on Pearl Harbor?" Several people in the courtroom laughed. Maria continued, "I also read the New York Times."

Mr. Thompson turned to the four men sitting behind the brightly polished table. Displaying a slightly victorious smile, he replied, "Yes, but the New York Times isn't a communist newspaper."

Thompson continued questioning her, raising his voice, "Do you attend church? Do you believe in God? Are there any friends of yours that are communists in this country?"

He stopped, then moved close to Maria, making sure he had the full attention of the four men sitting behind the table. He stated, "In 1946, you attended a seminar in the Catskills called The Institute of World Affairs. Did you know that was a communist organization?"

Maria corrected him, "It is not a communist organization. You are thinking of The United World Affairs Institute, that is a communist organization."

"How do you know that?" he demanded.

"I read it in the Russian newspaper," Maria stated.

The audience laughed. The chairman banged his gavel on the table, demanding order.

Maria felt she was a target for the Justice Department as the prosecutor continued, "I did attend that seminar. President McCracken of Vassar College said that it would be an honor for the College to have me attend. I took that as a compliment and attended out of respect to her and the college. It isn't my fault that you are confusing the institute with another organization with a similar name."

Mr. Thompson, visibly annoyed, snapped, "This is something that you will have to prove."

Maria refused, "I'm not proving anything. You go and look it up in your FBI files. You have more resources than I do."

Mr. Thompson changed the direction of his questioning, "How about your parents in Czechoslovakia. Are they communists?"

Maria sighed, "You don't know what you are saying to ask me such a question. My father is a Greek Catholic Priest. He would be excommunicated the moment he became a communist."

The questioning continued, becoming more intense hour after hour. Tears filled Maria's eyes. She stared out into the audience, her thoughts drifted. Mr. Thompson stuck his finger close to her face. She watched his lips move, but heard nothing.

Epilogue

For risking her life daily and for helping the American members of the Dawes Team, the only successful OSS operation in Slovakia during World War II, Maria was:

1) recommended for the Distinguished Service Cross and refused because she was a woman; 2) recommended for the Silver Star and refused because she was not a US citizen; 3) the only woman in the history of the US to receive the Bronze Medal with full military honors at West Point with the cadet corps passing in review.

Then Maria: 1) received only $50.00 a month as payment for all her efforts in trying to save downed pilots and American and British soldiers; 2) was hounded by West Point for not paying her room bill when she was supposed to be their guest; 3) was left stranded in the US without family, friends or money; 4) was dragged before the Justice Department during the McCarthy era, to answer charges that she was a communist; 5) facing deportation, finally sued the US Government to win status as a citizen.

In 1964, Czechoslovakia held their twenty-year reunion of the Uprising. The puppet communist government in power decided to hold a celebration. All of the Russians, generals and outstanding military soldiers, were invited to attend an awards ceremony in the city of Banska Bystrica.

An invitation was forwarded to Washington, DC, requesting McGregor, Lain, Catlos and Dunlevy attend. They were to receive decorations for their efforts in aiding the Uprising.

The four of them honored Washington's request and met there on 1 September 1964. On their way to Czechoslovakia, their first question to the government officials in Washington was, "Where is Maria?" She was not invited.

The four of them arrived in Banska Bystrica and were taken to a large hotel just outside the city. They were told by their government guide to be ready for the awards ceremony in the morning.

The following morning, they dressed in their new coats and ties. A Russian officer knocked at their door and escorted them to an awaiting bus. They drove into the city, entering the rear of a mass gathering. Thousands of people filled the square, waiting to see the heros receive their medals.

An officer stopped the bus at the rear of the crowd, ordered the driver to open the door and get off. He departed into the throngs of people, never to be seen again. The Americans left the bus on their own.

Mac, Lain, Catlos and Dunlevy looked over the heads of the people and watched while the Russians received their awards. The four of them moved slowly through the crowd. It was impossible. As they approached the stage, the ceremony ended.

The Czechoslovakian people were left with the thought that the Russians were the only people who helped them, since they were the only ones on the stage. The Russian officials apologized to Mac and the others and suggested that a second ceremony be held.

The next morning, they were taken to Tri Duby Airfield, just south of the city, by a different officer. Only Russians attended the ceremony at the airfield. There wasn't a Czechoslovakian civilian in sight. The ceremony took several minutes, during which the Russian dignitaries were lifeless. The four Americans were soon standing alone. They stood, amazed, holding back their laughter. Then they gathered in a small circle and threw their arms around each other, laughing.

MARIA ZIMA: Won her suite against the US Government and became a citizen. She married Commander Peck and has a son and daughter. She now lives in Southern California.

The pilots captured in the village, after being turned in by the minister, were executed on Christmas morning 1944, by the Ukrainian Division.

The minister died in January 1945 from a fever of unknown origin.

HOLT GREEN, Lt., USN: Executed at Mauthausen 24 January 1945.

JAMES GAUL, Lt., USN: Executed at Mauthausen 24 January 1945.

EDWARD BARANSKI, Capt., USA: Executed at Mauthausen 24 January 1945.

KENNETH LAIN, Capt., USA: Liberated from prisoner of war camp.

WILLIAM MCGREGOR, Capt., USA: Liberated from prisoner-of-war camp. Settled in the Santa Fe, New Mexico. Owns and operates his own cattle ranch.

TIBOR KESZTHELYI, 1st Lt., USA: Executed at Mathausen 24 January 1945.

LANE MILLER, 1st Lt., USA: Executed at Mauthausen 24 January 1945.

FRANCIS PERRY, 1st Lt., USA: Executed at Mauthausen 24 January 1945.

J. G. MICAN, 2nd Lt., USA: Executed at Mauthausen 24 January 1945.

NELSON B. PARIS, military photographer: Executed at Mauthausen 24 January 1945.

CHARLES HELLER, Sgt., USA: Executed at Mauthausen 24 January 1945.

STEVE CATLOS, Sgt., USA: Liberated from Russian detention camp 1945. Returned home.

JOSEPH HORVATH, Sgt., USA: Captured at Polomka 26 December 1944. Missing in action, never heard from again.

ROBERT BROWN, Cpl. USA: Captured at Polomka 26 December 1944. Missing in action, never heard from again.

KENNETH DUNLEVY, Pvt., USA: Liberated from Russian detention camp 1945. Returned home.

JOHN SCHWARTZ, Pvt., USA: Rescued from German prisoner-of-war camp. Was under suspicion for destroying the radios of the Dawes Team and for aiding and abetting the enemy. After the radios were destroyed, Schwartz carried with him his cipher and his signal plan, which fell into Gestapo hands. None of the charges could be proved, further investigations were halted.

JOSEPH MORTON, associated press correspondent: Executed at Mauthausen 24 January 1945.

FRED MAYER, American Jew: Interrupted mid-transmission, presumed dead.

HANS WYNBERG, Dutch Jew: Interrupted mid-transmission, presumed dead.

FRANZ WEBER, German soldier: Missing in action with Mayer and Wynberg, presumed dead.

JANO VLASAK, Slovak soldier: Forced into the German Army, killed by Luftwaffe strafing, Carpathian Mountains, 1945.

ALEXIE SEVELENKO, Major, Red Army: Lived through the War and was promoted to General.

OLGA ZIMA, Czechoslovakian Partisan: Carried her fight for freedom against the Russians. Missing in action in the Carpathian Mountains, presumed dead, 1948.

STUDENKO, Major, Red Army: Fought to the streets of Berlin. Returned to Russia as a national hero.

TAMARA, Lt., Red Army: Husband died of war wounds. She returned to Russia alone.

MISO SOPHO, Collaborator, border guard: Killed in 1945, while hiding in a cellar from the Red Army.

THE CHERNYS, Czechoslovakian civilians: Turned their home into a hospital twice during the War. Treated Czech's, Germans and Russians. Both died of old age in 1950.

JULIUS GOLDBERGER, Czechoslovakian civilian: Remained through the War in his beloved land. His lumber mill was taken over by the Russians and he was forced, again, to be a manager in his own factory.

MARSHA, Czechoslovakian civilian: Survived the War and remained in Banska Bystrica, organizing the Communist Party.

PUCHYS, JAN AND HELENA, Czechoslovakian teachers: When their school reopened under the control of the district commissar, they were forced to teach the new Communist Party curriculum.

POLACK, Head of Czechoslovakian Secret Service: Picked up by the Gestapo in late 1944. Reported missing and presumed dead.

MADAME ZOLKOFF, Russian aristocrat, Czechoslovakian citizen: Survived the War and opened a new dress shop in Banska Bystrica.

MASLOV, Major, Red Army: Killed in action while fighting with the mountain Partisans.

ANNA, Czechoslovakian citizen: Was last seen in 1944 speeding away in a CFI staff car headed for a ski resort in the Carpathian Mountains.

SCHOENESEIFFEN, Dr., Sturmbann Fuhrer: Responsible for the torturing of the Dawes Team at Mauthausen Prison. Present location unknown.

TOST, Dr., German doctor: Member of the interrogation unit sent to Mauthsusen from Berlin. Tortured Dawes Team. Present location unknown.

ERNST KELTENBRUNNER, Chief of Beichsicherheitshauptar: Signed the order to execute the Dawes Team. Presently in British custody in London.

ARBECKER, Criminal Commissioner at the RSHA Berlin: Participated in the brutal interrogation of the Dawes Team. Present location unknown.

GEORGE BECHMAYER, Member of the SS staff at Mauthausen: Responsible for brutal torturing of Dawes Team. Committed suicide.

WERNER MULLER, Interpreter for the RSHA group from Berlin: Translated between RSHA and the Dawes Team. Identified nine members of the Dawes Team, both by name and photograph. Was present throughout the entire interrogation and witnessed the torture techniques of the SS. Presented himself to the Nurenberg Trials to testify against Nazis who executed members of the Dawes Team.

MARIAN RUBIN, American civilian nurse: Captured and executed at Mauthausen 1945.

WILHELM ORNSTEIN, Jewish prisoner in charge of body disposal: Mauthausen Prison. Lived through the War in Mauthausen Prison. Presented himself to the Nurenberg Trials to testify against SS atrocities committed at Mauthausen. Returned to his home in Poland, where he presently lives.

KARL ARMBRUST, Sturmbann Fuhrer, SS: Carried radio for Maria through check point. In charge of temporary prisoner-of-war camp. Escaped Allied forces and returned to Germany.

NICOLAI, Sgt., Red Army: Assigned to guard the Dawes Team in Russian territory. Escaped from the Russian Army to Vienna, Austria. Picked up by the NKVD and returned to Russia. Presumed dead.

The events and the characters in this book are real. Names, where appropriate, have been changed by the author.

This book is history. It is what actually happened. To say otherwise would be to plunge a dagger into the heart of a sad reality.

To Order More . . .

To order additional copies of **They Died In Silence**, please complete the form below and mail it with your check or money order to:

**Dillard Publishing
300 Carlsbad Village Drive
Suite 108-A
Carlsbad, California 92008-2999**

Enclose $15.00 for each book, plus $2.00 per book for shipping and handling. (California residents please include sales tax.)

ORDER FORM

Please send me ____ copies of **They Died In Silence**.

My check for $_____ is enclosed.

Make checks payable to: **Dillard Publishing**

Name_____

Address_____

City_____State____Zip_____